EMIL AND KATHLEEN SICK SERIES
IN WESTERN HISTORY AND BIOGRAPHY

With support from the Center for the Study of the Pacific Northwest at the University of Washington, the Sick Series in Western History and Biography features scholarly books on the peoples and issues that have defined and shaped the American West. Through intellectually challenging and engaging books of general interest, the series seeks to deepen and expand our understanding of the American West as a region and its role in the making of the United States and the modern world.

JEN CORRINNE BROWN

TROUT CULTURE

HOW FLY FISHING FOREVER CHANGED
THE ROCKY MOUNTAIN WEST

CENTER FOR THE STUDY
OF THE PACIFIC NORTHWEST

in association with

UNIVERSITY OF WASHINGTON PRESS
Seattle and London

© 2015 by the University of Washington Press
Printed and bound in the United States of America
Design by Thomas Eykemans
19 18 17 16 15   5 4 3 2 1

CENTER FOR THE STUDY OF THE PACIFIC NORTHWEST
PO Box 353587
Seattle, WA 98195, USA

UNIVERSITY OF WASHINGTON PRESS
www.washington.edu/uwpress

LIBRARY OF CONGRESS CATALOGING-IN-PUBLICATION DATA
Brown, Jen Corrinne, 1980–
Trout culture : how fly fishing forever changed the Rocky Mountain West /
Jen Corrinne Brown.
    pages cm. — (Emil and Kathleen Sick series in western history and biography)
Includes bibliographical references and index.
ISBN 978-0-295-99457-4 (hard cover : alk. paper)
1. Fishing—West (U.S.)—History.
2. Fishing—Social aspects—West (U.S.)
3. Trout fishing—West (U.S.)
4. Fly fishing—West (U.S.)
5. West (U.S.)—Description and travel.
I. Center for the Study of the Pacific Northwest.
II. Title.
SH464.W4B76 2015   639.2'7570978—dc23   2014034908

Parts of chapters 3, 4, and the epilogue originally appeared in "Trash Fish: Native Fish Species in a Rocky Mountain Trout Culture," *Western Historical Quarterly* 45 (Spring 2014): 37–58. Copyright by the Western History Association. Reprinted by permission.

For Brian

CONTENTS

ACKNOWLEDGMENTS

I WOULD LIKE TO THANK MANY FRIENDS, FAMILY, AND FACULTY members for their support and guidance over the years. To begin with, financial assistance from the Washington State University History Department and Graduate School as well as a travel grant from the American Heritage Center and a summer award from the Charles Redd Center for Western Studies made much of the research which formed the basis of this book possible. I found friendly archivists and librarians throughout my western travels, but even more so at home during my frequent visits to Manuscripts, Archives, and Special Collections in the Washington State University–Pullman Libraries. Pat Mueller, Trevor Bond, and the rest of the staff there were very helpful.

I would also like to thank the Washington State University History Department faculty for their guidance and support in the writing process. Special thanks to David Pietz and Orlan Svingen for their encouragement and insightful comments. Above all, Jeff Sanders set high standards, creating a model for excellent teaching and clear writing.

I am also thankful for a good group of friends and colleagues in Pullman who were fun and supportive, including Beth Erdey and Jason Williams, Grant Fruhwirth, Torsten and Cheryl Homberger, Rachael Johnson, Carrie Kyser, Stephanie and Nathan Roberts, and Nathan Sowry. Additionally, Lee Ann Powell graciously commented on every chapter and provided good company during a final year of teaching and writing in Richland, while Katy Fry, Lesley Moerschel, and Shawna Herzog gave valuable feedback on different sections.

Special thanks to my family as well. While my extended family of aunts, uncles, and cousins is much too large to list here by name, I would like to thank Susan, Clifford, my twin sister Jes (I look forward to outfishing your boyfriend every visit), Doug, Jonalyn, Simon, Patrick, Isabella, and Olivia.

In revising the book and moving across the country (twice), I have met many new colleagues and friends. At Texas A&M University–Corpus Christi, Eliza Martin and David Blanke insightfully commented on various revised chapters and Department Chair Peter Moore was helpful and supportive. Adam and Keren Costanzo and Michael and Neda Jin offered good company.

I would also like to thank the anonymous reviewers as well as Ranjit Arab, Mary C. Ribesky, Amanda Gibson, Tom Eykemans, and the others whose hard work at the University of Washington Press made this book possible.

Across the world and the West, anglers, fisheries managers, and conservationists are working hard to save rivers and trout. I would like to thank them for their efforts. I also wanted to give a shout out to Captain Steve Utley and Don Alcala in Corpus Christi for sharing their knowledge of saltwater fly fishing and promoting conservation in their community outreach classes at Texas A&M University–Corpus Christi.

This book is dedicated to Brian Pauwels, one of the most considerate people I have ever met, whose love and cheer helped me finish.

ACKNOWLEDGMENTS

TROUT CULTURE

Norman Maclean, *A River Runs Through It, and Other Stories* (Chicago: University of Chicago Press, 1976).

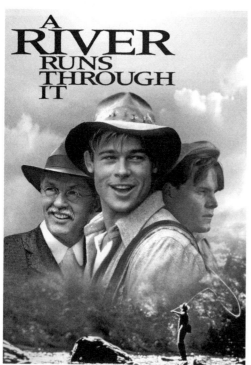

Notable examples of western trout iconography, *A River Runs Through It* and its 1992 film version, seen here, have helped create a West known for fly fishing and trout. *A River* joined nineteenth-century railroad circulars and sporting literature as well as twentieth-century promotional material, fishing books, and advertisements from fly shops, outfitters, and tackle manufacturers in selling regional fishing and trout. *A River Runs Through It* ©1992 Allied Filmmakers, N.V. All rights reserved. COURTESY OF TRISTAR PICTURES.

Introduction

FLY FISHING, LIKE OTHER ASPECTS OF THE ROMANTICIZED American West, has taken on a larger-than-life appearance. No one sells this western mythology as shamelessly as westerners. Sculptures and artwork of fish and fishermen (but rarely women) line streets and city parks. Advertisements and exaggerated images dot the Rocky Mountain landscape and occupy the imaginations of tourists and visitors. Billboards outside of Idaho Falls, Bozeman, and countless other communities advertise waders, drift boats, and fly shops. Microbrew labels feature fishing-related themes, perhaps taking a little too seriously Norman Maclean's maxim about fishing and beer: "you will have to realize that in Montana drinking beer does not count as drinking."[1] The poster from the Robert Redford adaption of *A River Runs Through It* shows a Brad Pitt stand-in casting beautifully in the middle of a river.[2] All of this iconography proclaims the West to be where the trout are. Big trout.

The exciting and picturesque sport can be distilled down to just a unique method of catching fish. Ever wonder what all the commotion over fly fishing is about? Basically, bug puppets. Author and fly fisher David James Duncan describes those little concoctions of feathers, string, fur, and hook that fly fishers use to lure trout as bug puppets.[3] The puppet imitates an aquatic or terrestrial insect, or, in fishing parlance, trout food. The fly fisher—the puppeteer—mimics insect movements in the water, attempting to trick trout into eating the fly. It seems wonderfully simple. However, the imagery of fly fishing suggests not just a sport but rather a religious experience, a transformative western adventure and, mainly, a nostalgic and simplified view of the past.

This book, then, overturns the biggest fish story ever told. It uncovers the true tale of Rocky Mountain trout, a story rarely heard. In reality, the exceptional (and oversold) trout fisheries of the West are neither wild nor natural,

The Rocky Mountain West.
Map by Carrie Lynn Kyser.

but now exist because of drastic and complicated environmental and social changes. The billboards and beer labels belie a history in which anglers and fisheries managers introduced nonnative trout; stocked billions of hatchery fish; attempted to limit the fish use of Native Americans, lower classes, and immigrants; dumped toxins into rivers to kill off millions of native fish; and, in at least one instance, wrested the ownership and control of a river from a western tribe. The history is not entirely a disaster, either. Many anglers and fisheries managers also fought against pollution, protected fish and rivers, and held views on conservation remarkably ahead of their times, thereby playing an important role in addressing environmental issues in the late nineteenth and early twentieth centuries. The iconography of western fly fishing and the nostalgia for majestic trout streams were not timeless features of the West, but rather the product of anglers, fisheries managers, tourists, guides, local business people, and regional boosters and their century-long profound manipulation of the Rocky Mountain environment.

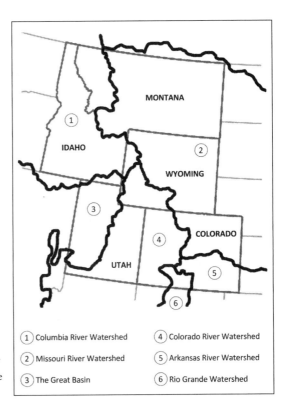

Major watersheds of the Rocky Mountain West. Map by Carrie Lynn Kyser.

① Columbia River Watershed   ④ Colorado River Watershed

② Missouri River Watershed   ⑤ Arkansas River Watershed

③ The Great Basin   ⑥ Rio Grande Watershed

The remade trout fisheries of the inland mountain West sit in large reservoirs and in tiny high country lakes; they run through breathtaking valleys surrounded by mountains, through mundane suburbia, and through high plains. Since state entities manage fish and rivers, this book looks at the five mountain states known for their trout and fly fishing opportunities: Montana, Idaho, Utah, Wyoming, and Colorado. Western watersheds clearly do not fit into these neat state boundaries, but state agencies manage fisheries and much of the source material comes from these entities, thereby requiring a more strict definition of place and region. The states in question and their fisheries are therefore noticeably diverse. Known for snowcapped peaks and extremes in weather, the Rocky Mountains are a succession of smaller ranges that give much of the region its distinguished topography, including basin and range, foothills, and prairie. High, semiarid valleys drain the towering mountains nearby. Tall cottonwoods and stands of trees often line the banks of clear, swift, and rock-lined rivers.

Other trout streams, flowing cold and clear from dams, seem out of place on the treeless steppes of central Wyoming and eastern Colorado. Trout now live in rivers and lakes throughout national forests, national parks, wilderness areas, and backyards. The region is big, but not empty. It is strewn with ranches, farms, vacation homes, and sprawled-out cities like Denver, Salt Lake City, Boise, Jackson, Cheyenne, and Missoula.

The diverse landscapes contain a mix of people, many of whom like to fish, hike, and spend their time outdoors. "The real people of the West," Wallace Stegner once observed, "are infrequently cowboys and never myths."[4] Still, on lakes up in high mountain cirques, it is not unheard of to see the occasional party of old timers riding horses, sporting vintage fiberglass fly rods, and (from personal experience) giving other fly fishers excellent advice about choice of fly patterns. Anglers also visit the West for the fishing. In the warm summer months, guides frequently row tourists down the larger rivers while guides and locals alike sometimes laugh at the "dudes." Tourists come for the sublime experiences that the popular, blue-ribbon trout rivers have to offer. Locals fish these rivers, but they also find out-of-the-way places without the crowds. Even after a few fishing-themed microbrews, they still guard their secret spots. On the smaller creeks and urban waters overlooked by tourists, anglers come across other residents with fly gear, spin gear, or some weird local combination of the two. All of these anglers take advantage of nineteenth-century environmental changes that created a West with many types of trout, a virtual troutopia.

Western trout, while often steeped in local lore and regional nostalgia, tell an important story of the changing human relationships to the natural world that extends far beyond the American Rockies. Today's fishy West can be understood only within a larger network of global processes and transnational exchanges, particularly during the nineteenth and early twentieth centuries.[5] In this larger history, the region became part of the rise of outdoor recreation and sport around the world, processes caused by industrialization and imperialism. Middle classes around the Western world legitimized their own leisure and the consumption of nature during this era. Rocky Mountain anglers played their part, remaking western waters for better fishing and helping to define conservation solutions based upon transnational sporting culture. Significantly, in doing so, they adapted national and international conservation practices to fit regional conditions. Here, fishing remains distinct from the history of conservation and hunting, with the harsh control that hunters had over non-sports-men. Western fish conservation focused on the very common technique of angling (fishing with a hook and line) and restocking fisheries with hatchery fish. As such, fish conservation laws were relatively mild compared to hunting laws, and often went unenforced.[6] The growth of state conservation and the influence of a transnational sporting culture had worldwide magnitude.

Unlike the Pacific Northwest, once famously defined by Timothy Egan as "wherever the salmon can get to," it becomes problematic to define a region based on the presence of trout. With the exception of Antarctica, trout species were introduced and subsequently naturalized on every continent for sport fishing purposes during the nineteenth and twentieth centuries. The long history of fly fishing confuses matters even more. Angling has existed for thousands of years, with evidence dating back to the Paleolithic era. Humans angled long before they invented agriculture, used the wheel, or wrote their stories. As a form of angling, fly fishing has a definitive written record dating back to 200 A D, when the Roman Claudius Aelianus first described Macedonian fly fishing in *De Natura Animalium*.[7] If trout live almost everywhere and fly fishing has an expansive history, why do they seem so western?

This question is rooted in the construction of place. From the mid-nineteenth century to the present, westerners physically and ideologically refashioned the region. They introduced preferred trout species, based largely upon Euroamerican sporting traditions. In the industrial age, steamships and railroads allowed fish culturalists to exchange favored fish species and transport fish eggs to far-off destinations, like the American Rockies. Over time, many trout species became naturalized in coldwater lakes and streams.[8] Yet, trout's existence in the West did not automatically make a place.

Westerners gave meaning to new species, inventing social, cultural, political, and economic trout in the region.[9] During the twentieth century's first half, they formed a new fly fishing culture, generating distinctly regional flies and methods. They also marketed Rocky Mountain trout and sold the trout-fishing experience.[10] Cultural and economic power translated to political sway. In the twentieth century's second half, anglers and their allies in state fish and game departments won court cases, protested (and occasionally won) against new dams, and brought water pollution and habitat protection to the forefront of western environmental issues. Their actions confirmed the importance of trout in the region.

All of this highlights a central theme of western history and this book: place matters. The ways in which humans create and define places have a much broader import. As westerners linked trout to the Rocky Mountains, this conception of place and region produced mixed consequences, sometimes beneficial and sometimes problematic for both people and fish. Creating and maintaining trout fisheries required a striking amount of human control over nature. Fish culturalists, state agencies, and federal hatcheries planted billions of trout, devastating native ecosystems. In the trout aesthetic developed by the mid-twentieth century, many native fish became regarded as "trash fish" to be discarded and ignored in this new regional culture.

The chapters that follow are not meant to comprehensively detail this environmental history, but rather to give readers a short, accessible narrative of the changes to Rocky Mountain fisheries. Chapter 1 explores the origins of western sport fishing and its sources in imperialism, industrialization, and leisure. In the nineteenth century, a transnational angling fraternity developed, particularly between the United States and Great Britain. These middle- and upper-class anglers, like fly pattern expert Mary Orvis Marbury and Colorado conservation writer Lewis B. France, defined a new sporting ethic. As industrialization and imperialism transformed the world, the same anglers benefited, both in their newfound social status and in the tackle revolution it produced. But their focus on angling—that easy and often-used fishing method—as a sporting technique meant they could never quite control angling or conservation, as illustrated by the diverseness of fishing in the western territorial era.

Moving to a more regional level, chapter 2 examines the construction of hatcheries and conservation laws in the inland West, showing the importance of regional conditions in shaping national and transnational factors. Starting in earnest during the 1870s and 1880s, private fish culturalists and enthusiasts along with state and federal agencies artificially propagated both native and nonnative trout species. New regulations accompanied the expansion of the hatchery system. This chapter complicates recent conservation history, finding both local approval and local rejection of state-led conservation among all classes. The introductions of nonnative trout also laid the groundwork for a future region celebrated for trout fishing.

Chapter 3 investigates the emergence of a Rocky Mountain trout culture and economy from the 1920s to the 1950s, its democratic character, and its environmental transformations. The creation of western fly fishing traditions, from Franz Pott and Ted Trueblood to countless other western guides, fly tiers, and anglers, marked the growth of the western tourism and recreation industry. Westerners, tourists, and fish managers remade nonnative trout and non-local practices into something distinctly regional. This Rocky Mountain trout aesthetic relied on an entrenched hatchery system that privileged nonnative fish.

The development of a regional trout economy, chapter 4 argues, caused neglect and mistreatment of native coarse fish (non-trout fish species) by anglers and fisheries managers alike. Starting with the roots of these prejudices in Euroamerican fishing culture, the treatment of coarse fish, which became known as "trash fish" by the mid-twentieth century, worsened with the rise of western trout fisheries. In this context, fish managers frequently dynamited, netted, and dumped fish toxicants in numerous western waters, attempting to improve trout populations.

Testifying to the widespread manipulation of fisheries, chapter 5 focuses on irrigation and dam building in the twentieth century. New West met Old West as anglers and fish managers adapted to the region's irrigation system and water law. Post–World War II dams were even more consequential. While damming coastal rivers proved deadly to fish, bottom-release dams on inland rivers ironically created bigger trout in greater numbers than naturally possible. These tailwater fisheries also produced native fish declines, crowding, and user conflicts. The disturbing tensions confirm the controversial nature of romanticized trout fishing and the need to address this history.

The wild trout era of the 1960s and 1970s, as addressed in chapter 6, concludes this history. Years of environmental change naturalized nonnative trout, creating self-sustaining populations throughout the region that were deemed "wild" in an era that celebrated the natural world. The modern environmental movement inspired western anglers and fisheries managers to reimagine their interactions with nature. As a result, they started to dismantle the western hatchery system after discovering hatchery fish actually caused wild fish declines. The new focus became the protection of habitat and environmental health for the naturalized populations of nonnative and native trout. The Rocky Mountain trout culture, economy, and fisheries management have continued in this form to the present, with a now uneasy priority given to nonnative trout, the culmination of more than a century of environmental and social transformations.

The history of western fishing lends crucial background and context to the worldwide presence of nonnative species—and the environmental mess accompanying them. Nonnative trout have wreaked havoc on native ecosystems; the International Union for Conservation of Nature ranks both brown trout and rainbow trout among "100 of the World's Worst Invasive Alien Species."[11] Combined with habitat destruction, the introduction of nonnative species caused native fish declines throughout the world during the twentieth century.[12] These trends are only amplified in the West, where many native fish populations such as cutthroat trout, bull trout, and fluvial Arctic grayling have bleak prospects. Once one of the most abundant North American fish, cutthroat trout occupy little of their former range that historically extended throughout the western part of the continent. Of the fourteen subspecies, two are extinct (yellowfin cutthroat trout and Alvord cutthroat trout); one is endangered (Paiute cutthroat trout); five more are considered threatened (westslope cutthroat trout, greenback cutthroat trout, Rio Grande cutthroat trout, Lahontan cutthroat trout, and Humboldt cutthroat trout); and three others are considered to have vulnerable populations (Yellowstone cutthroat trout, Colorado River cutthroat trout, and coastal cutthroat trout).[13] Bull trout populations in Idaho and Montana have experienced similar declines, with threatened and vulnerable populations.[14] And fluvial Arctic grayling, once abundant in Michigan and Montana, now occupy only one section of one river in the contiguous United States: the upper Big Hole River in southwest Montana.[15] These at-risk species, unfortunately, represent only a portion of the Salmonidae family. Dozens more fish native to the Rocky Mountain West are extinct, endangered, threatened, or vulnerable.

Importantly, native fish survival and regional sustainability rely on the same people who benefit from nonnative trout. Anglers, tourists, outfitters, local businesses, tourism boards, and fisheries managers still celebrate the West's nonnative trout while commercial boosterism suggests an experience with pristine nature in the Rockies. These stakeholders could protect imperiled native fish and habitats. This is, after all, Wallace Stegner's "native home of hope." When Stegner famously wished for a West that lived up to its beautiful environs, he asked residents to rethink how they understood themselves:

> Angry as one may be at what heedless men have done and still do to a noble habitat, one cannot be pessimistic about the West. This is the native home of hope. When it fully learns that cooperation, not rugged individualism, is the quality that most characterizes and preserves it, then it will have achieved itself and outlived its origins. Then it has a chance to create a society to match its scenery.[16]

Anglers, fisheries managers, and others have historically overlooked native species, but their livelihoods rest on redefining themselves to create a more sustainable West.

This blind spot goes far beyond individual fishing preferences. During the twentieth century, westerners and tourists developed a multi-million-dollar industry based on the opportunities to catch nonnative trout in the Rocky Mountains. The lucrative tourism and recreation industry provides little incentive to reevaluate the region's problematic association with nonnative trout. With the current scientific and ethical concerns about declines in native species and the need to preserve biodiversity, at some point in the near future, western anglers, guides, regional boosters, and fisheries managers will need to protect native fish much more than they do now. In short, they need to come to terms with history.

I share the history of Rocky Mountain fish and fishing with the hope that anglers, conservationists, environmentalists, and fisheries managers address this entrenched trout culture and economy in their continued work to save rivers and fish. As a fly fishing and conservation sage, Roderick Haig-Brown believed the sport's charms included knowing a river: "[A river] has its own life and its own beauty, and the creatures it nourishes are alive and beautiful also. Perhaps fishing is, for me, only an excuse to be near rivers. If so, I'm glad I thought of it."[17] Likewise, protecting western waters and fish means knowing the past as much as the rivers we love.

Headwaters

I N ONE OF FLY FISHING'S MOST CURIOUS AND INVENTIVE EPI-
sodes, after running out of flies while fishing, nineteenth-century
Scotsman John Wilson improvised a makeshift fly pattern by reportedly tying buttercup petals and grass on a hook. An eccentric professor at
Edinburgh, Wilson wrote, taught philosophy, and fished.[1] His delightfully
odd flower-petal combination apparently caught fish, and Wilson later
replaced the buttercups and grass with more durable yellow silk and feathers, naming the popular fly pattern the "Professor."[2] In an era marked by
its transnational exchanges, Wilson's whimsical fly (in the non-buttercup
version) for Scottish fish became a popular late-nineteenth-century pattern on Rocky Mountain waters, and perhaps was even used to imitate
stone flies, abundant western aquatic insects.[3] Such fascinating interchanges illustrated how national and international processes helped give
form to Rocky Mountain fishing.[4]

Nineteenth-century imperialism and industrial capitalism served as
the headwaters—the source—of sport and environmental change in the
American West. Industrialization represented a break from the past, transforming how people worked, lived, and played. In industrialized nations
such as Britain and the United States, a growing middle class benefited
from more leisure time and disposable incomes. They looked to outdoor
recreation and fishing for leisure and escape. Since sport was no longer
within the reach of only the wealthy, the middle classes legitimized their
actions by celebrating angling (fishing with a hook and line) and leisure
for its own sake.

Imperialism, too, had transformative powers. Western civilization continued to expand, gaining land and natural resources from military and
political conquest. Imperialism was also a cultural endeavor, bringing the
language of empire, religion, and new ways of interacting with nature to

other regions. Naturalizing leisure and the "sport" of fishing became part of the imperial process and settler colonialism.

Despite the growing control of leisure-class anglers, the range of fishing traditions and the endgame of actually catching a fish ensured that angling could never be completely defined as sport. Unlike baseball, tennis, golf, and many other games, angling evolved as a way to gather food. Angling itself had diverse roots and varied meanings; fishing with a hook and line embodied a simple and effective method to catch fish throughout history. Angling's widespread use and unsophisticated gear requirements meant that it could never entirely become an elite sporting activity. Even so, leisure-class anglers tried to assert claims of superiority through new hook-and-line laws and through their gear.

Middle- and upper-class white anglers in the transnational angling community sought to set themselves apart from lower classes and other races through their use of new tackle, brandishing new rods, reels, fly lines, and colorful flies created by global trade and industrialization. From 1860 to 1900, a tackle revolution improved fly fishing gear. After new rounds of imperialism in the nineteenth century, Euroamerican anglers had an excess of bird feathers, bamboo, and more exotic materials from across the globe to fashion into fishing gear. No wonder, then, that a fly fisherman, the creative John Wilson, reportedly first described the British Empire's vastness as one "on which the sun never sets."[5]

Throughout the world, however, angling had varied practitioners who placed different meanings, whether sport or subsistence, on catching fish with a hook and line. In his history of the Columbia River, *The Organic Machine* (1995), Richard White explored how energy and work connected humans and nature along the Columbia. White argued that race, class, and gender divided space, excluding Chinese, Indians, and other groups from the river or relegating them to indoor cannery work. Conversely, upper-class white tourists like Rudyard Kipling enjoyed spending leisure time in nature: "Out of doors, class as well as race divided the river. Kipling, in retreating to a rod and reel, took his salmon on the Willamette. In selecting how and where he fished, he gave away his class. How and where men caught fish reflected a class struggle." Kipling used angling as a restorative activity that would reconnect him with nature, a relationship he saw as alienated by machines and the modern world.[6] Yet angling did not necessarily always reveal class or class struggles. Kipling's fancy rod and reel, as imagined by historian Paul Schullery, certainly marked his elite status. When Kipling, the quintessential imperial apologist (and late-nineteenth-century fly fishing tourist) fished the American Far West during the late nineteenth century, Schullery noted that Kipling "brought the world" with him:

> His rod was probably made of "Calcutta" bamboo from India, split and glued into an excellent casting instrument by one of many British or American rod makers. His line was almost certainly silk from India or Persia, plaited to perfection in some European or American tackle factory. His leaders would have been silkworm gut from Italy, Sicily, Portugal, or (most likely) Spain. His flies could have contained feathers and furs from six continents, tied on Irish, English, or Norwegian hooks, in patterns representing several centuries of British fly-pattern theorizing.[7]

The Calcutta bamboo rod, the silk fly line, the exotic feathers in his flies placed Kipling in a transnational angling community that enjoyed sport and leisure. For others, however, fishing with a hook and line meant something altogether different, reflecting angling's different roots and traditions. Class, then, sometimes manifested itself not in *how* or necessarily *where* people fished, but in the significance they attached to the gear and activity, whether for sport, subsistence, or a combination of meanings, as the diversity of anglers demonstrates.[8]

Historically, angling represented a commonly used fishing method, practices that were not limited to Euroamerican elites but used by almost everyone. It has been a simple way to catch fish for millennia. Archeologists in East Timor recently uncovered the world's oldest fish hook, dating back to 42,000 BP![9] The limited gear needed and the fact that many anglers could easily make their own lines, hooks, and rods meant that it was broadly practiced. Even after the advent of industrialization and world trade that created demand for split bamboo rods, silk lines, and colorful feathers, some elite sportsmen still conveniently fashioned a pole out of nearby trees or willows when they arrived at their fishing spot.[10] With angling's non-elite origins, elite attempts to redefine hook-and-line fishing into a sport could never succeed completely because of its simplicity in gear (pole, line, hook) and its effectiveness in catching fish. Fly fishing also developed among Europe's lower classes and those who fished for a living.[11] European fly fishing continued to have common practitioners up into the nineteenth century, when British angler Sir Humphry Davy observed peasants fly fishing in Austria, Germany, Switzerland, and the western Balkan Peninsula. As an ardent upper-class angler, Davy attempted to distance himself from peasants catching fish the same way, qualifying his observation by noting the peasants fly fished "though always with rude tackle."[12] Despite Davy's attempts to slight lower-class fly fishing, he observed the almost universal use of fly fishing in Europe.

Use of a hook and line was not restricted to Anglo or European peoples, or their colonists elsewhere. In Japan, peasants used the Tenkara tradition of fly fishing for centuries, and it was promoted among the warrior class during the Tokugawa period as a peacetime activity.[13] Other cultures also fished with similar tackle. Long before the nineteenth-century fishing tackle revolution allowed Kipling to find refuge in nature on the Willamette River with his rod and reel, Chinese fishermen used the same gear. In ancient China, men occasionally fished with silk lines and bamboo poles.[14] Later, Chinese anglers invented fishing reels, centuries before Europeans.[15] The tackle may have been similar, but the meanings diverged. Kipling's role justifying imperialism clouded his views toward other races and fishing cultures, setting up British traditions, including angling, as superior. Kipling's contemporaries, too, strove to distinguish their sport (and, by extension, themselves) from nonwhite hook-and-line fishing.

In the rampant nationalism and imperialism among European nations and the United States during the latter half of the nineteenth century, some British anglers took the opportunity to define their sport as more progressed. In *A Handbook of Angling* (1853), sporting writer Edward Fitzgibbon maintained that British citizens and colonists had perfected outdoor sports like angling, while fishing with a hook and line among other cultures lagged behind: "At first the modes of practicing it were exceedingly rude, and they still remain so amongst uncivilized nations."[16] These ideas continued throughout the era. Another compatriot acknowledged the widespread use of hook-and-line fishing throughout the world, but again differentiated between "civilized" and "uncivilized" angling. To him, barbless hooks like the Inuit bone hooks displayed at the London Fisheries Exhibition of 1883 represented an inferior society: "Probably centuries of use and observation lay between the first hook and the hook which by an advance of thought was furnished with a barb."[17] To this angler, barbed hooks reinforced the supremacy of British men.

In order to define their sport, Americans took cues from the British. The first American book on angling looked to well-known English authors such as Izaak Walton for a description of the sport's purpose.[18] To many in the leisure class, fishing with a hook and line signified civilization. In the midst of dramatic social and economic upheavals during the nineteenth century, the middle class sought to maintain its sometimes seemingly fragile economic and social status by defining citizenship through the shifting concept of whiteness to contend with immigration and industrialization.[19] As the American leisure class tried to strengthen these claims to whiteness and superiority, they renewed connections to their British angling peers to create a Western angling community. Sport and whiteness connected Western civilization, as one American sporting writer maintained: "Indeed, the Anglo-Saxon race have followed angling with an energy and a zest far beyond any other nation."[20] Race helped define angling as a white, leisure-class endeavor.

Gender could be used in the same way. Within the social and economic transformations of the late nineteenth century, middle-class men became concerned with challenges to their authority. Economic downturns, fewer career opportunities, labor unrest, increasing immigration, women's movements for equality, and a new disease called "neurasthenia" all threatened to undermine white, middle-class male power. A sort of nervous mental disorder, neurasthenia plagued middle-class professionals working in the modern world. Many men turned to the outdoors and exercise to strengthen their bodies and manhood.[21] Within this worldview, some saw angling as a way to confirm their masculinity. One British sporting writer believed outdoor recreation provided a solution to the "mental exhaustion" of businessmen.[22] An American counterpart, notable conservationist and politician Robert Barnwell Roosevelt (Teddy's uncle), considered the health benefits of angling and being outdoors, connecting physical strength to national strength: "Our ancestors had in a thinly settled country as much physical labor as their bodies needed, but their descendants are suffering for the want of out door [sic] exercise."[23] Some anglers linked angling to masculinity in order to combat the age's social turbulence.

Mirroring the paradoxes within gender roles themselves, femininity could also be used to mark angling as a leisure-class activity, its participants set apart from other races and lower classes who fished for food or

Fishing represented a respectable sport for women, but in keeping with gender norms, they often fished in regular clothes. As traveling missionaries in Wyoming during the early 1900s, Annette B. and W. B. D. Gray sometimes found time to go fishing. Here, Annette shows off a trout. W. B. D. & Annette B. Gray Papers, American Heritage Center, University of Wyoming.

market. Angling represented a respectable sport for Victorian women, as long as they maintained proper gender boundaries (hence the vast number of early photographs of women in dresses, skirts, and other seemingly inappropriate fishing garb). Women anglers also contributed to sporting periodicals, wrote books, and ran fly-tying businesses, giving them authority within the sport.[24] Mary Orvis Marbury's famed treatise on American fly patterns, *Favorite Flies and Their Histories* (1892), demonstrated that part of women's acceptance into the angling world rested on an element of consumerism and class. The daughter of renowned tackle maker Charles Orvis, Mary Marbury saw her readership (and customers of her father's business) as a leisure class: "The object of this treatise is to aid those who fish and observe for pleasure,—who seek fresh vigor and strength in a pursuit which occupies mind and body in the open air, and yields excitement without worriment."[25] Marbury and other women's angling expertise offered them a way to exercise agency that also provided legitimacy to the sport itself.

As some Americans used gender to situate angling within middle-class conceptions of nature, they also brought this sport and leisure westward. In the West, agents of empire proved to be zealous anglers. The officer-sportsmen, as well as the enlisted men, stationed at western garrisons from Fort Laramie to Fort Missoula fished enthusiastically during and after the territorial period. Throughout the Rocky Mountains, fishing provided recreation near remote outposts as well as varied food on long marches. "Tamarack," one of the many military men that corresponded with Mary Orvis Marbury about American fly patterns, reported the excitement that fishing generated among his company during a march from Utah to Fort Missoula in 1877. After seeing pools of trout in one encampment along the Snake River, the men rushed to get their gear: "Immediately every one [sic] who had a hook and line hunted them up, picked up the first stick he could find for a 'pole,' and got ready for business; but there were neither flies nor hoppers to be had." While the other men used salted pork for bait, Tamarack improvised with a piece of red yarn, catching one small native Yellowstone cutthroat trout. He then cut it up for bait to catch fourteen more trout, seeming to relish both the trout dinner and, in a competitive spirit, the jealousy of the company's less successful fishermen.[26]

While regulars enjoyed fishing for the food, sport, and spirited rivalry, elite officers appeared more likely to contribute to national sporting periodicals on western aspects of natural history and fish life, angling methods, and conservation. Soldiers stationed in the West wrote regularly in eastern sporting periodicals like *Forest and Stream*. Some of the first regional boosters, they extolled western fishing and hunting opportunities. Stationed at various posts, sportsman and bird collector Major Charles Bendire routinely shared his western experiences with an eastern audience. During the Bannock War of 1878, Bendire traveled through central Idaho and the headwaters of the Salmon River. Saying remarkably little about the war itself, he described the region in terms of sporting prospects: "The upper Salmon River country must be a sportsman's paradise, both as regards fish and game."[27] Another officer-sportsman used his time near Lake Coeur d'Alene to glorify the area's natural attractions in a two-part article. He claimed the lake offered excellent fishing with abundant types of fish, stating, "The catch is often fabulous."[28] From the viewpoint of officer-sportsmen who promoted western sport, the region offered virgin sporting opportunities with no apparent competition from the native inhabitants. Their writings helped popularize the Rocky Mountains as a place for play and as a tourist destination.

Oddly enough, fishing even played a role in western campaigns. During the 1876 Sioux War, General George Crook's column marched north from Wyoming's Fort Fetterman in part of a three-column search for the Sioux and Northern Cheyenne. As with any enthusiastic sportsman taking a trip to trout country, Crook brought along his gear, in this case, expensive split bamboo rods.[29] Throughout the campaign, the troops fished during seemingly every spare moment, so much so that a captain in Crook's command called several of the other officers "trout maniacs." The captain noted, however, that fishing was not confined solely to a few enthusiasts: "they had many followers in their gentle lunacy, which, before the hot weather had ended, spread throughout the whole command."[30] The fishing continued even after meeting warriors led by Crazy Horse at the Battle of the Rosebud.

Both sides suffered casualties in the battle, and while Crook's column went back to its previous camp on Goose Creek to wait for reinforcements, the Sioux and Northern Cheyenne fighters joined the larger force at the Little Bighorn River. At the same time Custer and the Seventh Cavalry met their demise, Crook's men were hauling in loads of cutthroat trout at Goose Creek. This has led historians to speculate on the battle's outcome, had Crook not spent his time after the Battle of the Rosebud waiting for reinforcements and, of course, fishing.[31] At the Battle of the Little Bighorn, Captain Frederick Benteen's leadership saved the other half of Custer's command from meeting the same fate. An avid fly fisherman, Benteen also saw fighting in the Nez Perce War the following year. Incredibly, at the Battle of Canyon Creek he led a cavalry charge armed with only a fly rod, apparently a first and last for military history, reminiscent more of a MASH episode than a serious skirmish.[32] Fish stories aside, as the enforcer of a federal policy aimed at dispossessing and assimilating Native Americans, the western military presence opened the door for settlement, environmental change, and new ways of viewing nature through the lens of leisure.

Americans legitimized both empire and leisure by expressing supposed superiority. Leisure-class anglers contrasted their angling to the methods used by Native Americans or other subsistence fishers. One popular American fishing writer described indigenous spear fishing as "cruel and wasteful." In his opinion, wasteful sportsmen and market fishermen ran the risk of crossing racial lines by not following a sporting code of conduct: "though it cannot be wondered at in the untutored savage, cannot be reprehended too severely when practiced, as it is universally by the civilized white man, for purposes of reckless sport or illicit and dishonorable gain."[33] Widely read author Thaddeus Norris also criticized Native American fishers for fish declines due to their "unfair" fishing techniques. His casual racism despised indigenous fishing methods: "for the red man . . . was a destructive fisher; his weirs and traps at the time of their autumnal descent, the spear on the spawning beds, and his snare or loop, were murderous implements."[34] Norris also took aim at lower-class rural anglers:

> No fish affords as much sport to the angler as the Brook Trout; whether
> he is fished for by the country urchin, who ties his knotted horsehair-line
> to his alder-pole, and 'snakes out' the speckled fellows by the caving-bank
> of the meadow brook, and from under the overhanging branches of the
> wooded stream; or by the scientific angler, who delivers his flies attached
> to his nine-foot leader—straight out and lightly—from his well-balanced
> rod, and kills his fish artistically.[35]

To be fair, not all elite anglers blamed fish declines on lower-class, rural anglers. Robert Barnwell Roosevelt countered that "in spite of what elderly gentlemen may say to the contrary, an ignorant countryman, with his sapling rod and coarse tackle, never takes the largest fish nor the greatest in quantity."[36] Yet, leisure-class anglers increasingly separated sport from subsistence. When other classes and races fished with the same hook-and-line technique, it became harder to justify this contempt.

Sometimes, angling's diverse practitioners had interesting meetings. At the turn of the twentieth century, American dry fly prophet Theodore Gordon had benefited from the modern tackle revolution and decades of exchanges between American and British anglers that refined the sport of fly fishing. Yet angling still could not be classified as an exclusive Euroamerican, middle- to upper-class fishing technique. Gordon related a story of a chance encounter with a little African American girl along an upstate New York stream: "[she] had been trying to open the trout season with a stick and a string. I did not wish to poach upon her pool, but as a matter of form, dropped my fly at the edge of the stone and not three feet from the small maiden's toes. It was seized at once by a half-pound native [brook] trout, which had been lurking under her pedestal, and I am not sure who was more surprised, the child or myself."[37] In Gordon's eagerness to catch the trout, he encroached upon her spot, knowingly violating an unwritten code of sporting conduct, perhaps thinking the girl's stick and string proved no match for his dry fly skills. Gordon's story shows that despite all the sporting literature, hook-and-line fishing represented a simple and efficient way to catch trout, simultaneously existing as an elite sport and a rural pastime that put food on the table.

Despite the efforts of middle-class anglers to distinguish sport from subsistence, angling had existed for thousands of years with surprisingly varied roots and practitioners. Many classes and races angled for fish. Sometimes cultural syncretism even produced new fishing techniques. Native Americans occasionally employed fishing poles, lines, and various lures and baits.[38] Their methods influenced American fly fishing. White anglers embraced the use of deer hair and hairwing flies, which stemmed from indigenous fishing techniques on eastern waters.[39] Rocky Mountain fly fishers built on these roots, incorporating deer and elk hair into the western fly-tying tradition that developed in the early twentieth century. The absorption of indigenous flies into mainstream American fly fishing illustrates the complicated development of sport, one not solely shaped by Euroamerican traditions, but rather one influenced by indigenous cultures and adapted to local conditions and needs.

Everyone wanted to catch fish when they angled, but many placed different significance on the activity. The leisure class characterized angling by the effort, not the outcome. Indeed, one adage reflects the sometimes difficult sport: "That's why they call it 'going fishing' instead of 'going catching.'"[40] For lower-class and indigenous people, the catching was seemingly more important than the fishing and they employed a variety of (remarkably similar) methods, from hook and line to net and dynamite.

Before and after the territorial era, western tribes often supplemented their hunting and gathering with fishing. Within the diverse cultures and landscapes of the Rocky Mountain region, fishing varied greatly from place to place. The amount of indigenous fishing depended on location and access to fish. The Crows of central Montana rarely fished, but occasionally added fish to their buffalo diet or ate fish during hard times.[41] Comparatively, Idaho tribes which lived along anadromous salmon and steelhead runs (fish that live in the ocean and spawn in freshwater rivers) developed more of a fishing culture and obviously ate and traded more fish. The Lemhi Shoshone-Bannock practiced diverse methods from spears and gorges (straight hooks that would gorge a fish, used with or without bait) to traps, weirs, and baskets, as well as baited bone and wood hooks. They also traded dried fish with regional neighbors like the Crow, Flathead, Wind River Shoshone-Bannock, Northern Paiute, and occasionally the Nez Perce.[42] In the Bonneville Basin, Ute bands also relied a great deal on fish and described themselves by location or food; near Utah Lake they defined themselves as "fish eaters" and the Sevier Lake band, "close to water."[43] The Fish Eaters ate Bonneville cutthroat trout, Utah suckers, June suckers, and Utah chubs.[44] The access to numerous fish meant the band consumed twice as much fish as other Ute bands in western Colorado. Like other indigenous people, the Fish Eaters caught fish with nets, baskets, weirs, spears, and arrows. They also grabbed them with their hands, contemporarily known as guddling or tickling.[45] Other western tribes also incorporated fishing into their seasonal subsistence activities. In addition to subsistence fishing, some natives guided tourists or engaged in market fishing.[46]

From the 1860s to the 1910s, dynamite represented a popular and effective fishing method, especially for miners and railroad workers who had ready access to explosives. One Colorado angler complained that explosives had "nearly depopulated the waters" by 1889.[47] Another elite sportsman worried about its use in Wyoming: "Not satisfied with destroying the game, the greedy settlers are ruining the fishing in Snake River."[48] And at the turn of the twentieth century, Utah officials still listed dynamite as one of the major factors that impeded their fish cultural work.[49] Native Americans also sometimes used explosives. One unspecified band raised the ire of eastern sportsmen by spending a summer in the 1880s along Lake Pend Oreille dynamiting fish for regional city markets.[50]

Besides dynamite, settlers occasionally used nets, seines, and weirs to capture fish. One early Yellowstone tourist complained that locals used spears and nets to catch trout from Henry's Lake, perhaps exaggerating—as fishermen do—that six hundred to seven hundred pounds of fish were taken nightly by spearing.[51] In another case, locals near Leadville,

Lewis B. France's (a.k.a. "Bourgeois") *Mountain Trails and Parks in Colorado* focused on fly fishing. In his writings and actions, France promoted angling and fish conservation during early statehood. Of the former, France wrote that "a combination of art and science may be desirable, but if one may not have both I prefer the art." France, *Mountain Trails and Parks in Colorado*, 2nd ed. (Denver, CO: Chain, Hardy, 1888), 213. Gallup Collection, Manuscripts, Archives, and Special Collections (MASC), Washington State University Libraries, Pullman.

Colorado, used pitchforks (a modern take on a trident?) to catch spawning yellowfin cutthroat trout running into the streams from Twin Lakes.[52] Hunger thus brought forth seemingly odd catching techniques, a point recognized but not respected by the leisure class.

With angling as a widely practiced activity and the assortment of other fishing methods, many middle- and upper-class anglers demonstrated their social position through their fishing tackle and new consumer goods. Industrialization, world trade, and imperialism made the tackle revolution possible. Venturing west during the Colorado gold rush as a young lawyer, Lewis B. France spent decades fly fishing regional waters. From the 1880s onward, he promoted Rocky Mountain fish and fishing in sporting periodicals and books while simultaneously enjoying his fancy Hiram Leonard split bamboo rod, his innovative Orvis reel, and his role in re-creating eastern civilization along the Rocky Mountain front.[53] If France's expensive gear failed to signify his class position, he advertised it not so subtly with the pen name "Bourgeois." As such, he upheld fly fishing as a "noble fellowship" that revolved around civilized sport.[54] The nineteenth-century tackle revolution, enjoyed only by those who could afford it, allowed this transnational consumer-oriented leisure class to characterize its angling as vastly different from that of the so-called country urchins, lower classes, immigrants, and other races.[55]

Industrialization remade humans' relationships with the environment. Railroads and steam power increasingly interconnected the nineteenth-century world. The transportation revolution shipped goods, people, and natural resources much faster than had been possible in previous eras of human history that relied solely on animal power.[56] In the Rocky Mountains, railroads linked minerals, timber, animals, and other resources to distant markets, all of which promoted western industry. Railroads also contributed to leisure, allowing western anglers to connect to their peers in the eastern United States and Europe while shuttling tourists west to find nature in the Rockies.

Industrialization and mechanization also allowed gear makers to create precise rods, new reels, and better hooks, while imperialism and global trade brought a dizzying array of exotic materials into use for rods, lines, and flies. In turn, the new gear changed the way people fished, providing for longer casts, new fishing techniques, and the rise of modern dry fly fishing.[57] Nineteenth-century fly fishing, then, represented much more than a recreational activity in nature—it symbolized the ever-changing ways the modern world shaped everyday life. For middle-class sporting types, that meant buying new fly fishing gear. Victorian-era fly fishers drew pleasure from the unequal colonial trade, making birds, animals, silkworms, and plants from far-off places into instruments to catch fish.

Industrial capitalism transformed fly fishing into a modern activity, updating all facets of the sport, especially flies. Yet the term "bug puppet" fails to capture the complexity of fishing with flies. Flies are classed generally in two categories: imitators and attractors. Imitators resemble bugs, attractors do not, yet fish still take both. Why? Like all great philosophical quandaries—fly fishing or otherwise—this question continues to be debated.[58] Popular in the nineteenth-century Atlantic world, fancy flies like the Professor fall under the attractor category; they do not look like a natural insect, or much of anything, really. If an imitator fly is an insect doppelganger, a fancy fly is a bug puppet on acid.

The Jock Scott, a well-known British fly pattern for Atlantic salmon, exemplifies the garishness that characterized mid- to late-nineteenth-century fancy flies.[59] The Jock Scott could hardly pass for an insect of any kind, flashing a mixture of silk, tinsel, and brightly colored feathers from wild and domesticated birds native to five continents. On top of local materials, the pattern's exotic feathers included those from toucan, red macaw, and blue macaw from South America; jungle cock and crow from India; black turkey, native to North America; bustard (one expert believed the Indian and African species were superior to those from Europe); and gallina, or guinea fowl, of which the best varieties reportedly came from the Philippines, Africa, and Madagascar.[60] In addition to the difficulty of acquiring the tropical feathers, the multiplicity of other materials incorporated into the pattern required a large amount of artistry and skill from the fly tier. Once tied, the results proved to be an ostentatious show of empire on a hook. The Jock Scott's popularity, however, lay mostly in the fact that it caught fish, not in its illustration of the empire's strength.

Other effective nineteenth-century fancy fly patterns also boasted colorful components from the realm's far reaches. One well-known London tackle maker listed over two pages of fly-tying materials that tiers needed in order to create various fly patterns. The items included both local and international birds and animals. More ordinary dressings came from the feathers of birds like chickens, mallards, pheasants, and blue jays, as well as sheep wool, pig hair, and rabbit fur. Yet the tackle maker specified that colorful feathers "of a most gaudy hue" made the best wings on salmon patterns. He identified bright, exotic feathers that came not only from the same birds as in the Jock Scott, but also from ostrich, scarlet ibis, bird-of-paradise, parrot, and cock-of-the-rock. He also added other unusual furs like black bear and sable to the list.[61] The sheer variety of materials available to Victorian fly tiers revealed the spatial inequalities produced by capitalism and new imperialism; like others in industrialized nations, anglers benefited from the exploitation of diverse environments.

These processes wrought change on a global level, and they also contributed to national and regional changes, including modifications to fly

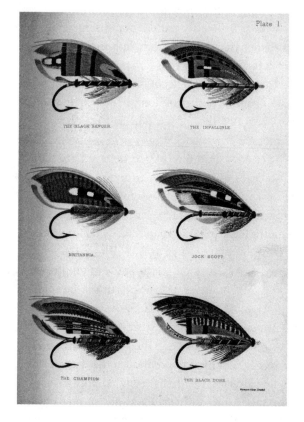

A fancy fly and attractor pattern, the Jock Scott was tied with a variety of exotic feathers. Geo. M. Kelson, *The Salmon Fly: How to Dress It and How to Use It* (London: privately printed, 1895), plate I. Gallup Collection, Manuscripts, Archives, and Special Collections (MASC), Washington State University Libraries, Pullman.

tying. While British and European fly fishers influenced American sport, by the mid-nineteenth century, American anglers had also developed their own sporting traditions and fly patterns. In writing the seminal *Favorite Flies and Their Histories* (1892), Mary Orvis Marbury relied on correspondence with anglers across the nation to record commonly used fancy flies from European patterns as well as newer, unique American bass flies that used many of the same exotic feathers.[62] She recorded popular patterns used by American anglers, providing readers with their histories, in addition to recipes and tips for fishing. Colorful illustrations of each fly highlighted the book, which contained dozens of plates that used chromo-

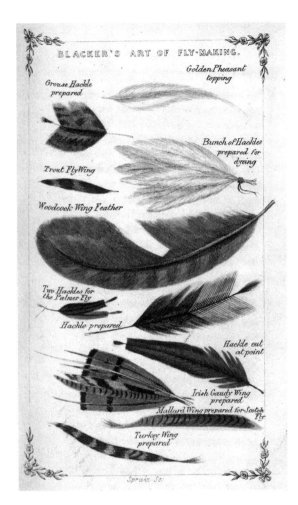

Some of the many types of materials used in nineteenth-century fly making. William Blacker, *Blacker's Art of Fly Making, &c, Comprising Angling, and Dyeing of Colours, with Engravings of Salmon and Trout Flies Shewing [sic] the Process of the Gentle Craft as Taught in the Pages. With Descriptions of Flies for the Season of the Year as They Come Out on the Water. Rewritten and Revised by the Author Blacker, Himself, Fishing Tackle Maker of 54, Dean St, Soho, London. 1855* (London, 1855), unnumbered plate, 34–35. Manuscripts, Archives, and Special Collections (MASC), Washington State University Libraries, Pullman.

lithography, a relatively new method of mass producing color illustrations. Marbury meant for the vivid prints and detailed descriptions to create conformity among fly patterns, at a time when American locales became linked through transportation improvements and an industrialized market economy.[63] Within this more close-knit society, Marbury's standardized local varieties of flies provided practical information to American fly fishers. The fancy fly patterns themselves, like the Jock Scott, depended on world trade and a bourgeois penchant for flair.

The dictates of fashion shaped the increasing globalization of trade and access to exotic feathers for fly-tying materials. For centuries, and especially during the late nineteenth century, birds adorned fashionable women's hats.[64] The styles provided seventeenth-century British tiers with ready access to flamingo, parakeet, and macaw feathers.[65] With bird hats back in vogue during the 1880s, middle-class Victorian women on both sides of the Atlantic could display their status and femininity in the fashionable, yet outrageous, hats.[66] Their male counterparts could simultaneously test their masculinity fly fishing for trout or salmon, while using an equally gaudy fancy fly pattern made from the same bird feathers from far-off lands. To complicate matters, fly fishing formed a respectable pursuit for Victorian ladies, producing countless theoretical permutations on feathers, flies, hats, and gender roles for present-day imaginations. The passing strange uses for bird parts likewise pointed to the commodification of nature inherent in a global exchange. However, the popularity of fancy flies and bird hats waned by the century's end. Notions of womanhood and morality led Victorian women to form Audubon clubs and rally to save the birds that sat on hats. The downfall of fancy flies, however, followed a different route.

The rise of industrial capitalism also brought new raw materials for fly lines and rods, eventually leading to the dry fly revolution and the sport's modern development, while making fancy flies passé. Imperial connections, however, remained in the form of silk lines as well as bamboo and greenheart rods. Small changes to late-nineteenth-century tackle produced large transformations in fishing techniques. Tackle like tapered, dressed silk lines, better rod materials manufactured with industrial methods, and the development of reels ushered in modern dry fly fishing. Improved gear allowed anglers longer, more precise casting and with the widespread incorporation of false casts, fly fishers could cast dry flies upstream into the wind.[67] Dry fly fishing represented an exciting method of floating flies on the water's surface, letting anglers watch more of the action. While present-day fly fishers rarely use bamboo rods or silk lines, they directly inherited these techniques, elevating dry fly fishing to almost mythic proportions. Growing up in a religious Montana family, fly fishing's bard, Norman Maclean, once imagined that Christ's disciples were fly fishermen, and "that John, the favorite, was a dry-fly fisherman."[68] This much-cherished dry fly tradition arose out of the tackle revolution caused by nineteenth-century industrialization and global capitalism.

The utilization of silk and silkworm gut in tapered fly lines and leaders marked a new era in casting. For centuries, European and American anglers had used horsehair braided and knotted together. Because it was easily obtainable from local sources, anglers often made their own lines from stallion tail hair (preferred over that of mares because urine weakened the strength of mare tail hair). Despite its handy acquisition, horsehair lines required multiple knots and the lines tended to fray, both of which hampered casting long distances.[69] The growth of the European silk industry and fashionable middle-class silk clothing, like the stylish bird hats, brought fly fishers better line material. By the eighteenth and nineteenth centuries, European and American anglers had slowly started incorporating silk into lines and silkworm gut into leaders, sometimes placing both silk and horsehair in the same line.[70] Before the post–Civil War development of a large and sophisticated American tackle industry, one American guidebook suggested a mixed line of hair and silk, imported from London.[71] Shortly thereafter, another American angler noted the increasing popularity of silk lines, which could be "imported from China, Spain, and Italy."[72] Coated with oil, dressed silk lines floated remarkably better than horsehair. Tapered and plaited by modern machines and strung onto modern rods, silk lines permitted nineteenth-century anglers to cast distances unimaginable to their horsehair-flinging ancestors.[73]

Tackle makers fashioned modern fly rods from exotic woods that were also available through world trade. In the mid- to late nineteenth century, trout rods became increasingly shorter and lighter, built with new materials such as greenheart and bamboo. Anglers could cast farther with these new rods and refined tackle, changing the sport itself and how people fished. American anglers frequently fished with split bamboo rods. Rod makers used bamboo species (a type of grass) from Calcutta and later Tonkin.[74] Alternatively, English anglers preferred greenheart rods, imported from imperial holdings in British Guiana, over split bamboo into the twentieth century. In addition to dynamic new materials, the fabrication of rods changed. Split bamboo rod makers created impressive fishing instruments through better machinery and planing techniques that allowed them to remove rough bamboo nodes, split the cane into six strips, then glue it back together.[75] Indeed, the era's best rod makers, like the famed Hiram Leonard, applied advances in machinery and newer industrial techniques to their craft. While Leonard catered to an upscale clientele like Lewis "Bourgeois" France, other manufacturers mass produced split bamboo,

The grasshopper in this whimsical versal letter from a chapter on angling for children in Genio C. Scott, *Fishing in American Waters* (New York: Harper and Brothers, 1869), 198, appears to be of leisure-class origins from his garb, but the rough nodes on his bamboo rod show a time before modern machinery and planing techniques transformed fly rods during the tackle revolution. Manuscripts, Archives, and Special Collections (MASC), Washington State University Libraries, Pullman.

making it more accessible to American anglers.[76] With these new rods, fly fishers casted farther and more accurately than before.

Tackle makers took other cues from the machine age to refine hooks and create better reels. Inventions abounded in an era of steel skyscrapers and railways, and growing industry in the United States, England, and Germany. Typewriters, telephones, lathes, and sewing machines all promised to make life easier, so much so that one contemporary observer remarked that mechanization was unbridled "like one of our mighty rivers."[77] In this era of rampant industrialization, tackle makers produced better hooks and modern reels. They made stronger hooks by using better finishing methods.[78] One modern rediscovery, the eyed hook, made dry fly fishing much easier. Previously, fly tiers tied silkworm gut directly onto the hook, then constructed the fly, a cumbersome, not-so-durable method. One late-nineteenth-century dry fly guru attributed successful dry fly fishing to eyed hooks.[79] As with hooks, the modern fishing reel came directly out of industrialization. Reels, like other mechanized inventions, benefited from better machining and gears.[80] Charles Orvis's 1874 patent marked modern reel technology as Orvis and his British and American counterparts designed reels that have changed little since then.[81]

In this world of mechanized leisure, Richard White has observed that Americans held an Emersonian outlook, embracing nature and machines at the same time: "Emerson reconciled nature with the busy, manipulative world of American capitalism. . . . Emerson could simultaneously rejoice in the ability of the machine to subjugate and control nature and in the

FISH AND TIDE IRRESISTIBLE.

Nineteenth-century Americans often embraced both the machine age and leisure. Genio C. Scott, *Fishing in American Waters* (New York: Harper and Brothers, 1869), 57. Manuscripts, Archives, and Special Collections (MASC), Washington State University Libraries, Pullman.

spiritual truth and inspiration nature provided."[82] Holding an Emersonian perspective, anglers embraced the machine-age inventions that ushered in dry fly fishing, the celebrated fishing method of Norman Maclean and favored disciples.

The rise of dry fly fishing ironically caused the decline of showy fancy fly patterns and the need for exotic feathers. Fly fishers usually tied dry flies as imitators (insect doppelgangers) meant to mimic adult insects floating on top of the water. Thus, the need for outrageous color schemes and exotic materials abated. Starting in the mid-nineteenth century, anglers on southern English chalk streams fished the modern dry fly, institutionalized with Frederic Halford's 1886 publication of *Floating Flies and How to Dress Them*.[83] Halford's practical, no-nonsense approach provided readers with the basic knowledge to tie and fish dry flies. The patterns described and illustrated in the book lacked all resemblance to their fancy fly cous-

Modern yet simple dry fly patterns from Frederic Halford's important book, *Floating Flies and How to Dress Them: A Treatise on the Most Modern Methods of Dressing Artificial Flies for Trout and Grayling with Fully Illustrated Directions and Containing Ninety Hand-Coloured Engravings of the Most Killing Patterns Together with a Few Hints to Dry-Fly Fishermen* (London: Sampson Low, Marston, Searle, and Rivington, 1886), plate 1. Manuscripts, Archives, and Special Collections (MASC), Washington State University Libraries, Pullman.

ins. Smaller flies with olive, gray, and toned-down colors dominated the plates and Halford explicitly stated dry fly fishing equaled the imitation of natural insects: "To define dry-fly fishing, I should describe it as presenting to the rising fish the best possible imitation of the insect on which he is feeding in its natural position."[84] The insistence on imitation meant fly tiers needed fewer exotic bird feathers. While Halford did mention some rare bird feathers, he privileged native birds and dyeing techniques.[85]

While the dry fly revolution came a bit later in the United States, it also quickly outdated colorful fancy flies. In America, the introduction of nonnative trout also prompted the dry fly's use; fly fishers needed less vivid feathers and flies to trick wary trout. As more selective feeders, the European brown trout that had naturalized in many American waters required fly fishers to refine their techniques.[86] In the Catskills, Theodore Gordon developed local dry fly patterns as he fished for both native brook

Frederic Halford followed the seminal *Floating Flies* with his later *Dry Fly Entomology*, which provided readers with practical information on insect life, like the mayfly nymphs carefully diagrammed here, and ways to copy it with imitator fly patterns. Halford, *Dry Fly Entomology: A Brief Description of the Leading Types of Natural Insects Serving as Food for Trout and Grayling with 100 Best Patterns of Floating Flies and the Various Methods of Dressing Them*, 2 vols. (London: Vinton, 1897), plate 1. Manuscripts, Archives, and Special Collections (MASC), Washington State University Libraries, Pullman.

trout and nonnative brown trout. Often deemed the father of American dry fly fishing, Gordon helped popularize the technique in eastern waters during the 1880s and 1890s. Contributing to both American and English sporting periodicals on fishing techniques and conservation, Gordon later addressed the decline of exotic birds. He called for bird preservation, arguing that fly tiers needed access to only a handful of feathers "in spite of the many tropical birds mentioned in all of the old books on salmon fly dressing."[87] He believed that local and domesticated birds provided more use to fly tiers, especially to those creating dry flies. Gordon's own fly patterns reflected this view. Dressed with a stripped peacock body, wood duck wings, and a dun-colored hackle, his Quill Gordon pattern imitated an adult mayfly of similar color. Somber by comparison, dry fly patterns quelled the need for flashy feathers while new lines, hooks, rods, and other tackle made it all possible.

As members of the leisure class capitalized on industrialization and imperialism, they consumed goods to demarcate class. They also used their political and economic sway to promote angling for conservation, classifying other fishing techniques as illegal poaching. Just like sporting ideals, early conservation regulations spread through empires. In the Rocky Mountains, territorial legislatures passed the first regulations that limited fishing, especially for trout and other game fishes, to use of a "rod and line" or "hook and line." These hook-and-line laws, which limited catches to one fish at a time, reflected the sporting ideals and political influence of a transnational angling community concerned with dynamite, nets, and other fishing methods of Native Americans and non-elite settlers. With the growth of sport, similar conservation regimes sprouted up throughout American territories and states (the government entity responsible for fish and game regulations) and the British realm.

Some of the earliest manifestations of angling laws came from eastern states. Ardent fly fisherman and silver-tongued politician Daniel Webster passed an 1822 Massachusetts law that prohibited fishing for brook trout with all but hook and line. As the sole bill introduced in his term as a state legislator, the sporting statute represented Webster's angling ethics, a sentiment shared by sportsmen throughout the world.[88] In Britain, where fish conservation came more from private landowners than the state, hook-and-line regulations existed only as informal ordinances. With the increasing popularity of nineteenth-century sport fishing, landowners found more money in charging elite anglers and middle-class sporting clubs than in renewing fishing leases for commercial fishermen using nets, weirs, and other gear. Middle-class angling clubs often rented waters, unable to afford individual leases on prime trout and salmon waters.[89] Often these clubs fixed rules as to the gear and methods, some of which became highly specific and restrictive over time.[90]

British settlers also brought angling regulations to the colonies, but conservation varied by colony. In New Zealand, where local acclimatization societies principally controlled fish and game matters, regulations bore the sporting ethics of the settlers who constituted these societies. Acclimatization societies imported new flora and fauna as well as enacted hook-and-line laws. Like other anglers, they regarded other fishing methods and devices as "unsportsmanlike."[91] In India, settlers used state power to set forth a fish conservation agenda and, like elsewhere, it reflected sporting ethics. Colonial officials often considered themselves sportsmen and criticized traditional indigenous uses of wildlife as unsporting and destructive. One official called for more state regulation over freshwater fisheries, lamenting both the resistance of other colonial officials and the techniques used by local fishers: "Every device that can be imagined is now called into action . . . the rivers are denuded of fish, so far as human agency can contrive it."[92] Prejudices such as these became incorporated into later conservation codes. Another colonial official wrote both sporting books and fisheries regulations in India. One of the first laws, the Bengal Act II of 1889 allowed angling, but limited public access to fisheries, laying the foundation for later laws. Subsequent laws that included the entirety of India outlawed dynamite and poison, but legalized nets.[93] Angling laws within fish conservation showed the prejudices and inequalities inherent in imperialism.

As American expansion progressed and people started settling the inland West, driven by gold strikes in the Rocky Mountains, territorial assemblies laid the foundation for the later development of a trout culture. Early on, legislatures enacted laws that restricted fishing methods to the use of a hook and line. Soon after one hundred thousand miners overran the Colorado goldfields, the newly created Colorado Territory outlawed fishing by "seine, net, basket, or trap" in 1861 and clarified the law in 1872 to prohibit fishing for cutthroat trout with all but hook and line.[94] Aimed at native fishing techniques, this first law attempted to limit the indigenous fishing with government regulations. Not so coincidentally, Lewis B. France served as a clerk to the House Judicial Committee in that first legislature.[95] Neighboring territories followed Colorado's lead in territorial fish conservation, using similar language. Wyoming Territory enacted a hook-and-line law in 1869.[96] Utah's 1876 territorial legislature restricted fishing to "hook and line not exceeding three hooks to a line."[97]

Territorial legislators attempted to control fish destruction, but transformed sporting ideals to meet territorial conditions. Early Montana settler Granville Stuart illustrates the role of locals in early western conservation. At Montana's first territorial capital of Bannack, no more than a muddy, ramshackle mining camp that sprang up near the rich gold deposits along Grasshopper Creek, the first legislature outlawed fishing with nets, seines, and poisonous substances. The law also stated that "a rod or pole, line and hook, shall be the only lawful way trout can be caught in any of the streams of the territory."[98] Stuart represented Deer Lodge County in that first legislature. However, his role in passing the regulation remains unclear. Brothers Granville and James Stuart occasionally fished, among their various other pursuits as early Montana settlers. The Stuarts laid claim to one of the first gold strikes in southwestern Montana. As was common during the territorial period, Granville Stuart wore a variety of hats, in this case holding territorial offices, mining, mining the miners, trading, running cattle, playing vigilante, and writing pioneer history.[99]

As their joint diary reveals, the Stuarts also liked to fish. Granville recorded that they observed the Fourth of July, 1863, by feasting on trout: "James and Clabber, our Indian horse herder, caught twenty-five large trout and we celebrated the national day by having a fine dinner with trout as the principal dish."[100] A couple days later, Granville himself fished with grasshoppers as bait, catching thirty-five trout.[101] The diary says nothing about the type of gear, but the brothers and their horse herder certainly used a baited hook and line. The cultural mixing through fishing, intermarriage, and other territorial activities confirmed that race was less important before statehood.[102]

As territorial elites, Stuart and others brokered sporting values on a local level. Briefly living in Helena in the early 1880s, he worked for longtime friend, banker, sportsman, and later territorial governor Samuel T. Hauser. While there, Stuart served as president of the Helena Rod and Gun Club and became concerned with the decline of bison and the widespread hide trade.[103] During the same time period, Stuart also introduced a failed bill in the state legislature that would have established the state's first fish hatchery.[104] Stuart's actions show sporting values informed territorial conservation, but it was a complicated situation of fish use and conservation.

While expressing sporting ideals, hook-and-line laws also reflected community values in some locales. One US Fish Commission scientist noted that at Panguitch Lake, Utah, Mormon settlers had self-imposed hook-and-line regulations, prohibiting other methods "by common consent."[105] The widespread roots of angling for sport and for subsistence meant that angling laws could only try to temper larger fish catches, not outlaw fishing altogether. The value of Bonneville cutthroat as food prompted settlers to regulate their own subsistence and market use, in this case, allowing settlers to take only one fish at a time. The community-centered angling rules reveal an interesting sharing of conservation ideals among classes. To the reporting scientist, however, the regulation of methods proved inadequate: "This, however, is no hardship, since large captures are easily made with the hook, I myself having taken from thirty to forty pounds weight in a single hour's fishing."[106]

By the end of the nineteenth century, imperialism and industrial capitalism transformed the ways in which many people fished. These forces connected the Rocky Mountains with the rest of the world while aiding a tackle revolution that incorporated both new manufacturing techniques and colonial natural resources. Class inequalities manifested themselves in reshaping fly fishing gear, affordable only to some, while simultaneously allowing a leisure class in western nations to escape from the modern world into nature. Part of a transnational community, nineteenth-century anglers placed new meanings on their fishing methods and modern tackle, adding to a long history of angling. Leisure-class anglers employed gender ideals and new gear from the tackle revolution to set themselves apart from lower classes, immigrants, and nonwhite races who relied on fish for food or cash. As leisure-class anglers attempted to assert their power, they came across other practitioners of hook-and-line fishing, illustrating how elite sport could have only limited control over others.

Sporting ideals provided the headwaters of conservation regulations and environmental change in the Rocky Mountain West. For leisure-class anglers, sport equaled conservation. The limitations they placed on catching fish (the "sport"), as well as their time on the water, led them to find conservation solutions in the growing power of governments. While the territorial era angling laws went largely unenforced from the 1880s to the 1920s, the rise of state conservation transformed Rocky Mountain fisheries. Yet, at the regional level, leisure-class anglers never entirely controlled or defined conservation.

Trout Empire

I N 1885, A YOUNG OWEN WISTER TRAVELED TO A RANCH ON THE
Wyoming frontier to restore his health. From an elite eastern family,
the recent Harvard graduate, who had befriended Theodore Roosevelt at the university, had not yet become a famous writer. After suffering an illness that resembled that pesky neurasthenia, Wister set off west
to recover. He spent weeks hunting and fishing, wrangling, and drawing
in the western experience. The expanse of country surrounding Medicine
Bow and the characters he encountered there provided the material he later
used to write *The Virginian* (1902). The novel helped to create the cowboy
as the American archetype of freedom and rugged individualism.[1] Since
then, the West has loomed large in American popular culture, allowing
the nation to define itself through (white) progress, self-reliance, and freedom while obscuring the region's complicated and contested development.

Despite Wister's role in romanticizing western history, he witnessed
the region amidst large economic, environmental, and social changes.
During the nineteenth and early twentieth centuries, the Rocky Mountain
West became swept up in a global rearrangement of people and power—
and, incidentally, trout. Industrialization, better transportation and com-
munication networks, and steam transportation led to the development of
the West, as railroads shipped people, goods, and creatures to and from
the Rocky Mountains.

During that first Wyoming trip, Wister accompanied his host, cattle-
man Major Frank Wolcott, to pick up cans of live bass and trout at the
Medicine Bow rail station so they could plant the fish in nearby streams.
Wister described the unsuccessful journey home in his diary: "We started
off across the plains at two o'clock. At three we discovered we had lost our
way—but found it inside of thirty minutes. On the way home the sun killed
the trout, but the bass survived."[2] Their attempt to stock streams failed

even with willing labor and the railroad's ability to transport live fish long distances. Yet, Wister's story sheds light on the early contours of a trout culture and economy that involved not only the physical transformation of fish life, but also the composition of new meanings written onto these places. As part of an eastern elite concerned with the ills of civilization as well as the masculinity of its members, Wister envisioned the West as a vanishing rugged frontier while using it as an outdoor playground.[3] The latter simplified western history as much as Wister's cowboy hero. While fish never made an appearance in *The Virginian*, trout represented part of the late-nineteenth-century story in which westward expansion and industrialization transformed nature and leisure in the Rockies.

This chapter follows the attempts to physically and culturally rewrite the western landscape, starting with the western hatchery system that developed from the conservation movement and the transnational evolution of fish culture.[4] With the intention of saving fish, leisure-class anglers hoped to control the fishing practices of others, but as territorial angling laws indicated, they often did so through the lens of race, class, gender, and national identity.[5] In the midst of the conservation movement, they espoused limited catches defined by sporting ethics. Unlike the anti-democratic themes present within *The Virginian*, however, western fisheries show that the rise of state conservation had both elitist and non-sporting characteristics. In Wister's masterwork, the Virginian himself, the unnamed hero, emerged as a natural leader, an aristocratic cowboy in which Wister projected his class fears while attempting to naturalize class inequalities. The Virginian could wrangle cattle and lead men, just as the social status of Harvard-educated elites like Wister supposedly made them superior to lower classes.[6] In the Rocky Mountains, a more complicated story arose, as the sporting elite did not entirely define fish conservation.

For better or worse, western fish conservation has been connected to sport in interesting and complex ways. From the 1880s to the 1910s, numerous private, state, and federal fish culturalists and enthusiasts introduced nonnative brook, rainbow, and brown trout, prized sporting species. Fish culture work also brought about new regulations aimed at protecting fish, but these laws did not develop strictly from an elite sporting agenda. Sport fishing and subsistence fishing continued to exist simultaneously into the twentieth century. Regulations did garner resistance and did affect rural residents, but state power remained incomplete and opposition did not necessarily fall along class lines.[7] Locals rejected state conservation at times because it actually lowered fish populations or threatened the local fishery. Above all, state fish conservation developed gradually in the Rocky Mountain West; new laws and regulations therefore did not produce immediate, drastic changes to the lifeways of American Indians, settlers, and immigrants.[8] In the long run, these characteristics garnered even more support for state conservation. Over time, conservation work had lasting environmental effects, as Rocky Mountain waters developed into world-class nonnative trout fisheries.

The conservation movement expanded during the second half of the nineteenth century, as many Americans began to confront environmental problems stemming from the growth of industrial capitalism. George Perkins Marsh's bestselling *Man and Nature* (1864) provided a key text for those seeking to remake interactions with nature. Marsh's work as the Vermont fish commissioner trying to save the state's declining fisheries as well as his time abroad as an American diplomat (he spoke twenty languages fluently) provided him with the material to write a voluminous book on human destruction of the environment.[9] Marsh examined forestry, floods, soil erosion, fisheries, and other topics, using the environmental ruin of Europe and its ancient empires as an example to Americans. More than just a catalog of environmental decline, Marsh maintained his faith in humans and science and offered various solutions, including the artificial propagation of fish, a key factor in creating Rocky Mountain trout fisheries. After the book's wide publication, the conservation movement gained ground in the United States.

Hatcheries and human reproduction of fish became an important solution for declining fish populations, separating fish conservation from other aspects of the conservation movement. Later generations would discover that hatcheries provided an expensive way to cause declines in wild fish populations, but in the late nineteenth and early twentieth centuries, it represented an important solution to ailing fisheries. Fish culture and trout introductions found support among conservationists and the general public, who believed hatcheries had the capacity to save fish while creating better fishing.

Fish culture previously existed for thousands of years, but the nineteenth-century development of hatcheries and the artificial propagation of fish marked a new way of producing fish for human use. Ancient Chi-

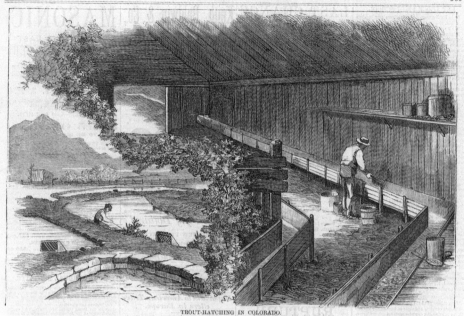

TROUT-HATCHING IN COLORADO.

nese, then Romans and their later counterparts, often raised fish in ponds or transported live fish to different waters. Artificial propagation of fish separated hatcheries from these early fish culture efforts. All hatcheries operated in similar ways. Fish culturalists first captured live spawning fish from the wild and took their eggs or milt (fish sperm). After collecting and mixing the eggs and milt, fish culturalists either shipped the fertilized eggs elsewhere or incubated them in a controlled environment with running water. The water temperature depended on the species of fish.[10] After hatching, the small fish (alevins) fed off yolk sacs attached to their body, but, as they grew, the yolk sacs disappeared and the small fish (now called fry) needed to be fed at the hatchery. Fish culturalists then planted the fry into depleted waters. Hatcheries also kept their own brood stocks of adult fish in larger ponds or raceways at the hatchery for later egg and milt collection, while supplementing frequently these stocks with egg collection from the wild. Hatcheries required clean running water, a fair amount of daily labor, fish food, and a belief in human superiority over nature. Hatcheries could transform nature's perceived inefficiency into a veritable

A *Harpers Weekly* article in 1874 about trout hatcheries in Colorado. Denver Public Library, Western History Collection, Z-3832.

An illustration showing how to collect fish eggs for hatchery use. Thaddeus Norris, *American Fish-Culture, Embracing All the Details of Artificial Breeding and Rearing of Trout: The Culture of Salmon, Shad and Other Fishes* (Philadelphia: Porter & Coates, 1868), unnumbered plate.

fish factory (France's first state hatchery was literally called a "piscifactoire"[11]). This production method for fish became incorporated into the conservation agenda, although conservation represented just one of the varied goals of fish culturalists.

Guided by a firm belief in progress, American fish culture enthusiasts first promoted hatcheries for repopulating depleted waters, increasing profits to agricultural producers, and providing a food source for the growing nation. The promises of the hatchery system prompted a rise in popularity. A reverend turned fish culturalist, Livingston Stone saw fish culture less as a factory system and more as an animal husbandry technique in which producers could profitably raise trout for market and bring down food prices.[12] On top of its money-making potential, fish culture could save declining fish populations, according to early conservationist and sporting writer Robert Barnwell Roosevelt and prominent fish culturalist Seth Green.[13] The lucrativeness of hatcheries encouraged a rise in private efforts during the mid-nineteenth century, including a venture from Samuel Colt, whose Colt .45 took on legendary proportions in the West, but his mid-nineteenth-century construction of a Connecticut hatchery received comparatively little notice as one of many such establishments.[14]

In the Rockies, fish culturalists often advocated for improvement of sport and leisure. During the western territorial period, fish culture remained a mostly private venture among a diverse group of individuals, with private hatcheries and stocking efforts both prevalent. Officer-sportsmen represented the vanguard in the transformation of Rocky Mountain waters. Not surprisingly, as enthusiastic anglers and western boosters, officer-sportsmen promoted western fish culture. One of the earliest Montana trout plantings took place near Fort Assiniboine around 1880, when soldiers reportedly stocked Beaver Creek, a favorite camping and picnicking destination for them and their families.[15] In Yellowstone National Park, angler and acting superintendent Captain Frazier Boutelle personally took responsibility for the development of fish culture there. An invitation to US Fish Commissioner Marshall McDonald to visit the park in 1889 led to US Fish Commission scientific studies and trout introductions. David Starr Jordan explained that McDonald believed more trout would attract visitors to Yellowstone: "It was made very evident from the observations of the Commissioner that much could be done towards enhancing the attractions of the great national park 'pleasuring ground' by the stocking of those of its various streams and lakes which are now destitute of fishes."[16] While 40 percent of the park's waters did not originally contain fish, trout introductions led to more fishing opportunities for tourists.[17]

Other individuals who promoted western fish culture varied from farmers and ranchers seeking to supplement incomes by raising food fish in ponds, to businessmen, lawyers, and doctors wishing to create more local sporting opportunities, and to military men and government officials who wanted to improve regional attractions like Yellowstone National Park. For instance, Owen Wister's first host, Major Frank Wolcott, took part in fish culture activities. Wolcott also helped found the politically powerful Wyoming Stock Growers Association. Composed of elite ranchers and politicians, the association—just like the Virginian—used violence to gain control of Wyoming ranges. Wolcott himself helped lead a group of hired detectives and vigilantes against smaller cattlemen they deemed "rustlers" during the Johnson County War of 1892. Wolcott's gang failed in their intended takeover after being surrounded by Johnson County residents and were only saved from probable death by being arrested by the

US cavalry.[18] For Wolcott, settlement and economic development meant not only controlling the range but also remaking the landscape for sport.

By the 1880s and 1890s, much of the burden for the production of trout shifted to state and federal agencies. Following France's lead, US hatcheries became a government enterprise, connected to the rhetoric of national greatness and economic independence in trying to feed a growing nation.[19] Despite the patriotic overtones, more practical and economic reasons also explained the shift to government-run hatcheries. Roosevelt and Green maintained that fish culture needed government aid because of the patchwork of ownership along streams as well as the legislation necessary to protect fish from water pollution and dams.[20] In response to such issues as well as the high costs of hatcheries, both state agencies and the US Fish Commission took up hatchery work in the United States. Their actions mirrored the growth of fish culture work throughout the world. As the first commissioner of the fledgling Fish Commission (and a protégé of George Perkins Marsh), Spencer Baird noted that most European nations as well as colonial holdings such as India, Java, and Australia already engaged in fish culture.[21] By the early twentieth century, even more nations, like Japan and Argentina, operated hatcheries.

In the Rockies, the US Fish Commission and state agencies expanded on the work of private enthusiasts. In order to acquire nonnative brook trout and brown trout for a new federal hatchery in Spearfish, South Dakota, (which also served the inland trout fisheries of the mountain states), the superintendent looked no further than the nearby creek to collect fish for the hatchery brood stock.[22] Many westerners also lobbied for the construction of these hatcheries not only for the conservation and sporting benefits, but also for the economic gains. Longtime Colorado Senator Henry M. Teller ran a private hatchery in Gilpin County and helped obtain key appropriations for the first western federal hatchery near Leadville.[23] By the early twentieth century, the US Fish Commission had built three trout hatcheries that served the region, in Leadville, Colorado (the second federal hatchery in the entire nation); Bozeman, Montana; and Spearfish, as well as various substations and egg collecting stations at points throughout the West, including at Yellowstone National Park and along the Madison River.

Between 1880 and 1908, Rocky Mountain states also built their own trout hatcheries to preserve fish populations and to encourage tourism and economic growth. A new fishing licensing system after 1900 chiefly bankrolled state hatcheries. State officials justified the fees by arguing the small cost of licenses created more fish because it paid for hatchery work.[24] License fees allowed state fish commissions (the precursors to modern fish and game departments) to expand their hatcheries. By the mid-twentieth century, the Rocky Mountain states each ran somewhere between ten and fifteen different hatcheries, most of which produced nonnative rainbow, brown, and brook trout and native cutthroat trout. Illustrating a common justification, one Utah official argued that a state hatchery would benefit residents for recreation purposes, as well as bring in tourist dollars:

> . . . with a capacity to hatch from 1,000,000 to 2,000,000 of trout fry per year, which could be placed in the numerous streams of the State with the most gratifying results, as a source of pleasure, recreation and food for the ever-increasing number of our citizens who go annually into the

The transformation of western fisheries involved nonnative trout introductions and new ideas of leisure in mountain scenery. Both photographer William Henry Jackson and artist Thomas Moran illustrated the sublime western landscape for eastern audiences. In this photograph, Moran (right) fishes Goose Creek near Sheridan, Wyoming, in 1892. Photograph by William Henry Jackson. Courtesy of History Colorado (William Henry Jackson Collection, scan #20101159).

mountains and canyons camping for the purpose of seeking health and
pleasure for themselves and families during the summer months. And if
our mountain streams were kept well stocked with trout, and our game
protected from inordinate slaughter, they would become, in a few years,
an alluring attraction for tourists, health-seekers and sportsmen from
other states, which would result in considerable revenue to our State
from this source, as the class of people who seek this kind of pleasure and
amusement are generally wealthy, and willing to spend their money lav-
ishly to get good fishing and shooting.[25]

The official pointed to the financial benefits reaped by Colorado and Wyoming in creating a tourist industry based upon good fishing, while lamenting that Utah residents increasingly sought fish and game in neighboring
states because of dwindling wildlife populations.[26]

Fishing served as a popular activity for Yellowstone National Park tourists. Before being
outlawed, anglers at Fishing Cone in Yellowstone Lake often tried to catch a fish from the lake,
then cook it in the hot spring while the fish was still on the line. Photograph by William Henry
Jackson. Courtesy of History Colorado (William Henry Jackson Collection, scan #20102762).

The popularity of western fishing prompted the introduction of non-native trout. In this photograph, anglers fish from a boat in a mountain lake. S. N. Leek Collection, American Heritage Center, University of Wyoming.

A man fishing from horseback. S. N. Leek Collection, American Heritage Center, University of Wyoming.

Hatchery work often quickly transformed western waters. Here, a young girl poses with a nonnative lake trout. S. N. Leek Collection, American Heritage Center, University of Wyoming.

A Utah state fish hatchery in 1908. Used by permission, Utah State Historical Society, all rights reserved.

Even as a government undertaking, hatcheries relied on western industrialization and labor from thousands of enthusiasts. Railroads played a key role in introducing nonnative trout to the Rocky Mountain West. While the first known Colorado fish introduction took place when seven sunfish were brought overland by oxcart in 1862, very few fish introductions occurred before the railroads.[27] Railroad companies freely hauled fish eggs and fry to their destinations, sometimes in specially outfitted "fish cars" designed to transport live fish. Fish car crews ensured the fish stayed alive, adding ice periodically to keep the water cool, as well as aerating the water to supply needed oxygen. Both federal and state governments owned fish cars. The US Fish Commission purchased its first fish car in 1881 and had four in operation by 1893, all traveling across the nation delivering fish and fish eggs for free to applicants.[28] Applicants received telegrams ahead of time to meet the train at the station. Sometimes they received only a "forced to plant en route" telegram; if the fish looked distressed or started dying, fish car or railroad employees would dump the cans of fish in the nearest body of water along the tracks. If the fish did arrive, the applicants then hauled the cans of fish by wagons or on horseback to their destinations in nearby waters and, like Wolcott and Wister, hoped that the fish would not die along the way. Assorted people took advantage of the US Fish Commission application process, ensuring popular support for the hatchery system.

In addition to labor and steam transportation, the development of western trout fisheries also depended upon national and transnational processes. Within the worldwide spread of fish culture, experts traded knowledge, techniques, and sometimes personnel. The nineteenth-century exchange of scientific thought, technology, and trout occurred in the midst of the great transatlantic migrations; approximately fifty million people left Europe in the nineteenth and early twentieth centuries. Many went to the United States, Argentina, Canada, New Zealand, Australia, and other prime trout habitats.[29] American fish culturalists gained new scientific findings from foreign hatcheries and exotic fish eggs, including European brown trout, the most prevalent fish currently in western rivers. Both private fish culturalists and the USFC under Baird's leadership routinely translated works from French, German, Russian, and other foreign fish culturalists.[30] Immigrants trained at European universities also brought their knowledge to the Americas. German immigrant Rudolph

Hessel, for instance, oversaw the US Fish Commission's short-lived carp program.[31]

Hatchery expertise and fish life flowed both in and out of the Rocky Mountains. In 1903 and 1904, the Argentine government employed two former US federal fish culturalists to help start a new federal hatchery program. One of these men previously worked as the fish culture division chief and the other was E. A. Tulian, an ex-superintendent of the Leadville hatchery in Colorado.[32] The US Fish Commission (which became the US Bureau of Fisheries in 1903) frequently shipped fish eggs outside of the country, including rainbow trout and brook trout eggs, during the late nineteenth and early twentieth centuries. These transnational exchanges remade the world's coldwater fisheries such as Rocky Mountains waters into nonnative trout fisheries.

Sport linked these environmental changes. Federal hatcheries had both political and sporting connections. A self-styled gentleman angler, Dr. James A. Henshall became the first superintendent of the Bozeman hatchery in 1896. Henshall invariably sported a starched shirt, stiff collar, and bold mustache throughout forty years of portraits. The doctor became a conservationist and fishing writer (best known for his *Book of the Black Bass* published in 1881). During Henshall's thirteen years at Bozeman, the station propagated native grayling and cutthroat trout, as well as introduced brook trout and rainbow trout to the area.[33] The angling officials of the USFC like Henshall played a significant part in Rocky Mountain trout introductions. Their work in creating sport fisheries proved effective over time. In Colorado, brook trout had become so numerous by 1904 that the US Fish Commission collected more eggs from streams near Leadville than it had from eastern waters in its native range. A large demand also existed for rainbow trout eggs among western applicants.[34]

But why trout? First, fish culturalists found it relatively easy to propagate trout in hatcheries compared to other fish species. The three most widely introduced trout species had widespread populations in the nineteenth century, from various brown trout morphs native to Europe and western Asia and brook trout found throughout eastern North America to rainbow trout with abundant native populations along the Pacific Coast of North America and the Kamchatka peninsula in Russia. These large ranges made it easy for many fish culturalists to collect spawning trout eggs and milt from nearby streams.

Second, anglers enjoyed the aesthetics of trout fishing. Allured by the sport, taste, and attractiveness of trout of all species, anglers throughout Europe, the United States, and colonial holdings played a key role in the creation of worldwide trout fisheries. One British angling writer and acclimatization promoter wrote that of all freshwater fish "there is none which affords so wide-spread and great an amount of sport to the angler as the [brown] trout."[35] His American counterparts celebrated the introduction of European brown trout, made through German and British connections to US Fish Commission scientists.

American fish culturalists also promoted and distributed their own native fish, including brook trout and rainbow trout. Livingston Stone explained in 1873 that brook trout was a popular freshwater game fish due to its food and game qualities as well as its ever important beauty: "He surpasses all other fish in grace of form, in beauty of coloring, in gentleness of expression, in fascination of manner, in gameness of spirit, in sweetness and firmness of flesh, and in general personal attractiveness."[36] The esteem for brook trout was later overshadowed by that for rainbow trout. In *American Food and Game Fishes* (1902), renowned fisheries scientists David Starr Jordan and Barton Warren Evermann discussed the distribution of popular game species throughout North America and the world. They observed that anglers considered rainbow trout "the greatest of all game-fishes" because of its "beauty of color, gracefulness of form and movement, sprightliness when in the water, reckless dash with which it springs from the water to meet the descending fly ere it strikes the surface, and the mad repeated leaps from the water when hooked." Such surprisingly flowery sporting values often privileged nonnative trout over native cutthroat varieties in Rocky Mountain states. Some anglers championed cutthroat trout, but in the nineteenth century they were a minority. Jordan and Evermann noted that most anglers saw various cutthroat varieties as "inferior in gaminess to the eastern brook trout."[37] As charismatic species, trout had many proponents.

Third, nineteenth-century conservationists sought to introduce species they saw as better suited to changing environments, operating under the assumption of the interchangeability of trout species.[38] Their early successes with trout introductions only affirmed these views. Rainbow trout can live in slightly warmer water and are easier to propagate in hatcheries than other trout. These characteristics, and its popularity as a game fish, gave rise to the spread of rainbow trout throughout the world.[39] Eastern fish culturalists often observed pollution and rising water temperatures due to industrialization and timber cutting. In these transformed environments, they believed rainbow to be more suitable: "[Rainbow trout] will serve stocking streams formerly inhabited by the brook trout (*Salvelinus fontinalis*), in which the latter no longer thrives, owing to the clearing of the lands at the sources of the streams, which has produced changed conditions in and along the waters not agreeable to the brook trout's wild nature. The rainbow is adapted to warmer and deeper waters."[40] While brook trout could no longer survive in the transformed environment of their native range, the species thrived in western waters. One federal official even believed brook trout were more fit for the Rocky Mountains than even native fish: "Observations at this station [Leadville, Colorado] point to the superiority of the brook trout over all others for Colorado waters, native varieties not being excepted."[41] From this viewpoint, native fish, like native peoples, represented relics to be swept aside by the white expansion across the continent. In terms of native fish, the foundational assumptions that guided settlement also shaped hatchery work.

Informal sporting codes and new laws accompanied hatchery activities. Leisure-class anglers played an important role in defining fish conservation and engaging in fish cultural activities. If their societal status provided them with an element of escape, their time on the water also brought the leisure class closer to the environmental degradation that followed the rise of the market economy and industrialization from which they benefited. Their first-hand experiences on the water prompted many anglers to support the late-nineteenth-century conservation movement. In the rise of conservation sentiment, European and American anglers incorporated ideas of self-control and limited catches to promote their sport, using print culture to disseminate ideas across the Atlantic and throughout colonial holdings.[42]

Throughout the nineteenth century, anglers proclaimed sporting ethics that imposed voluntary restrictions. Due to anglers' varied motivations and the awareness of rivers and fish populations, catching large numbers of fish was not necessarily important for the sport. British chemist and inventor Humphry Davy, for instance, advised fellow anglers to release smaller fishes under two pounds: "If every fish that took the May-fly were to be killed, there would be an end to the sport in the river, for none would remain for next year."[43] American anglers fostered similar values. One influential American angler insisted sport was not about taking fish, but about the pleasure derived from it, "not with the value or numbers of the victims, but with the difficulty of the capture, and the degree of skill, science, courage, or endurance, called forth in the act of taking."[44] Colorado gold rush lawyer and sporting writer Lewis B. France echoed British and eastern American views that anglers should temper their fish catches, stating, "The true sportsman does not go down stream and afield for the mere love of killing something."[45] Robert Barnwell Roosevelt wrote extensively on fishing and conservation in eastern North America during the 1860s and 1870s, arguing it was important to save fish "from total destruction."[46] Roosevelt and other sportsmen played an instrumental role in the 1871 creation of the US Fish Commission, the first US government agency to address conservation issues.[47] Conservation principles like the restrained use of resources had roots in sporting ethics, but anglers also disagreed on the extent of its role in the sport.

In the late nineteenth century, anglers debated the meaning of conservation within sporting periodicals such as *Forest and Stream*. Rocky Mountain anglers contributed to these discussions. "Millard" from Ariosa, Wyoming, defined the sport by its conservation principle, stating, "The essence of good angling is not to catch too many."[48] Similarly, if anglers kept an improvident catch, other sportsmen could censure them for waste. "Shoshone" bragged in an 1887 article about his fishing party's extravagant catches in Nevada. The group of upper-class men from Salt Lake City reportedly caught 100 trout before lunch and kept fishing through the afternoon. By the day's end, the party's most productive member caught well over that number alone. The group's luck may have been precipitated by a golden stonefly (large yellow insects) hatch, which usually tapers off by mid-afternoon: "The best results for the day were obtained by Mr. Beo. B. Brastow, of Salt Lake, who, with a Leonard split bamboo rod and three-fly leader, landed 133 fine trout. His favorite flies were the grizzly-king, brown-hackle, and royal-coachman. The yellow-bodied gray-hackle did good work in the morning, but seemed worthless after 2 o'clock."[49] A fellow angler quickly wrote in to the periodical, criticizing the wastefulness by asking, "What could these five sportsmen do with 150 to 200 lbs of trout out in the wilds of Nevada, having a larder already well stocked with game, in the month of August? Comment seems unnecessary."[50] Anglers argued in print culture over conservation within the sport and monitored each other, regardless of locale.

Print culture could also be employed on a more local level, reinforcing community values of moderate catches rather than elite sporting ideals. The local paper in the mining (now ghost) town of Ruby City, Idaho, called attention to the trout "fishing mania" sweeping the town in July 1868. The editor also used the opportunity to reprehend three men for taking too many: "We couldn't get a bite, for the reason that Jack McQuaid, Bill Gabriel and Dave Jackson bought up all the fishing tackle in town and went out there with a pack train yesterday and they wont [sic] leave a fish. Let us have a fish law passed next Legislature providing against such indiscriminate fish slaughter."[51] Like leisure-class anglers, rural residents also used print to gain support for conservation and check on community fish use. The example points to the complex development of western fish conservation, one in which sporting ethics did not solely define the conservation agenda.

Between 1890 and 1920, new regulations and better enforcement paralleled the rise of the western hatchery system, as fish culturalists quickly realized that they had to do more than just plant fish or catch fewer to maintain high populations. Westerners, however, accepted government control of conservation only on their terms. States enacted a host of new regulations to address fish declines, but these laws remained fairly lax.

At the turn of the century, mountain states had only small forces of game wardens, allowing residents to easily bypass fish and game laws if they wanted. Wyoming did not have an actual game warden until 1899. The law stated that the warden could appoint forest rangers as game wardens and assistant game wardens for counties, but only so long as he received a petition signed by fifty residents.[52] As such, early fish and game laws needed community assistance for enforcement, demonstrating an early disdain for many conservation regulations. A Swedish immigrant named Albert Nelson served three years as Wyoming's first game warden, attempting to enforce fish and game regulations for the entire state. As a young boy, he developed a fascination with the frontier after reading James Fenimore Cooper's *The Leatherstocking Tales*. After his parents died, he traveled to America and worked his way out West, landing in Wyoming. Once there, he worked variously for the railroad, on a ranch, as a guide, and later homesteaded. During his term as game warden, Nelson made numerous arrests, but he never achieved a conviction.[53] The next Wyoming state warden had a larger force, but the patrols only made twenty-three arrests and got twenty convictions.[54] Surrounding states had similar levels of enforcement, demonstrating that the rise of state conservation in the Rocky Mountains only slowly took root and did not immediately change how residents interacted with nature.

Other states also lacked strong game warden forces. After statehood in 1889, Montana law allowed county commissioners to hire one game warden per county, but no counties actually hired game wardens and ten years later only four counties had done so. Not until 1901 did the state finally hire its first game warden, who promptly hired eight deputies.[55] The first Idaho state game warden took his job in 1899 and relied on a force of unpaid county wardens who received part of the fine if there was a conviction. He noted that Ada, Custer, and Shoshone counties did not even bother to appoint wardens because it was "impossible to secure persons to act."[56] The Idaho state warden lamented the widespread disregard for fish and game laws: "Public sentiment seemed largely against the punishment of offenders, and convictions were almost impossible even for the most flagrant violations."[57] With earlier settlement and larger populations, Utah and Colorado had slightly bigger forces, but still had problems enforcing game and fish laws. In the late 1890s, the Utah state game warden observed a refusal among certain counties to appoint game wardens or turn in lawbreakers: "Eight counties only, out of the 27 in the State have reported violations of the Fish and Game Law in the last two years."[58] Utah, as well as Colorado, relied heavily on volunteers from sportsmen's clubs to help catch fish and game law violators. Even with volunteer forces, enforcement problems ran rampant. The small game warden forces which patrolled notably large geographical areas—the five states have a total area over 500,000 square miles, or roughly 327 million acres—exemplified the early lack of state authority in fish and game matters. The absence of control meant that game wardens relied on help from various classes to catch offenders.

Middle-class sportsmen and women, working-class fishermen, and lower-class rural residents turned in fish law transgressors. For instance, one Utah man disapproved of his brothers surreptitiously seining fish out of the Weber River at night and finally informed the state game warden of their activities after they refused to stop.[59] Rocky Mountain game wardens relied heavily on citizens reporting violations. The extra help revealed more than just a concern for preserving rivers and fish life. Nativism and racism also sometimes shaded public assistance and state enforcement of conservation laws.[60] In the Rocky Mountains, enforcement concerns arose over Indians, Japanese, and European immigrants. Some states even required expensive fishing licenses designed specifically for foreigners. In the early 1900s, a Utah game warden reported success in convicting "Japanese and foreign laborers" for fishing without licenses.[61] The uneven enforcement and targeting of certain groups exposed some important difficulties in the rise of state conservation.

A POACHER.

A poacher, as imagined by Genio C. Scott in *Fishing in American Waters* (New York: Harper and Brothers, 1869), 152. Manuscripts, Archives, and Special Collections (M A S C), Washington State University Libraries, Pullman.

Enforcement had other problems, as not all game wardens proved to be model patrolmen. Some game wardens received their job by political appointment, others violated laws themselves or neglected their duties. The gubernatorial appointment of game wardens became highly politicized. Political parties, sportsmen's clubs, and even labor unions routinely pressed governors and state game wardens to appoint their men to positions or endorsed game warden candidates.[62] Other game wardens failed to properly enforce game laws. One Utah fish commissioner criticized a county warden in 1911 for sleeping on duty.[63] The same commissioner had problems with a different county warden the next year, who reportedly fished closed waters while drunk, then bragged about it.[64] In Montana, one deputy game warden extorted money from a coal mining company along the Yellowstone River in return for not turning them in for violating pollution laws.[65] The small forces of not necessarily model patrolmen ensured that state conservation needed local advocates, otherwise people could skirt around the laws.

The laws, however, remained fairly lenient, illustrating that the gradual shift to government-led conservation did not abruptly end local fish use. State regulations accommodated subsistence fishing by the lower classes, showing that conservation regulations were not as transformative as larger economic changes in the West. To start, those early, unenforced territorial hook-and-line laws made no restriction on the amount of fish caught by angling. When states finally enacted creel limits, clearly stemming from sporting ideals and aimed at market fishing, they remained high enough to not impair subsistence fishing. In 1903, Wyoming set a daily catch limit at twenty pounds.[66] A 1909 Montana law restricted anglers' catches to twenty-five pounds per day.[67] By 1912, Utah had a fifteen-pound creel limit.[68] The allowances for fish continued to be high throughout the first half of the twentieth century. In 1921, Wyoming set its creel limit to fifteen pounds per day, and continued at this level for at least another twenty years.[69] Additionally, these creel limits were often intended to protect only trout and other "game" species, excluding other species like suckers. Utah's state game warden wanted the open season to be amended in 1901 because people used the open season to fish for trout under the guise of fishing for other species like suckers and chubs.[70] The liberal allowances permitted westerners to continue fishing for food throughout the twentieth century, one of the reasons why fishing remained popular among broad sections of society. These high catch limits, however, demonstrated that the evolving western economy and connections to national markets were probably more to blame than the rise of state conservation for the decline of subsistence use of fish and game. By the early twentieth century, rising incomes, shifting forms of labor that did not provide the time, and refrigeration and supermarkets all reduced subsistence fishing.

Some fisheries regulations, however, restricted fishing more rigidly than the lax creel limits by prohibiting fishing for parts of each year. In the intricacies of new conservation regulations, however, some lower-class locals criticized what they saw as class-based laws while others supported these stricter regulations. Before states created creel limits, they established fishing seasons to guard against overfishing as well as protect spawning fish. Some territories outlawed fishing between late fall and late spring. For example, an 1886 Wyoming law closed fishing from November 1 to June 1.[71] These seasons sometimes became a point of contention among local people, but they could also be ignored. In 1915, a newspaper publisher in Kellogg, Idaho, complained to the governor that a "great number of people" fished during the closed season, taking advantage of the fact that no game warden had been appointed to the region.[72]

Locals did more than resist controversial laws. They also became politically involved, asserting their right to decide fish and game matters. During the same year that Kellogg residents reportedly violated the closed season, Blaine County, Idaho, residents sent a petition to the governor asking him to veto a bill that would close fishing from November to June. They saw the measure as elitist: "This provision is more for the preservation of the fishing in the interests of a few city sportsmen, who would deny the right to the rural population to take fish at a time of year when they are not too busy to go fishing. The winter season is not the best time of year to fish and what few fish are taken at that time does not in any manner deplete the supply."[73] The petition reveals a clear class division as well as a concern among the lower classes to maintain fish populations. From this viewpoint, locals supported conservation, but on their own terms.

Not all rural residents opposed seasons or state regulations, even if seasons were less equitable than high creel limits. In 1916, for instance, the Farmers Union of Bonner and Boundary Counties, Idaho, wanted the Sandpoint hatchery to raise lake whitefish (important for their food and commercial value) and the state to enact a closed season yearly between September 1 and December 1.[74] These farmers sanctioned the same strict laws, hoping to benefit from abundant fish populations for food and perhaps market.

Some westerners rejected the class-based aspects of state conservation regulations. Yet with the growth of state-led conservation, resistance came from broad segments of society. Some opposition to conservation came not from local subsistence fishermen, but from the middle and upper classes, suggesting an early manifestation of the familiar western distrust of government. Fish commissioners and game wardens constantly complained about cases being dismissed by judges and county attorneys who refused to prosecute violators. The Wyoming game warden noted continuing problems in 1919 and 1920: "When these parties are taken before a Magistrate they are turned loose or fined and then the fine is remitted."[75] The Idaho state game warden earlier observed the apathy on the part of those responsible for prosecuting offenders: "Despite adequate evidence, prosecution has been seemingly lax. This is especially true in instances where the law breakers have been prominent citizens."[76] Utah experienced the same problems. County attorneys often "refused to prosecute cases" or judges imposed very small fines that fell under the minimum set by law.[77] The middle-class and elite rejection of state conservation through their refusal to prosecute cases pointed to a complex reasoning regarding the acceptance of and resistance to conservation regimes. In Colorado, the commissioner noted that county politics and some concern for fellow locals encouraged people to ignore disliked fish and game laws.[78] Local elites may have also resented government interference in what was seen as a local matter.

In addition to the loose enforcement and prosecution of fish laws on the part of local elites, many violators came from the ranks of the middle- to upper-class residents or tourists who rode the rails. In 1906, the Idaho state warden reported that a deputy warden "arrested three prominent citizens of Spokane, Washington, for fishing without licenses." The wardens used the embarrassing moment to sell more non-resident fishing licenses, which "materially increased" after the arrest of the respected Spokane men.[79] In the same way that elite anglers criticized immigrants, nonwhite races, and lower classes for contributing to fish declines, rural residents often attacked well-off outsiders (derided as "dudes") for needlessly keeping too many fish or game. The Colorado counties that had large game herds held strong local sentiment against market hunting and helped to enforce laws. In these counties, the state fish and game commissioner reported that locals believed the "game laws were made for the city 'dudes' and 'tourists' generally and not for the ranch men and other residents of these counties."[80] These Colorado residents, then, saw conservation regulations as supportive of their own community conservation sentiments, providing them with motivation to help game wardens catch outsiders who violated game laws.

Other aspects of the state conservation agenda remained in tune with the ideology of community-centered conservation. In the Rocky Mountain West, conservationists were forced to negotiate the industrialized western economy. In 1889, USFC scientist David Starr Jordan reported that Colorado mining polluted trout streams: "In some cases placer-mining and stamp-mills have filled the waters of otherwise clear streams with yellow or red clay, rendering them almost uninhabitable for trout. Parts of the upper Arkansas and Grand Rivers have been almost ruined as trout streams by mining operations."[81] In Montana, Barton Warren Evermann found little to no fish life in the Deer Lodge Valley due to the smelting and mining operations in upstream Butte and Anaconda.[82] Similar reports came in from all parts of the West. In response to these conditions, many fish culturalists believed protecting fish translated into protecting waters.[83]

Fish culturalists often called for strengthened water pollution laws. James A. Henshall took up the cause of water pollution both before his tenure at the Bozeman hatchery and after, when he edited and regularly contributed to a monthly column on the topic for the Izaak Walton League's *Outdoor America* in the early 1920s. In 1890, he cautioned fish culturalists to take "proper care and protection of the fish *and the water.*" Henshall blamed a variety of industrial sources for polluting eastern waters, from manufacturing and factories to sawmills and timber cutting, seeing it as not only a legal issue, but also an ethical one: "No man, or company of men, have the moral or legal right to pollute or poison the waters of any flowing stream."[84] To keep waters clean and save fish, he called for more legal protections. Following examples set by eastern states, western states established regulations to curb water pollution during the late nineteenth century.

Rocky Mountain fish laws attempted to address some of the concerns over market use of fish and the destruction of fish within the western extractive economy. States enacted laws that prohibited the sizable timber industry from dumping sawdust and poisonous materials in rivers, required dams to have fishways and irrigation ditches to have screens, and passed other statutes that combated declining fish populations due to industrial causes. The regulations attempted to stop pollution and environmental degradation from mining, the timber industry, and agriculture. Most inland western states also banned commercial fishing in some form.[85] Unfortunately, like some of the other laws, they were hard to enforce; in 1897, one Montanan complained of men "trout fishing and selling, in the open market, which is against the law."[86] These aspects of the state conservation agenda mirrored earlier community-centered conservation ethics, which often rejected individuals and corporations seeking to profit by using or harming public fish and wildlife. Like other fish conservation regulations, however, pollution laws went largely unenforced.[87] The lack of enforcement for environmental protections created tension between local populations and government agencies.

In some cases, like the collapse of fish populations caused by Sunbeam Dam in Idaho, locals rejected state conservation because it was ineffective in conserving fish populations or it actually caused declines. In central Idaho, the 1914 construction of the Sunbeam Dam by the Sunbeam Mining

Company cut off fish spawning runs to major tributaries and lakes in the upper Salmon River area near Stanley, subsequently ending both subsistence fishing and the region's burgeoning tourist industry. Locals looked to the Idaho Fish and Game Department to construct proper fish ladders for the dam, writing letters and sending petitions to various governors for over twenty years. Two years after construction, the county prosecutor joined in the fight, writing to the Idaho governor about the defunct fish ladder. He included a photograph of a rickety and broken wooden fishway and went on to say that the blocked fish runs hurt both local subsistence and the tourist economy: "The entire Stanley Basin country get practically all of their fish through the Salmon River and owing to the fact that this country is a great tourist country, for the entire Southeast, it is a matter in which we are all very much interested."[88] The letter articulated that a broad segment of the population stood to gain from effective fish conservation and locals around Stanley looked to the state for a solution.

Another citizen also complained about the lack of action over Sunbeam Dam: "I have repeatedly requested you to investigate the condition of the fish ladder at the dam . . . but up to date there has been nothing done. Your fish ladder has always been a farce and from all indications the Office of Game Warden should be abolished and the protection of game and fish left to the people."[89] In this case, this irate citizen saw the state lack of action as farcical and believed community-led conservation would better save fish. The local outcry continued until 1934, long after the Sunbeam Company went bankrupt, when the Idaho Fish and Game Department finally blew apart most of the dam with dynamite.[90] The remnants of the Sunbeam Dam, along with a healthy distrust of government, remain today. The outrage in the upper Salmon River country over the dam blocking fish runs shows that resistance to state conservation came from many levels for many reasons, including the fact that state conservation often proved ineffectual.

Many of the complaints surrounding fish conservation arose over the fish declines caused by the yearly egg-collecting activities of state and federal hatchery workers during spawning time. Hatcheries usually kept fish as brood stocks to continue producing fish, but they also operated egg-taking stations on rivers and lakes with large fish runs to supplement these stocks. Most yearly egg-collection efforts took hundreds of thousands or sometimes millions of eggs from spawning fish, leaving little for natural reproduction. Local residents often resented the accompanying fish declines. In the 1910s, for example, egg-collection efforts near Idaho Falls that led to declining fish runs incensed local businessmen concerned with the loss of tourist traffic and area trout fishing.[91] Many states also constructed traps and weirs to catch the spawning fish; these met resistance from locals because they blocked both spawning runs upstream and fishing access.

Federal egg collection near the Leadville hatchery exemplified the problems of egg collection. During the 1890s, hatchery employees built weirs at Twin Lakes to block yellowfin cutthroat (unique to these lakes) from migrating into streams during spawning season, then took eggs from the captured fish. The lack of spawning runs pushed locals from their traditional fishing grounds. They reacted by forming posses and attempting to dynamite the weirs, a sign of the gravity of the situation.[92] Leadville locals fought for what they believed was a customary right to the fish and highlighted the failures of state conservation to actually conserve and propagate more fish in certain instances (comparatively, at a Yellowstone egg-collection station, problems came not from irate locals, but from grizzly bears[93]). As it turned out, the Leadville residents were right. When the US Fish Commission discontinued yellowfin cutthroat egg collection in 1898 on account of declining populations, it was already too late.[94] The cutoff spawning runs combined with the introduction of rainbow trout into Twin Lakes spelled the end for the yellowfin cutthroat trout. By the early twentieth century, yellowfin cutthroat trout were extinct.[95] The mistakes of federal and state agencies in saving fish life supplied important, but often ignored, critiques of government resource management. Locals could be dismissed as backwards, especially those pitchfork-wielding Leadville fishers. Stemming from a variety of reasons, their resistance sometimes shaped state efforts and sometimes was overlooked by state "experts."

In the Rocky Mountains, state-run fish conservation eventually transformed regional waters into remarkable, and mostly nonnative, trout fisheries. In narrating their achievements in introducing trout to the region, fish culturalists celebrated the success of conquest itself. In 1912, one federal official looked back on the work accomplished, boasting that the intermountain West "is today the angler's paradise." He based his Edenic descriptions primarily on the existence, ironically, of nonnative fish: "Colorado and Wyoming's reputations are upheld largely by the magnificent rainbows found in the larger streams. Brook trout have become so plentiful and widely distributed that many people are inclined to think them indigenous."[96] Wister reminds us, however, that these trout fisheries did not spring up overnight, but slowly found success.

During the rise of government-sponsored conservation from the 1880s to the 1910s, hatcheries and more detailed fishing regulations transformed Rocky Mountain fish life. This growth of state-led conservation offered a complicated history. Westerners of all classes and groups sometimes resisted elite control of resources, sometimes resisted government jurisdiction, and sometimes resisted government inadequacies in preserving fisheries. Additionally, elite sportsmen did not solely dictate the agenda of state conservation, as broad segments of the public also lent their support or voiced complaints. This advocacy and the slow development of state management helps to explain the remarkably democratic character of later western trout conservation that assisted in the protection of regional rivers and fish from continued environmental degradation.

In the years following the Great War, social transatlantic connections declined. Guided partially by these earlier exchanges, the environmental transformations of the nineteenth and early twentieth centuries laid the foundation for creation of a Rocky Mountain trout culture from the 1920s to the 1950s. While western waters could be described earlier as paradise, it was not until this later time that a strong trout-fishing culture, and an economy based on it, flourished. The successes of trout introductions and this new regional economy yielded a key justification for western hatchery expansion from the 1910s to the 1930s. This enlarged system further remade Rocky Mountain rivers and lakes. As western hatcheries grew, so did the regional boosterism that sold western waters as fishing destinations. During the mid-twentieth century, anglers, conservationists, and boosters shaped the inland West into a trout place, illustrating both the environmental changes and the cultural compositions that created place and region over time.

Trout Culture

IS THERE REALLY A TED TRUEBLOOD?" ASKED OUTDOOR HUMOR-
ist Ed Zern in the October 1962 issue of *Field & Stream*. In his comi-
cal "exposé" of Trueblood, Zern told readers that *Field & Stream*
editors concocted the popular Trueblood character, developing the per-
sona because no one in real life spent most of their time hunting and fishing. Zern then described an imaginary conversation with the magazine's
editors, who made up the too-good-to-be-true name, his "All-American"
family who hunted and fished with him, the town of Nampa, Idaho, and
even Trueblood's famed bird dog Joe to begin "an editorial hoax that
has lasted nearly two decades." The article quickly sparked controversy,
outraging some of Trueblood's faithful readers who failed to recognize
Zern's tongue-in-cheek humor—and the fact that Nampa, Idaho, actually
existed.[1] Amused by the whole affair, Ted Trueblood remained one of the
most widely-read outdoor writers of his time.

As the magazine's longtime fishing editor, Trueblood exemplified the
prevalence of western fishing during the early to mid-twentieth century.
Born in Boise in 1913, Trueblood grew up on a nearby homestead, and like
many westerners, came of age in the outdoors. He eventually landed a job
at *Field & Stream*, enabling him to write while spending the majority of his
time in the rivers and mountains he loved, often accompanied by his wife
Ellen, two sons Dan and Jack, and of course the bird dog Joe. As a popular columnist, Trueblood captured the imaginations of new generations of
anglers, especially in the Rocky Mountains, by promoting western fishing, making fly fishing accessible, and advocating for conservation and the
protection of rivers. His columns in the 1950s frequently defended catch-
and-release fishing and wilderness ethics.[2] By promoting western fishing,
Trueblood helped form a Rocky Mountain trout culture.

Taking advantage of the trout introductions and conservation framework built during the previous era, westerners and anglers like Ted True-blood helped to develop a New Western regional identity and economy based on nonnative trout fishing and outdoor recreation from the 1920s to the 1950s. During these years, scientists and government professionals, anglers, outfitters, and regional boosters generated a western trout aesthetic that, despite its local character, paradoxically privileged nonnative trout. The realities of a trout place held significant environmental costs for ignored western native fish that continually declined throughout the twentieth century.

With help from the automobile and magazines like *Field & Stream*, Rocky Mountain fishing and tourism became ever more prominent starting in the 1920s and again after World War II. Like Ted Trueblood and his all-American family, countless others in the West spent their extra time outside; during this era, one-quarter to one-third of residents in Rocky Mountain states bought fishing licenses each year, in addition to numerous tourists, making western fishing remarkably popular.[3] The creation of regional fly fishing traditions as well as a growing tourist economy marked the importance of nonnative trout in this transition, while fishing books and booster materials sold the West and its fish to tourists and newcomers. The additional fishing pressure spurred state and federal agencies to expand the western hatchery system and shift stocking practices to ensure plentiful trout fishing. By the 1950s, the Rocky Mountain trout culture was complete, resulting in the transformation of almost every single lake, river, and creek in the Rocky Mountains that could sustain trout. A trout culture, indeed.

The previous trout introductions and fish cultural work of the nineteenth and early twentieth centuries added to the popularity of western fishing. At the turn of the twentieth century, westerners fished frequently, heading out on nearby streams, rivers, and lakes for recreation and the sometimes added bonus of dinner. Before the widespread use of the automobile in the 1920s, many fished near home or relied on available modes of transportation like horses or the railroad. In the 1910s, the Utah fish and game commissioner noted the popularity of fishing in Salt Lake City and the surrounding region:

> It has been a most common occurrence to see men and women on street cars, having been for an afternoon only on a trip for recreation, and possessed of a successful catch. On the railroad trains, on the wagon roads,

Anglers relied on the available forms of transportation to get them to the river. Here, a group of men fish the South Platte River with makeshift poles; a couple of them hold bicycles. Photograph by Charles S. Lillybridge. Courtesy of History Colorado (Charles S. Lillybridge Collection, scan #20002305).

in the canyons and over the country generally, people on camping trips, all have fishing tackle and fish also. The country stores in all of the counties carry a stock of fishing tackle, because people are delighted to fish.[4]

Various people fished throughout the West. From Coeur d'Alene, residents frequently took weekend or Sunday trips on a steamer around the lake or connected to the St. Joe and St. Maries rivers.[5] Kellogg area locals also customarily fished on Sundays; one observer noted it was a "usual outing."[6] Other western anglers rode trains to their favorite fishing spots. Sunday excursion trains (often called fishing trains) with affordable fares embarked from cities and towns throughout the West like Denver, Butte, and Great Falls. The Butte train headed south along the Big Hole River, often carrying upwards of 500 passengers on summer Sundays. Dillon, Montana, anglers fished the Beaverhead River through town or frequently took the southbound train to the river's upper stretches, hopping off at

A fish train along the Rio De Las Animas River in Colorado. An African-American porter stands in the background while white leisure seekers fish and sit on rocks. Photograph by William Henry Jackson. Courtesy of History Colorado (William Henry Jackson Collection, scan #20103593).

A fish train near Chipeta Falls in the Black Canyon of the Gunnison, Colorado. Photograph by William Henry Jackson. Courtesy of History Colorado (William Henry Jackson Collection, scan #20103612).

the tiny platform called Grayling Station, which was named after the good grayling fishing in that section of the river. After fishing, the anglers flagged down the northbound train to get back into town.[7] While fishing near home remained popular among a variety of people, only leisure-class tourists could afford the expensive rail fares for a western vacation during the railroad era.

Lured by aggrandized railroad advertising, these tourists sought trout as enthusiastically as local anglers. Railroads sold western trout fishing to wealthy easterners looking to escape during the industrial age. This boosterism contributed to ideas of place that connected the Rocky Mountains with trout, starting an advertising campaign that snowballed in the coming decades. Railroad circulars started a publicity campaign that connected the West with nonnative trout. The best fishing, of course, depended on which line tourists traveled. The Colorado and Southern Railway championed the Colorado trout streams that ran along its lines.[8] The Great Northern believed the "finest of trout fishing is to be found in western Montana, Idaho and Washington."[9] And the Union Pacific argued Wyoming had "the finest trout fishing to be found anywhere on the globe."[10] Nineteenth- and early-twentieth-century railroad booster literature commonly emphasized the West's romantic beauty and the opportunity to escape to places filled with trout and game, but empty of people and the trappings of civilization.

One booklet from the Union Pacific Railroad advertised trout fishing in Colorado and Wyoming by following the story of an eastern business-man who identified himself more as a fly fisherman than a desk clerk. Clearly aimed at a middle-class, male, eastern audience, it sold escapism through the thrill of catching trout in a romanticized nature: "With such beatific visions whirling in his head, the impatient angler closes his book, and, with a long-drawn sigh, turns back to the work-a-day world, to await the arrival of the hour when he may again sally forth in the pursuit of his favorite pastime—trouting in the enchanting fastnesses of the Colorado or Wyoming wilds."[11] The narrative followed the listless businessman as he restored himself on a trout fishing vacation, conveniently along the lines of the Union Pacific. In Wyoming, his fishing party relied on the guiding services of "a rugged Swede," Henry Olson, to row them down the river, while the businessman engaged in a masculine, life-and-death struggle landing a large trout. The fishermen likened themselves to the manly guide while discounting the sporting prowess of the party's women. One picture showed three women holding the stringer of trout they caught. The cap-tion reads, "A String of Speckled Beauties—The Fish, I Mean."[12] The pic-ture demonstrated that the women, in their formal attire, could catch fish while maintaining proper gender boundaries. The author, however, chose to emphasize how fishing could seemingly restore masculinity, in order to sell more rail tickets.

As did many of the railroad pamphlets, the Union Pacific booklet described the region, the rivers, the game laws, and travel accommoda-tions, while assuring readers that hatchery activities ensured well-stocked streams filled with both native cutthroat and nonnative rainbow and east-ern brook trout. The author mustered up some pretty lofty language—even for booster literature—to describe the trout fishing: "There is nothing like it. Trout fishing is a symphony; all is harmony; one can enjoy the sky, the air, the mountains, the pines, the tackle and the fish. It is the highest branch of the delicate art."[13] With varying degrees of extravagant descriptions, this and other railroad circulars sold the region as a trout-fishing destination.

Railroads and their agents also helped transform western fisheries in the mid- to late nineteenth century, making it easier to introduce nonnative rainbow, brown, and brook trout across the region. Railroad companies transported fish eggs and fry at free or reduced rates and sometimes even requested that state agencies introduce trout along their lines. For instance, the Northern Pacific Railroad sought to get Lake Pend Oreille stocked with a variety of fish other than just the native trout, in order to make the area more attractive to tourists in the early twentieth century.[14] Railroad employees and ticket agents also doubled as liaisons to anglers who rode the fishing trains, sending in fishing reports to nearby cities or applying for fish to be stocked. In the early 1900s, the passenger agent for the Denver and Rio Grande Railway applied yearly for cutthroat or brook trout from federal hatcheries, planting them in the nearby waters like the Provo River.[15] Railroads did not promote trout fishing out of some kind of corporate benevolence—they also hoped to profit from tourist fares and publicized Rocky Mountain fishing.

The widespread introductions and environmental manipulation that attracted railroad tourists, however, took their toll on native fish populations. Some fish culturalists and resource managers started to rethink the hatchery system during the twentieth century. Their concerns went largely unheeded in the midst of a burgeoning trout culture and economy. In 1918, an aging, nearly blind Dr. James A. Henshall read a paper from a young, then unknown federal forester named Aldo Leopold. Leopold's paper was short, simple, and characteristically visionary. During his time in the Southwest, Leopold noticed that various nonnative trout had been "indiscriminately mixed" with native cutthroat trout, leading to hybridization and infertility, as well as brown trout feeding upon other species and "becoming predominant."[16] These observations led to new trout-stocking rules within national forests in Arizona and New Mexico. The guidelines set forth that appropriate species should go in suitable waters and multiple species should not be stocked together. Leopold placed high value on native fish: "Stocked waters will not be further mixed. Restock with the best adapted species, *the native species always preferred.*"[17] Eventually, these ideas developed into his land ethic, which placed humans in a community of life in which decisions needed to go beyond economics, as Leopold stated in *A Sand County Almanac*: "Examine each question in terms of what is ethically and esthetically right, as well as what is economically expedient. A thing is right when it tends to preserve the integrity, stability and beauty of the biotic community. It is wrong when it tends otherwise."[18] Leopold represented one of many twentieth-century anglers and resource managers who questioned the haphazard introductions of nonnative trout demanded by many anglers and tourists.

Former Bozeman hatchery superintendent James A. Henshall also worried about the fate of native fish as rainbow, brook, and brown trout started to comprise the majority of fish populations in Rocky Mountain waters in the twentieth century. Aldo Leopold's "Mixing Trout in Western Waters" inspired Henshall to rethink his time in the West and his role in transforming the fisheries of the upper Missouri River basin. Long since gone from Bozeman and his hatchery job and now living back in Cincinnati, writing his autobiography for *Forest and Stream* and devoting his time to water pollution issues, Henshall lamented the decline of native fish, particularly arctic grayling and westslope cutthroat trout, due to various reasons, not in the least, the introduction of new fish species. He also questioned his part in introducing nonnative trout, stating, "There was no good reason or valid excuse, except that applicants asked for brook, rainbow or steelhead trout, and they were supplied."[19] Henshall's extensive knowledge—"an angling experience of seventy years, and an experience of fifty years as a fish culturalist and naturalist"—gave him an almost unparalleled perspective of the field. He believed Leopold's ideas mirrored "all practical fish culturalists who have given the matter earnest thought and consideration."[20] The experiences of Henshall, Leopold, and others reveal that nonnative trout varieties had already started to surpass native cutthroat trout populations and that trout were not as interchangeable as once imagined by earlier generations of fish culturalists.

Fish managers learned hard lessons in the decline of cutthroat trout and tried unsuccessfully to combat the problem with hatcheries. By the 1920s, yellowfin cutthroat trout were gone. Henshall recalled that westslope cutthroat had already become scarce in Bridger Creek near the Bozeman hatchery by the time he left in 1909.[21] Other cutthroat subspecies' populations throughout the Rocky Mountains started to decline by the early to mid-twentieth century, with their ranges restricted to headwaters and mountain streams. To address the problem, state fish managers continued to stock cutthroat trout, which further intermixed hatchery or nonnative varieties of cutthroat trout with the unique cutthroat trout subspecies found in the West's different watersheds. Federal fish culturalists also reared more cutthroat trout. One fish culturalist observed in 1930 that the species had declined throughout its range and called for the establishment of a hatchery brood stock.[22] Likewise, the US Bureau of Fisheries continued to annually take three to twenty million cutthroat eggs from Yellowstone National Park in the early twentieth century. During the early to mid-twentieth century, most fish agencies continued stocking native and nonnative trout, focusing most of their attention on supplying popular rainbow, brown, and brook trout for a demanding public. The National Park Service, however, provided a notable exception—the only federal or state agency chiefly concerned with native trout in the rise of the Rocky Mountains' trout culture and economy.

The National Park Service created a progressive native fish policy within park borders starting in the 1930s in response to its agency mandates as well as native fish declines within national parks and throughout the West. Fears of hybridization of cutthroat and rainbow trout as well as a desire to protect the last holdouts of native fisheries and barren waters prompted the park service to curtail nonnative fish stocking.[23] But by the time the NPS reversed its native fish policy in the 1930s, nonnative trout had already established themselves in Glacier, Yellowstone, Rocky Mountain, and other national parks after decades of trout stocking. Of course, park service management need not be romanticized either. From the late 1920s to 1932, Yellowstone employees turned to smashing pelican eggs to lower the numbers of pelicans eating trout, trout reserved for tourists, not pelicans.[24] Even with a forward-looking native fish policy, national park managers continued to manipulate fisheries for visitors during the twentieth century, while surrounding states and other federal agencies embarked on predominantly nonnative trout policies.

Environmental change stemmed from the increasing importance of trout among growing numbers of western anglers and tourists. With the rise in automobile ownership during the 1920s, fishing became more democratic. Better standards of living, higher incomes, and the advent of affordable automobiles allowed more Americans to spend time and money on leisure and to enjoy living the good life sold by an increasing consumer culture.[25] In the adventurous spirit of the Roaring Twenties, many Ameri-

Automobiles democratized fishing in places farther from home, but the growing numbers of anglers also alarmed fisheries managers. In this photograph, two men pose in a Stanley Steamer automobile with a fishing pole. Photograph by L. C. McClure. Denver Public Library, Western History Collection, call #MCC-998.

Auto camping and fishing in the Big Horn Mountains, Wyoming. Hugo Janssen Photographs, American Heritage Center, University of Wyoming.

cans drew on their new economic prosperity to head outdoors. The automobile democratized this new travel and tourism, providing better access to regional trout and rivers.[26]

Western anglers and tourists could look for trout farther from home with automobile travel and its accompanying western road building. Tourists increasingly headed to national forests: "The increased use of automobiles by touring parties, and the movement to construct good roads through the forest reservations are causing more people to seek the reservations each year, and angling is one of the principal attractions."[27] Cars made tourism and outdoor recreation even more populist.

In the early to mid-twentieth century, the rise of western fly fishing traditions came out of the popularity of fishing and its increasing importance in the western economy. At once cosmopolitan and provincial, fly fishing has both international roots and a distinctive regional approach in the Rocky Mountains. Fly fishing may seem western but it dates back centuries, even millennia, with diverse origins in Europe, Japan, and elsewhere. Yet despite its international lineage, fly fishing by its very nature engenders a uniquely local character. A fly fisher's choice of flies depends largely on local conditions; seasons and weather, water conditions, the time of day, and various other factors all help determine insect hatches and corresponding flies.

While sporting goods stores and tackle shops existed in scattered towns and cities at the turn of century, their numbers grew in the 1910s and 1920s. The expanding numbers of anglers provided jobs for numerous professional fly tiers, who developed regional fly fishing customs. Relying on local and regional experiences, western tiers created homegrown traditions. Westerners frequently weaved hackles and fly bodies or incorporated readily available deer and elk hair into flies; the hair provided useful buoyancy in swift mountain waters and became a hallmark of Rocky Mountain fly patterns. Many western flies imitate stone flies, abundant insects in regional rivers. Many westerners fish differently, often using weighted nymph patterns and large streamers beneath the water's surface, a method considered by many easterners (and dry fly snobs, for that matter) as just short of poaching.[28] In Missoula, former wigmaker Franz B. Pott patented the handwoven bodies and hackles in his popular "Mite" series of flies in 1925.[29] Montana anglers fished the complex woven flies frequently and other professional fly tiers like Butte's Wilbur "Bugs" Beaty and George F. Grant and Livingston's Dan Bailey created their own versions in later years.[30] Fly shops and regional tying traditions continued to evolve from the 1920s to the 1940s.

As this industry grew, so did its advertisements and boosterism. In the 1920s and 1930s, local and state governments sold road building and the expansion of western infrastructure to tourists. They often promoted trout fishing and outdoor recreation, extolling the conveniences of newly built roads and highways. One 1940 Montana brochure opened up to a picture of Glacier and other typical tourism scenes. A key attraction proved to be the abundant fishing: "Montana has 32,000 miles of trout streams, 4,600 miles of improved highways."[31] Advertisements had to balance these connections with their portrayals of a wild West, drawing a fine line between modern conveniences and rugged western experience waiting to be had. A later Wyoming tract dealt with the dilemma by promoting both: "More than 20,000 miles of streams and over 5,000 lakes make Wyoming a fishing paradise. . . . Your car will take you right to the well-stocked water's edge. Or you can venture into seldom-fished wilderness areas."[32] Other states portrayed their hatchery system as yet another modern amenity. An Idaho pamphlet unabashedly claimed that Idaho had "more fish and game than any other state," publicizing the millions of trout, from native cut-throat to nonnative rainbow, brown, and brook trout, stocked yearly in major rivers and their tributaries.[33] In selling the West, regional boosters catered to tourists' desires, whether they be modern amenities or nostalgia for an imagined past. Environmental changes like road building and the growing hatchery system offered important attractions.

Like boosters, sporting writers also sold Rocky Mountain trout. The vast body of angling literature written over the last two centuries prompted one sporting commentator to wryly observe that "some of the best fishing is done not in water, but in print." In the twentieth century, many of these books connected the Rocky Mountains to trout fishing. In *Some Western Fishing* (1926), W. W. Crosby argued that rainbow and brook trout fishing in Glacier National Park and in Colorado surpassed trout fishing anywhere else in the world.[34] Similarly, Bertram D. Lackey's *Outwitting Trout with a Fly: Letters of a Western Angler* (1929) promoted fly fishing and western conservation through an Izaak Walton–style dialogue between two anglers, describing the various native and nonnative trout species available to California anglers.[35] In the years following, other authors, including Zane Grey, continued to write about western fishing, selling the region to tourists and novice anglers.

With the growing cultural and economic importance of trout, fish managers expanded hatchery activities, stocked more and larger trout, and continued their control over nature to ensure good fishing. The increasing numbers of anglers and their use of the automobile both alarmed fishery managers and affirmed their work in the 1920s. One federal fish cultural-ist blamed cars in his belief that "interior streams and lakes in all parts of the country have been heavily overfished."[36] Fish managers trusted that increased hatchery production supplied the solution. One Utah official outlined this optimistic view of fisheries management: "And while in times past Nature was able, with a limited population and inadequate trans-portation to keep a normal balance of wild life, our present conditions demand a broad constructive program of restocking in order to maintain something like the requisite amount of fish and game to satisfy the ever increasing demand."[37] With views such as these, fish managers enlarged the western hatchery system.

Starting in the late 1910s and 1920s, new hatcheries helped fish manag-ers stock national forests throughout the Rockies, planting tens of millions of trout yearly to accommodate tourists and anglers. State and federal agencies often worked with the US Forest Service from the 1920s to the 1950s to stock trout for increasing numbers of auto campers and anglers heading out into forest lands. During the 1920s alone, management agencies put thirty-five to forty million trout in national forest waters annually.[38] The Forest Service justified the astounding numbers through both the intrinsic recreational worth and the economic value of trout fishing. One Forest Service administrator, for instance, wrote of the incalculable value of mountain vacations, allowing broad segments of the public to get "away from the heat and grind of the cities or the everyday routine of rural occupations." He went on, however, to quote another source that had estimated 2.5 billion dollars would be spent in 1925 alone on automobile camping and tourism.[39] The optimistic forecasts justified increased hatchery work and trout stocking.

Fish agencies both expanded the number of hatcheries and attempted to make their work more efficient during the 1920s. Longtime Spearfish hatchery superintendent D. C. Booth called for not more, but more efficient, hatcheries and larger fish to meet the growing demands in the 1920s: "Good roads and the auto are responsible for the depletion of the game trout from many of the best trout streams and unless this condition is met by a greatly increased output of fingerling and yearling trout each year, good trout fishing will soon be hard to find."[40] Booth believed that effective stocking practices would address growing fishing pressures. His views echoed a larger shift in hatchery practices.

In the 1920s, fish management agencies started planting larger fish, not just the eggs or small fry prevalent in the nineteenth century. This management move reflected years of debate over efficient and economical ways to stock fish as well as the influence of the new consumer culture of the era.[41] As early as 1886, American fish culturalists wrote about raising larger fish. One federal hatchery superintendent argued that planted eggs and fry had poor survival percentages, but larger fish could better adapt: "At partial maturity, however, their vitality is far greater than in infancy."[42] These debates continued into the twentieth century. By the 1920s, this practice became more accepted. In 1925, the fish culture division chief at the US Bureau of Fisheries argued mature hatchery fish allowed agencies to better address automobiles and increased fishing, the development of more agricultural land, and the continued deforestation that had all negatively affected game fish populations in the era.[43] Other fish managers and anglers agreed.

Rocky Mountain states undertook the planting of larger fish at different times during the early to mid-twentieth century. In the late 1920s, the Utah Fish and Game Department started releasing fish around ten inches long, which could be caught by anglers immediately after planting.[44] Fish managers deemed planted fish longer than nine inches or so "catchable trout" or "catchable-sized trout." These catchable trout provided the mainstay in what was described as "put-and-take" stocking programs in which fish managers stocked trout in popular waters and anglers caught them soon after (sometimes even lining up and waiting for the hatchery truck). Excluding Utah, the Rocky Mountain states did not run large-scale put-and-take stocking programs until after World War II.

Western fish and game departments, however, employed other methods in their attempts to meet the growing demand from anglers. In the 1920s and 1930s, sporting clubs cooperated with state and federal agencies to plant larger fish, operating rearing ponds that grew hatchery fry into mature fish. In the mid-1920s, Wyoming constructed rearing ponds for fry, producing fish up to six inches in length.[45] They received help from sporting clubs which raised around one million fish in rearing ponds, then planted in state rivers in the late 1920s.[46] The work offered a simple solution. In *A Remedy for Disappearing Game Fishes* (1930), President Herbert Hoover articulated this viewpoint. Hoover believed that planting bigger fish would solve the declining game fish problem throughout the nation: "Artificial hatching can be made successful if the fingerlings are carried through infancy to childhood."[47] He therefore called for the Izaak Walton League and other sporting clubs to maintain "nurseries" to lower mortality rates of hatchery fish. The hands-off approach in which individual anglers and sporting clubs addressed declining fish populations reflected the same stance taken by the Hoover administration with the Great Depression. However, Hoover's concerns went beyond increasing fish populations. He considered fishing restorative to the soul and promoted the sport among all classes of men, while failing to mention women anglers.[48] Reading as a homily on morality in the modern world (although perhaps not as blatant as his 1963 book *Fishing for Fun—And to Wash Your Soul*), Hoover's and others' earlier calls to action sparked a brief-lived movement among sporting clubs to operate rearing ponds in the 1920s and 1930s.

Fisheries managers not only created artificial fish populations to meet the growing popularity of fishing, but they also tried to manipulate environments to produce more fish. During the 1930s, agencies began stream "improvement" projects. Popular among both managers and anglers, stream improvement involved creating more trout habitat by planting willows and other plants to stabilize stream banks, prevent erosion, and create shade. Dams and deflectors like logs, rocks, and unnatural materials were installed to make trout pools deeper and larger. Managers also added curves and riffles to the streambed itself. Finally, they dammed headwater streams, creating reservoirs to stabilize stream flows and mitigate floods.[49] All of this work reflected two central assumptions of the era's fisheries management. First, officials believed they could effectively control nature. Second, many felt that they needed to react somehow to the growing numbers of anglers. As one US Bureau of Fisheries employee put it: "Nature alone has been no match for the drain caused by man's fishing activity."[50]

While tourism declined slightly, westerners continued fishing during the Great Depression. Working-class conservationist and fly tier George Grant recalled catching fish for his family and neighbors in Butte.[51] Sometimes residents could not even afford fishing licenses. In the midst of the depression, one elderly woman wrote to the governor of Idaho requesting fishing licenses for her and her friends, "We have no car and are all widdows [sic] and love to fish. Mrs. Paul Gourley is 67 and Mrs. Green 62."[52] The governor obliged. Like the three fishing widows, westerners looked to the land to provide in lean times.

The popularity of trout fishing, whether for food or fun, contributed to the growing fishing economy and Rocky Mountain fishing traditions. During the mid-twentieth century, the western trout industry continued to expand and to cater to wealthy tourists. Most fly shops also doubled as outfitters, employing fishing guides on popular western rivers during tourist season. Dan Bailey ran a longtime fly shop and outfitting service in Livingston, having moved to Montana in the 1930s after reading a newspaper article about the good fishing in the trout-stocked waters there. His yearly catalog sold flies and fishing gear—and promoted the same views of the West that had lured Bailey out in the first place. From the 1920s to the 1970s, fishing shops often employed women tiers to meet customer demands. Many Livingston housewives worked in Bailey's shop.[53] Likewise, former wigmaker Franz Pott hired young college women from the

University of Montana to help with the craft.[54] Western fly shops confirmed the importance of trout in the regional economy.

The accompanying fly fishing traditions also evolved. Rocky Mountain fly patterns frequently mimicked the salmonflies and stone flies that were prevalent in large western rivers and trout favored as food, two of the reasons that John Wilson's buttercup-and-grass turned fancy fly pattern (the Professor) may have been popular in the nineteenth-century West. The giant insects live underwater most of the year. As the water drops in the late spring, they come out of the water to hatch, gaining two pairs of wings to reproduce and lay eggs on the water's surface. Westerners and tourists have mythologized these late spring and summer hatches almost as much as trout and fly fishing in the Rocky Mountains. Needless to say, fly fishers have tied their flies to imitate both the underwater nymph and the hatched adult form. Immortalized in *A River Runs Through It*, Missoula tier Norman Means's Bunyan Bugs represented a popular western dry fly; the pattern had colored cork with painted-on patterns and simple hair wings extending out each side.

Other Rocky Mountain fly patterns were also adapted to regional conditions. The western fly fishing tradition arose, in part, with the need to conform eastern and European flies to Rocky Mountain trout streams. Some tiers relied on local materials. Longtime Missoula shop owner and member of the Western Montana Fish and Game Association, Jack Boehme originally tied his popular fly, the Picket Pin, out of ground squirrel tail. Other patterns used badger hair; for instance, Franz Pott weaved badger hair into some of his popular Mite patterns.[55] After the postwar rise of spin fishing, some patterns never regained their popularity or were lost to posterity; other patterns continued to be fished and adapted on western rivers.[56] Renowned Jackson Hole guide Jack Dennis observed in the 1970s that certain fly patterns like the Trude remained common. He described regional fly styles that often included more hackle and stiffer tails, needed for buoyancy on swift western rivers. The patterns were often tied larger than their eastern counterparts, like the stone fly nymphs and dry flies so popular in the West.[57] Dennis noted that many Colorado anglers such as Jim Poor often adapted or "westernized" fly patterns, like the Colorado Captain.[58] Trout fishing's status among residents and tourists helped sustain a regional service economy in which new fishing practices arose.

The fishing industry also became dependent on a hatchery system and

A group of men enjoying some beer after fishing. Photograph taken in the early twentieth century by Charles S. Lillybridge. Courtesy of History Colorado (Charles S. Lillybridge Collection, scan #20001361).

widespread environmental changes. Federal and state governments built many new federal and state hatcheries from the mid-1910s to the 1930s to meet the demand of the expanding tourist and recreation economy. During the Great Depression, New Deal programs funded this expansion by building roads, campgrounds, recreational facilities, and the occasional hatchery on public lands. Rocky Mountain state agencies controlled numerous hatcheries that produced tens of millions of trout yearly. By 1929, Colorado operated fifteen different hatcheries; Idaho had eleven; Montana had fourteen; and Utah and Wyoming had eight. The yearly output totaled over one hundred million trout.[59] State agencies additionally started more rear-

Western anglers fantasize about stone fly and salmonfly hatches. This is the adult form of a giant salmonfly, *Pteronarcys californica*. Photograph by author.

A true western fly pattern, the Brown and Orange Colorback, designed and tied by George F. Grant and meant to imitate the nymph form of a giant salmonfly. Photograph by Stephanie Roberts.

Western retailers such as this Denver hardware store took advantage of fly fishing's popularity in the interwar years. Denver Public Library, Western History Collection, call #x-24445.

ing ponds. For example, members of the Wyoming Division of the Izaak Walton League of America and other sporting clubs, Civilian Conservation Corps and Works Progress Administration workers, and employees of the Wyoming Game and Fish Department all constructed more Wyoming rearing ponds during the 1930s.[60] States also began to develop special strains of rainbow trout, branding the species. Fish culturalists bred fish for color, size, behavior, and other characteristics valued by anglers.[61]

On top of state work, the federal government enlarged its own hatcheries. During the mid-twentieth century, the US Bureau of Fisheries pumped even more trout into Rocky Mountain waters. By 1935, the agency ran six main stations in Bozeman, Montana; Leadville, Colorado; Spearfish, South Dakota; Hagerman, Idaho; Saratoga, Wyoming; and Springville, Utah, and numerous substations and egg-collecting stations, all producing trout for the region.[62] The Bureau of Fisheries justified expansion of hatcheries because of conservation as well as the economic prominence of trout fishing: "The increasing importance of this type of recreation and the opening of new and better roads to the waters makes necessary the expansion of game fish cultural facilities. The work has also a monetary value, visible in the income from licenses, expenditures for guides, boats, bait, tackle, lodging, transportation, and the various other items which go to make up the cost of a fishing trip."[63] The cultural and economic importance of trout served as grounds to remake Rocky Mountain fisheries.

From the 1920s to 1950s, western anglers and fish agencies expanded this regional trout culture into wilderness areas. They introduced millions of nonnative trout in previously barren mountain lakes. This work took place amid a growing wilderness movement and received little criticism from it. Started by middle- and upper-class easterners, the Wilderness Society sought to preserve forest lands from what they saw as hordes of tourists and auto campers building roads.[64] Yet wilderness ethics also found support among westerners of varied backgrounds, including Finis Mitchell, a Wyoming resident who helped stock high country lakes in the Wind River Mountains.

Finis Mitchell's work illustrates the democratic character of trout introductions that transformed wilderness environments in the Rockies. The Rocky Mountains contain thousands of high country lakes, nestled in mountain cirques at high elevations. Ninety-five percent of high western lakes originally did not contain fish due to barriers formed by the Pleistocene ice age.[65] But the western trout culture changed all that, dramatically transforming high country lakes during the midcentury: "Of the estimated 16,000 naturally fishless mountain lakes in the western US, the majority of which are located within national parks and wilderness areas, 60% of lakes and 95% of larger deeper lakes now contain nonnative trout."[66] Fishing enthusiasts and fish managers converted these mountain lakes into trout fisheries.

Growing up on a failing Wyoming homestead near the Wind River Range, the Mitchell family supplemented its existence through hunting and fishing. Finis Mitchell remembered, "We were poorer than church mice. We lived on antelope meat, potatoes and fish."[67] Mitchell's fascination with the Wind Rivers began in 1909 when, as a young boy, he accompanied his father into the mountains on an elk hunt.[68] For the rest of his life, he spent much of his time climbing, fishing, and taking photographs in the range. As an adult, Mitchell worked for the Union Pacific Railroad until he was laid off during the Great Depression. Like many Americans, he turned to the land for a livelihood, in this case, opening a fish camp near Mud Lake in the Bridger National Forest.[69] Mitchell used this experience to promote the value of American wilderness, later writing:

Throughout this century I've roamed this wilderness, communing with nature, observing other creatures along with myself, merely desiring to live and let live. Because of this aloneness, I've learned to love, not only those of my own kind, but all life within a wilderness; the birds, the beasts, the trees, the flowers, and the grasses of the land. Only in wilderness, it seems, is man's love so thoroughly and completely returned, so unselfishly shared.[70]

His time in the forested mountains led him to appreciate nature as a whole and the importance of protecting land from further development. Mitchell also took this opportunity to stock trout in the barren lakes high in the Wind Rivers. One of thousands of enthusiasts who gave free labor to state and federal hatcheries, Mitchell perhaps took this to an extreme, planting 2.5 million brook, rainbow, cutthroat, golden, or brown trout in 314 lakes during the 1930s.[71]

Even with the advent of the automobile and massive road building in the national forests, high country lake stocking before World War II had to be powered by animals and humans. High mountain lakes often were inaccessible to pack animals, requiring a tremendous amount of human labor to create high elevation trout fisheries. In Glacier National Park, many of the first introductions in 1922 had to be packed in by National Park Service and US Bureau of Fisheries employees. The men carried these heavy packs of fish and also ice through the park, into high elevations, to stock barren lakes in the park, while coming across the occasional grizzly bear. That first summer, they stocked eight streams and twelve lakes with two million cutthroat trout eggs.[72] To plant trout in a lake in Wyoming's Medicine Bow National Forest in 1925, two forest rangers had to slide down a steep scree slope with the cans of trout perched in their laps. It took them nearly two hours to hike back up.[73]

Even with horses, the work was hard. Finis Mitchell used a string of pack horses to transform Wind River lakes. Under an agreement with Wyoming's Daniel hatchery superintendent, the state hatchery delivered milk cans of trout to their Mud Lake base camp. Mitchell would then load six horses with a can on each side. The milk cans, filled with one thousand trout fingerling each, were covered in burlap, and the movement of the horses would aerate the water, ensuring the fish would not die on the way. While the workers loaded each horse, someone would have to lead the already-loaded horses around to ensure aeration. Once on the trail, they would have to occasionally stop along a stream to refill the water lost through the burlap cover because of the horses' movement. After reaching the lake, the cans would be poured in the water.[74] Some trout died on the journey or after being planted, but many of these early introductions were successful, expanding the region's fisheries.

The nation's entry into World War II and the postwar era marked the end of the hard times for many and ushered in vast changes in the American West. Yet not everyone welcomed the new residents due to war mobilization. The Utah fish and game commissioner complained in 1946 of newcomers who did not share the same outdoor traditions and conservation ethics: "During the war and the period of adjustment following, we have had an ingress of thousands of out-of-state people who have not taken with any too much pride the fine fishing and hunting that we have been able to furnish. In many instances, we have found the war industrial workers to be among our most promiscuous law offenders."[75] To the regret of some residents, the Rocky Mountains became even more of a tourist destination.

Inland states saw a tremendous increase in outdoor recreation and tourism during the postwar years. Many of these new anglers took up spin fishing or came from regions without fly fishing traditions, representing a break from earlier eras. Spin fishing was easier to learn and less complicated for casting than fly fishing because it relied on the weight of the lure to shoot line out from a free-spooling reel.[76] Improved by World War II–era technological innovations and inexpensive manufacturing, spin fishing reflected postwar mass production and mass consumption, and it was not until the 1970s that fly fishing started to regain its popularity. The numbers of trout fishers grew throughout the mid-twentieth century, giving rise to an outdoor recreation and tourism economy that also flourished in the region. State and local governments, chambers of commerce, fly shops and outfitters, all sold Rocky Mountain trout fishing in the postwar era. To attract visitors, the "West play[ed] West" as historian Earl Pomeroy described it in the 1950s, promoting a mythical region and idea more from television westerns than reality.[77]

If nineteenth-century accounts of successful nonnative trout introductions echoed the optimism of westward expansion, post–World War II descriptions of a region filled with naturalized trout ignored the messiness of conquest in favor of a triumphal mythology. In the postwar years, Rocky Mountain tourist advertisements frequently played on the Cold War fascination with the frontier, which offered Americans a sanitized version of history. Familiar in their simple morality (good guys wearing white hats) and masculinity, television westerns propped frontier history on a pedestal.[78] State travel and tourism boards took advantage of this imagined past to promote their states. In the *Wyoming Historical Handbook* (1950), the Wyoming Travel Commission wrote a watered-down state history. Briefly touching on the native inhabitants, the fur trade, and the decline of the buffalo, the pamphlet glorified the state's development, from being the first state to grant women suffrage to having important cattle, coal, and oil industries.[79] Of course, no western tourism tract could be complete without an overview of the outdoor attractions. Wyoming's fish and game proved to be a key feature. Booster materials characteristically presented their states as better than others: "The entire state of Wyoming constitutes a fish and game paradise unsurpassed by any other section or state in the nation." In this large area, anglers could find abundant native and nonnative fish, including "eight trout species."[80] To extol the virtues of western trout streams, boosters sometimes turned to a nostalgic past to create a new regional identity.

Conversely, postwar fishing and guide books tended to rely less on mythologized history and more on the realities of catching trout. After World War II, the literature focused on western trout grew rapidly, marketing to the mass of tourists and outdoor recreationalists. Postwar fishing books obviously promoted Rocky Mountain trout. Ray Bergman's popular, if prosaically named, *Trout* went through three editions and dozens of reprintings from 1938 to 1976. While not constrained to the West, Bergman used many experiences in Rocky Mountain states and Yellowstone National Park to provide a how-to guide to growing numbers of anglers. The second edition in 1952 added chapters on spin fishing to cater to its postwar popularity. Other authors wrote solely on the West, taking advantage of the growing tourism industry. In *Western Trout* (1948), Syl MacDowell observed that trout had become "big business" in the West, where there were higher proportions of western residents fishing compared to their eastern counterparts as well as a multi-million-dollar tourist industry. Trout fishing's cultural and economic value translated into political importance: "One U.S. Senator from the West launched his political career on a campaign pledge to plant fish in an important voting district. There are a great many other instances in which angling has become a political issue. Western trout are important in business and politics. They are represented in Chamber of Commerce meetings, in trade forums, and in law-making assemblies."[81] The political realities of Rocky Mountain trout underscored the importance of the growing industry.

Unlike the booster literature published by these political bodies, fishing writers often promoted limited catches and other conservation ethics. In *Fishing in the West* (1950), wilderness defender Arthur Carhart warned against believing chamber of commerce descriptions of streams "teeming with trout" without considering the dam building and environmental degradation of the postwar era.[82] The fishing in print, however, still sold a West with trout. The growing tourism and fishing industries in the Rocky Mountains over time show that midcentury boosterism represented more than just extravagant claims, but a material reality of pretty good trout fishing.

The portrayals of western nature as a place for play, however, obscured the profound manipulation of fish and rivers over time. By the 1940s, the

Stocked by foot, horseback, and later airplanes like this one unloading trout fry, many mountain lakes now hold a variety of nonnative trout species. Used by permission, Utah State Historical Society, all rights reserved.

Rocky Mountain states had all shifted their hatchery practices to ensure good fishing for the loads of postwar recreationalists. All these management techniques served to further the environmental change in Rocky Mountain fisheries. At the war's end, most sporting clubs had already discontinued their rearing pond work. Plagued by problems with funding and productivity, state agencies found it more efficient to raise trout themselves rather than use those from amateur-run ponds. In the 1940s, officials in Wyoming and other western states reported a large number of failures of rearing ponds and their subsequent abandonment.[83] Similarly, stream improvement projects declined after falling short of their promised transformations. A large spring runoff could easily undo the work, as Utah managers observed in 1940: "In many instances, the flood waters washed the barriers and deflectors out of the streams and in other instances the changes made seemed to have an upsetting effect upon the whole stream bed and in no way helped the habitat for fish."[84] States replaced these endeavors with more hatchery work.

In the postwar years, management agencies overtook the work once cooperatively done by both the government and private anglers, like wilderness trout stocking and other introductions that had been the joint venture of both anglers and agencies. Stocking barren mountain lakes continued after World War II, aided by aircraft instead of horses, mules, and anglers. In the postwar era, airplanes and helicopters became more accessible for civilian use, while veterans could use their wartime skills to remake fish life in wilderness lakes. Aircraft made the task easier, cheaper, and more efficient.[85] Of the eight hundred or so originally barren high-elevation Colorado lakes that now hold trout, most were aerially stocked in the 1950s.[86] Despite the recent uncertainty about adding fish where they previously did not exist, few people at the time objected to this practice. High country lakes are still routinely stocked using aircraft; more than seven thousand western lakes are currently maintained through these methods.[87]

Perhaps the most transformative for Rocky Mountains fisheries, however, was not wilderness stocking, but rather the rise of put-and-take fisheries management. In the postwar era, western states routinely stocked catchable-sized trout, mostly rainbow trout, as part of massive put-and-take stocking programs. Like the mass-produced spin fishing gear of the postwar period, these larger, mass-produced fish catered to a new consumerist mentality in America.[88] State agencies willingly catered to these new fishing demands.[89] Illustrating that this new concept in fisheries management relied on the same outlook of previous generations of fish culturalists, one Utah state fish commissioner proudly observed that "fisheries management is nothing more than aquatic farming."[90] Anglers and new generations of fisheries managers would later criticize and, in some places, stop stocking catchable-sized trout. During the 1940s and 1950s, however, put-and-take stocking epitomized the continued hubris of western hatchery management and the new postwar views that nature could be produced and consumed like other commodities in the Cold War economy.

With hatcheries and a trout-fishing culture, tourists, western anglers, and fish managers all constructed an inland West known for its trout-fishing opportunities during the early and mid-twentieth century. In the railroad era, fishing represented a common pastime for many westerners and small numbers of elite tourists who could afford the spendy fares to the West. Over time, however, fishing and tourism became more democratic, with the help of rising standards of living and increasing automobile ownership. In the Rocky Mountains, growth of the fishing industry started regional fly fishing traditions in the 1920s and 1930s, which were somewhat surpassed by the popularity of spin fishing in the post–World War II era. Regardless of tackle, anglers and tourists demanded good trout fishing throughout the twentieth century. The cultural and economic changes in the region show how the importance of nonnative trout overpowered concerns about native fish in the Rocky Mountains. Rather than focus on saving declining native trout and other fish species, fish managers scaled up the western hatchery system to continue stocking more and larger nonnative rainbow, brown, and brook trout. The extent of the manipulation demonstrated that trout fishing, like other outdoor recreation activities, had profound environmental consequences. The next chapter demonstrates that this reckoning of place held even more environmental costs, by examining how anglers and managers ignored or mistreated other native fish. This Rocky Mountain trout culture shaped and amplified an earlier hostility toward non-trout species that stemmed from British and eastern American sporting ideals. In this manner, local and regional people and environments yet again modified larger ideas and processes at the expense of native fish and ecosystems.

Trash Fish

I N NORMAN MACLEAN'S ANTHEM TO FAMILY AND FLY FISHING, *A River Runs Through It*, Montana fishing in the 1930s meant catching trout, gigantic nonnative ones, to be specific. The 1976 book, and the Robert Redford film adaptation in 1992, helped foster a mythologized image of western trout fishing among readers, moviegoers, and inspired tourists. In one part of the novella, Norman and his brother Paul reluctantly take Norman's hungover brother-in-law Neal fishing. The brother-in-law's failure to catch trout illustrates an animosity toward native fish among Montana anglers during the rise of the West's trout culture:

> "What are you doing?" I asked.
>
> It took him some time to arrange an answer. "I have been fishing," he said finally. Then he tried over again for greater accuracy. "I have been fishing and not feeling well," he said.
>
> "This dead water isn't much of a place to fish, is it?" I asked.
>
> "Why," he said, "look at all those fish at the bottom of the hole."
>
> "Those are squaw fish and suckers," I told him, without looking.
>
> "What's a sucker?" he asked, and so became the first native of Montana ever to sit on a rock and ask what a sucker was.[1]

Here, Maclean uses suckers and squawfish (two disliked native species) to serve as a humorous apologue: as a double-sweater-wearing "fancy Dan," Neal did not quite fit in trout country. Neither did suckers, squawfish, and other native coarse fish, according to many trout fishers in the creation of a Rocky Mountain trout culture.

In a West now romanticized for its trout and fly fishing opportunities, the expectation of pristine nature has obscured decades of environmental change, so much so that readers automatically accept Maclean's authority and that rainbow trout belong in his Montana. These assumptions stem from the actions of anglers, fisheries managers, tourists, regional boosters, and local business people who had built a regional culture and economy based upon nonnative trout fishing by the mid-twentieth century. This historical creation of place proved detrimental to native fish. The ways in which many anglers, tourists, and fish managers understood place—the West as a manufactured trouty place—turned out deadly for native, non-trout species. The poor treatment of native coarse fish (simply defined by Euroamerican angling culture as most other fish species besides trout and salmon) reveals a historical trend that began in the late nineteenth century and has continued, at least in part, until today.[2] I argue that the historical creation and understanding of place also influenced the treatment of fish.

Coarse fish have occupied a contested place within sporting culture since the nineteenth century, when English and eastern American anglers frequently debated the food and game merits of coarse fish versus "game" fish like trout and salmon. While some anglers deliberately sought coarse fish species and championed their sport and food value, most others fished for the more appealing species of trout and salmon. In these arguments, class determined quarry; many middle- and upper-class anglers on both sides of the Atlantic defined their class and sport by the species they pursued. They privileged beautiful trout, a charismatic microfauna of the animal world, over the dull, scaly, sucker-mouthed coarse fish. Such seemingly trivial cosmetic judgments played a deathly serious role in the treatment of coarse fish and ultimately helped to determine state fisheries management practices in the Rocky Mountain West by the late nineteenth century. While individual anglers could choose to ignore or throw away these disliked coarse fish, starting in the 1890s, state management agencies codified these prejudices through regulations and management techniques, resulting in far more systematic harm. Anglers, hatcheries, and fish managers perpetuated a trout-fishing aesthetic, derived from European roots, refined on eastern rivers, and then superimposed on the western landscape.

As transnational sporting ideals influenced western anglers and fish managers, the previous uses and positive perspectives of native fish eventually eroded. Homogeneous fisheries management and nonnative hatchery trout replaced the early regional importance of native western fish. In this new region, endemic species and subspecies no longer mattered, like those unheeded suckers and squawfish in Norman Maclean's story. By the mid-twentieth century, coarse fish came to be known as "trash fish." The new terminology illustrated the growing importance of nonnative trout and the marginalization of other native fish in a lucrative sport-fishing economy.

Within this emerging trout context, fish managers aimed to improve fishing and reshape fisheries by controlling these "trash fish" populations that they believed competed with trout. To do so, they turned to a wide range of techniques, from dynamite and nets to fish toxicants. The institutionalized trout culture within fisheries management continued its eradication work, even inventing new fish toxicants to kill "trash fish," despite the 1960s rise of environmentalism that championed wild animals and ecological health. By midcentury, the eradication programs and continued disputes over coarse fish revealed that, in this trout culture, some fish were more equal than others.

The current grim status of native fish compared to that of the celebrated trout demands a reexamination of the Rocky Mountain West's connection to nonnative trout and the legacy of its trout culture. In the twentieth century, native coarse fish populations crashed. The Utah Lake sculpin, the Snake River sucker, and a subspecies of the June sucker are extinct. Other species are close to the same fate. The American Fisheries Society considers the following endangered: white sturgeon, pallid sturgeon, humpback chub, bonytail, Virgin River chub, least chub, peppered chub, woundfin, Colorado pikeminnow, Kendall Warm Springs dace, June sucker, and the razorback sucker. Dozens more are listed as threatened or vulnerable.[3] These coarse fish may never return to their historic populations and are on the brink of extinction. Nevertheless, the story of some western coarse species cannot be told in a simple tale of decline. Some coarse fish continue to have large populations, but remain more susceptible to population crashes in a region that has privileged trout.

Mountain whitefish serve as an indicator species of the poor treatment of native "non-game" fish in western rivers that had been transformed into lucrative sport-fishing destinations that relied on nonnative trout by the mid-twentieth century.[4] Yet, compared to the above extinct and endangered species, mountain whitefish have accomplished an astonishing feat during the twentieth century: with some key exceptions, mountain whitefish have survived and resisted the years of habitat change, the mistreatment from anglers who considered them trash fish, and government agencies' failure to manage coarse species in their focus on trout. Many western waters like the Beaverhead River in southwest Montana still contain sizable populations, to the annoyance of some trout fishers. Mountain whitefish, however, are on the verge of disappearing from the Big Lost River, one of the isolated Sinks Drainages that holds a genetically divergent population, near Arco, Idaho. By 2005, the adult mountain whitefish numbers there had dropped to only 1.5 percent of their historic population. When the population declined precipitously, the Idaho Fish and Game Department lowered the daily catch limit and started to worry about the species' future there because small populations run the risk of extinction through genetic inbreeding. Fisheries managers struggled to understand the decline and scrambled to find suitable management practices since few scientific studies exist on mountain whitefish.[5]

The Big Lost River dilemma indicates yet another problem of being a coarse fish in a trout world. As a coarse fish with generally high populations throughout the West, mountain whitefish were overlooked in the Big Lost River. Few scientific studies or management strategies have focused on coarse fish because managers historically privileged trout over trash fish. This deficiency now makes it hard for fisheries managers to catch up when a species starts to decline.[6]

The poor treatment of coarse fish in modern fisheries management dates back centuries. Its origins are in the intellectual and class history of British angling, which directly influenced Rocky Mountain sport and management by elevating trout over coarse fish. British anglers often upheld trout and salmon as favored prey. However, by the eighteenth and nineteenth centuries, enclosure laws and high rents on good fishing waters had created a class divide between game fishing (trout and salmon) and coarse fishing in Britain. Seeking profit in a developing capitalist world, landowners fenced traditional pastures and forests as well as pushed commercial fishermen and lower classes from traditional fishing waters. Good fishing waters that contained game fish like trout and salmon demanded high rents that only elite anglers and urban middle-class clubs could pay. Unable to afford access to trout and salmon waters, the lower and working classes resorted to fishing for coarse fish.[7] Longtime angling editor of the authoritative sporting periodical the *Field*, Francis Francis observed a British contempt for coarse fish in 1863. As an elite angler, Francis connected coarse fish to poorer classes and Jews in England.[8] Influenced by their own concerns with race and class, Francis and others within the British sporting establishment attempted to set themselves apart by trout fishing. For their part, working-class anglers often resented being expelled from nearby trout and game-fish waters.[9] Class, then, defined quarry. However, as one British sport historian has noted, the game and coarse fish divide was "never absolute."[10]

Sport-fishing culture in no way remained homogenous, and a few anglers of all classes constantly disagreed about the value of coarse fish. Anglers' esteem for species depended on location and individual preferences, despite being shaded by the social context of Euroamerican sporting ideals. In one instance, on a fishing trip that included friends (and the editors of England's most-read sporting magazines), R. B. Marston of the *Fishing Gazette* and William Senior (a.k.a "Red Spinner") of the *Field*, Senior demonstrated the sport to be had in coarse fishing. After Marston's wife landed a roach, one of those disliked coarse fish, on a dry fly and was annoyed, Senior tried for the rest of the day to recreate the achievement.[11] The anecdote illustrates that anglers' individual experiences also played a role in valuing coarse fish. Senior's editorial role advanced the sport of angling, but he defied mainstream definitions of game and coarse to find sport. Similar debates and ambiguities over coarse fish arose on the other side of the Atlantic, contributing to Rocky Mountain sport and fisheries management and illustrating the importance of local and regional dynamics in shaping transnational ideas and processes.

Although limited access to trout waters did not plague American anglers since fish and game belonged to the public, coarse fishing has never really been a part of the mainstream fishing culture. British sporting culture influenced American anglers and their ideas about coarse fish; American sporting culture also valued trout rather than coarse fish. British immigrant Henry William Herbert did the most to bring these sporting ideals to an American audience, while helping to create a uniquely American angling tradition based on brook trout. In one of the earliest American angling books, he defined both game and coarse fishing. Game fish had a fighting spirit and good taste. Coarse fish, on the other hand, held little value for the angler: "The truth is, that nowhere under the canopy of Heaven are the genus *Cyprinus* worthy to be accounted sporting fishes, and nowhere are they eatable." He went on to say that the smaller coarse fish like shiners, roach, and dace only provided sport to "schoolboys and young ladies."[12] For Herbert, social standing and the species of fish pursued helped to define sport fishing.

Other American writers echoed British sentiments about class within definitions of game fish. Charles Hallock used his position as founding editor of *Forest and Stream* to also bring British sporting ideals to his American readers. Not surprisingly, Hallock scorned coarse fish, defining game fish as the highest class of fish in 1873, comparing them to gentlemen while connecting coarse fish to the "vulgar" lower classes: "They may flash with tinsel and tawdry attire; they may strike with the brute force of a blacksmith, or exhibit the dexterity of a prize-fighter, but their low breeding and vulgar quality cannot be mistaken. Their haunts, their very food and manner of eating, betray their grossness."[13] The anthropomorphic class undertones obscure whether Hallock despised coarse fish or the lower classes more. He wrote at a time when the rise of industrial capitalism transformed both the landscape and relations between social classes. Concerns over the volatile Gilded Age economy in which wealth could be gained or lost, the turmoil of the growing labor movement, and the new waves of immigrants to the eastern seaboard made men like Hallock uneasy and obsessed with maintaining their privileged status. In Hallock's estimation, not even the nouveaux riches (or coarse fish, whatever the case may be) could hide their lower status in tinsel or intrepid spirit. Like their British counterparts, Hallock and his peers saw coarse fish as suitable only for the lower classes.

Other American anglers, like their British counterparts, complicated these definitions. Unlike some of his contemporaries, author Genio C. Scott portrayed fishing as a more democratic venture in America, but he still privileged brook trout over other fish: "Trouting is an abiding and universal source of pleasure to all classes and conditions of men and boys— ay, and of ladies also." Scott called coarse fish "leather-mouthed fishes" and stated they "are not generally regarded as gamy, though good sport for ladies and youth."[14] Although he did see a place for coarse fish within the sport, Scott based his view on the assumption that they could only be enjoyed by seemingly inferior anglers. Gender frequently shaped definitions of sport and quarry; as chapter 1 illustrates, ideas of masculinity did not entirely dictate sport in the nineteenth century. Often, anglers simply liked trout more. This preference turned out to be significant, since prejudices against coarse fish shaped the hatchery system and the rise of state conservation in the West during the late nineteenth century.

In eastern states as well as the Rocky Mountains, the state-led conservation system, influenced by sport-fishing ideals and funded by anglers' license fees, protected game fish while ignoring coarse fish or "non-game" fish. Starting in the nineteenth century, private and state fish culturalists stocked billions of preferred trout species in western waters, based largely upon Euroamerican sporting traditions. Western native fish like mountain whitefish, suckers, chubs, and other coarse fish shared similar characteristics and thus comparable prestige with the coarse fish of Britain and the eastern United States. So while fish culturalists introduced and artificially propagated almost every conceivable trout species in western waters, they rarely produced the coarse fish disliked by some sport fishers. Instead, conservationists centered on protecting and creating more trout and other esteemed game fish, prized for both their sport and food qualities.

Western state fish agencies often directed regulations toward protecting only trout and other game species while excluding coarse fish. For instance, an early Utah law, representative of other western state regulations, prohibited fishing during certain winter and spawning months, but only for trout.[15] By 1912, Utah had added a fifteen-pound daily catch limit, which did not apply to coarse fish.[16] Other western states also enacted liberal daily catch limits that ignored coarse fish populations. The nascent state conservation laws that favored game species, however, did not preclude coarse fish use, illustrating a lingering divide between sport and state management and common uses of fish into the twentieth century.

During the territorial period and continuing to the mid-twentieth century, numerous Rocky Mountain coarse fish species held food and game value for natives and settlers alike. Anglers and scientists also debated these values and uses throughout the period. Yet, the sporting values that privileged trout eventually won out. By midcentury, management practices upheld a Rocky Mountain trout culture while ignoring earlier coarse fish proponents.

The types of coarse fish varied by watershed in the West, but they all became subject to the same treatment in the region's trout culture. Mountain whitefish represent one of the most abundant native species and are related closely to trout as part of the Salmonidae family, as revealed by their adipose fins (trout, salmon, char, whitefishes, and grayling).[17] Other western coarse fish species, however, inhabit particular drainages and belong mostly to the Cyprinidae family (including carp, minnows, chubs, and pikeminnow) or the Catostomidae family (suckers). The distribution and large populations of these native species ensured their importance as food and game fish in the nineteenth and early twentieth centuries.

Known for their salmon cultures, Plateau tribes utilized other native species—those defined as coarse fish by Euroamerican sporting culture—to a lesser extent. The Nez Perce took bridgelip suckers, largescale suckers, mountain suckers, longnose suckers, mountain whitefish, and sturgeon and lamprey, in addition to salmon and steelhead.[18] Shoshone-Bannock captured a variety of species, including pikeminnow, suckers, chub, resident trout, lamprey, sturgeon, and mountain whitefish.[19] Other regional tribes also caught numerous types of fish. Reaching lengths of twelve to seventeen inches, the largescale sucker provided a frequent food fish for the Salish of western Montana.[20] Natives in other watersheds also utilized coarse fish, like the Bonneville Basin's Ute bands. Utah's large freshwater lakes held abundant populations of coarse fish (locally called "common fish" in the nineteenth and early twentieth century, a designation that was later replaced with "trash fish" like elsewhere in the West). Utah Lake held native Bonneville cutthroat trout, Utah chubs, Utah suckers, June suckers (endemic to Utah Lake and the Provo River), and other coarse species that provided important food sources to Ute bands originally inhabiting the area and the Mormons who came later.[21] Both settlers and natives often consumed coarse fish.

Non-sporting elite westerners frequently ate mountain whitefish during the nineteenth and twentieth centuries. Star Valley, Wyoming, residents, for instance, traditionally seined for mountain whitefish up into the 1930s.[22] This culinary value often translated into market value. Up until World War I, mountain whitefish could be found in regional markets. Sometimes labeled "mountain herring" to showcase its supposed taste, vendors sold mountain whitefish in city markets like Salt Lake City frequently during the nineteenth century.[23] During one particularly large spawning run in 1895 at Payette Lakes, locals near McCall, Idaho, captured the fish with seines, pitchforks, and shovels by the "wagonload," selling them in Boise and other nearby towns.[24] Settlers were not the only ones to take advantage of regional fish markets. In the early 1900s, Blackfeet Indians seined whitefish, selling them to lodges in Glacier National Park to earn extra money.[25] Western residents appreciated mountain whitefish and other native coarse fish for their food and market value. The abundant uses of coarse fish up until the mid-twentieth century illustrate how the rise of a western trout culture changed the values of these native fish. Westerners, however, disagreed on the food, market, and game value of coarse fish, as indicated by the conflicting values of Colorado pikeminnow.

The inland West has two native species in the pikeminnow genus: northern pikeminnow of the Columbia Basin, now seen as a nuisance predatory species, enough so that the Bonneville Power Administration now pays bounties for its capture, and Colorado pikeminnow of the upper Colorado Basin, which has been listed as an endangered species since 1967. In the upper Colorado Basin of Utah, Colorado, and Wyoming, many locals saw Colorado pikeminnow as a prized food and game fish, especially since it grew up to eighty pounds, the largest of American Cyprinid species.[26] In the early twentieth century, they used different lures, baits, and occasionally artificial flies to catch these monstrous freshwater fish. The baits included worms and fish chunks, as well as unconventional baits (to put it mildly) like chicken parts, swallows, rabbits, or frogs.[27] Yes, rabbits. Seeking Colorado pikeminnow through diverse means, numerous locals developed high opinions of the species, both in terms of game and food. The widespread use showed the early regional importance of coarse fish. Class, however, did not entirely define the wide-ranging opinions of coarse fish.

In the early twentieth century, a small minority of upper Colorado Basin locals disliked Colorado pikeminnow. Some people refused to eat them because of taste and boniness, feeding them to pigs, chickens, and cats or using them as fertilizer instead. Although Colorado pikeminnow represented the most important native species, many residents had lower opinions of the other endemic species such as razorback suckers, humpback chubs, and bonytail chubs.[28] One Utah resident recalled that his family found little use for any native Colorado River species: "See we take them, seine them out of the river and dump them on the lawn, let them die on the banks, we get a gunny sack full and use them for fertilizer, or whatever. If you couldn't eat them, what good were they anyway."[29] Based on food preferences, some westerners embraced the introductions of new game fish. Other locals had no choice. According to one resident, Colorado pikeminnow and bonytail "began to disappear" by the 1930s.[30]

As native fish declined, trout multiplied. Sporting culture and scientific management eventually subsumed earlier values with the rise of a Rocky Mountain culture and economy that valued these new trout.

Like the broader Euroamerican sporting culture, nineteenth- and early twentieth-century western anglers and scientists ranked different native and nonnative trout species based upon their sporting and food values. In this trout hierarchy, coarse fish usually ranked lower. Those who disliked western fish often parroted their English and eastern US counterparts, believing that in a masculine, white sporting culture, coarse fish were only suitable for lower classes, other races, women and children, or, in the case of Norman Maclean, foppish brothers-in-law. Anglers who liked coarse fish based their opinions on personal experiences, questioning mainstream sporting culture. Angler-scientists who worked in state fish and game agencies or the US Fish Commission also viewed coarse fish differently. These myriad views, however, started to fade away by the mid-twentieth century as conserving economically and culturally important trout became paramount to fish agencies.

Rocky Mountain watersheds held distinct native fish that were underprivileged as non-game species and contested within angling culture. Suckers had the dual dilemma of being disliked as both food and game fishes by most anglers. In their definitive *American Food and Game Fishes* (1902) renowned ichthyologists and former US Fish Commission scientists David Starr Jordan and Barton Warren Evermann frankly stated that no sucker species held any game qualities and that they ranked low as food due to their boniness.[31] Western anglers tended to agree with this estimation. Colorado anglers reportedly detested white suckers, as one scientist observed at Twin Lakes: "As food fish, the sucker does not stand very high in the estimation of local fishermen, consequently little attention is paid to it except as bait for trout."[32] Smaller-sized coarse fish held little value for anglers.

Often lumped under the generic term "minnows," small coarse fish held little sport or food importance, unless as bait or sport fitting for children. Easy to catch, minnows' small sizes made them manageable for children, even with makeshift gear, but they were met with disdain among sportsmen for precisely that reason: they were easy quarry. Jordan and Evermann noted that various chub species were "of little importance except as boy's fishes. With a few exceptions they are species of the Western States, and are perhaps most valuable to the Indians or in those regions where better fish are rare."[33]

Western anglers relegated minnows and small coarse fish to bait for game fish or children's prey, but disputed the game qualities of other western coarse fish like mountain whitefish. As a widespread western species, mountain whitefish had both supporters and detractors in the sporting community. In the early 1890s, some Montana anglers complained of the fish's "sluggish" habits, especially during warm weather, which gave them "a bad reputation."[34] Other sportsmen valued the fish for food and game. Writing under the unassuming pen name "Bourgeois," Colorado lawyer Lewis B. France observed that the sizable mountain whitefish populations in the state's White River occasionally annoyed trout fishers. He defended the fish, stating: "Why they should be a source of vexation of any one is a mystery. The fish is beautiful in contour, more slender than the trout, has a delicate mouth, rises eagerly to the fly, and its meat is delicious."[35] While class and social status colored some anglers' views toward coarse fish, France and his fellow elite sportsmen's admiration of mountain whitefish revealed that personal preference shaped their ever-significant estimations of fish.

Forgotten in the region's later economy and culture that privileged nonnative trout, these positive sentiments about coarse fish demonstrate how science and fisheries management displaced diverse fishing cultures with a homogenized trout culture. The historically shifting local and common names of the pikeminnow genus illustrate the influence of trout angling ideals within state-led conservation, which sought to create uniformity within knowledge of species. Pikeminnow had the common name of "squawfish" until 1998, when it was changed by the American Fisheries Society due to its offensive nature.[36] Squawfish as a common name, however, evolved over time to reflect sporting culture in scientific management. Scottish explorer and naturalist John Richardson first described the northern species in 1836 for Euroamerican audiences, listing the common name as Columbia River Dace.[37] In 1891, Barton Warren Evermann noted on a US Fish Commission expedition that in the Flathead Lake region, the locals called northern pikeminnow "squawfish."[38] The vernacular's origin remains unknown.

Northern pikeminnow in other locales had different common names. Idaho settlers called them "yellowbellies" near Redfish Lakes and "chub," "big-mouth," and "box-head," elsewhere in Idaho, all references—albeit not so creative—to their appearance.[39] Likewise, settlers in the upper Colorado Basin referred to Colorado pikeminnow as "white salmon," or occasionally "whitefish" or "salmon," all titles that denoted its size and importance as food.[40] Regardless of the other common names, eventually all pikeminnow species became known as squawfish, although exactly when is unclear. Jordan and Evermann's 1902 tome on game and food fish continued to list Colorado pikeminnow as "white salmon," but applied "squawfish" to northern pikeminnow over its other common names, stating, "This fish is highly esteemed by the Indians, hence its most popular name."[41] Over time, the scientific establishment deemed all pikeminnow the disparaging "squawfish." Regardless of the original meaning, the labeling shows the influence of race and gender within sporting ideals. In one strand of angling culture, codified by state conservation and western science, whiteness and masculinity could be demonstrated by the type of fish sought. Thus, squawfish did not fall under proper game fish.

As always, however, sportsmen contested these aspects of sporting culture. Despite its official status as an inferior coarse fish suitable only for Native American women, anglers and scientists often valued pikeminnow as a food and sport fish. On Barton Warren Evermann's first trip to the Flathead Lake region, northern pikeminnow failed to make a favorable impression on the USFC scientist: "They often prove quite an annoyance to him who is fishing for nobler game."[42] Several years later, however, Evermann changed his tune about the merits of northern pikeminnow. Under the auspices of "researching" Idaho's Redfish Lakes, he enjoyed the sport: "They would rise to the fly promptly, strike quickly, and fight vigorously for a few moments, after which they allowed themselves to be pulled in without much struggle." As for food, he described northern pikeminnow as "firm and sweet," but bony, adding their large size "reduces this objection to a minimum."[43] The mid-twentieth century focus on nonnative trout discredited these earlier positive views of western native fish that someday might be restored.

From approximately the 1920s to the 1950s, the creation of place, a trout culture, economy, and aesthetic, meant that coarse fish became even more disdained, as reflected in the era's popular usage of the term "trash fish," an expression sometimes still used today. Larger economic changes in the twentieth century allowed western consumers to buy frozen fish native to oceans and far-off waters, meaning coarse fishes' food value declined as well. Additionally, many residents began to prefer eating trout and other introduced species after the 1920s and 1930s. One Colorado man stated, "I like trout. Those damn suckers, they used to be so full of bones."[44] From this standpoint, coarse fish paled in comparison to nonnative trout. Simultaneously, trout grew in importance for Rocky Mountain sport fisheries, as illustrated by the species' centrality in *A River Runs Through It*. As western waters became linked to trout, anglers expected a certain fishing experience.

The evolution of a western trout culture translated into poor treatment of coarse fish by some anglers. Their actions became unofficially sanctioned by state agencies which, in the face of declining trout populations and habitat degradation, worked to remove coarse fish in an attempt to improve trout fisheries. The term "trash fish" perhaps reflected the fact that some anglers discarded coarse fish in the belief that they had no game or food merit and competed with trout. During the midcentury, state agencies increasingly reported that anglers threw away coarse fish. In the 1930s, California Fish and Game officials observed that Truckee River anglers disliked mountain whitefish: "At well-fished 'holes' it is not uncommon to see many whitefish strewn on the banks to rot. Many anglers throw away their entire catch of this species—believing it to be worthless"[45] The authors noted anglers often mistook the species for suckers, even though mountain whitefish, with their telltale adipose fin, are more closely related to trout. Episodes similar to the Truckee River rotting fish problem occurred throughout the midcentury West. The Wyoming state fish warden reported in 1941 that during the summer, anglers left piles of rotting mountain whitefish along the banks of the Salt, Snake, Shoshone, and Upper Wind rivers.[46] Harriet Wheatley, a well-to-do tourist, recounted that she and her husband rarely kept the species. At the behest of a guide in Jackson Hole, they supplied mountain whitefish to less discerning tourists staying in a local lodge. Wheatley and the other members of their fishing party delighted in filling their creels and she reported that, surprisingly, the mountain whitefish fought well and tasted good.[47]

Despite some positive fishing experiences, the widespread dislike of coarse fish shaped fisheries management in the twentieth century, and oftentimes turned violent. Funded by fishing license fees, state agencies institutionalized prejudices against coarse fish in their continuous work to maintain trout populations for recreational and food purposes during the twentieth century. In the face of increasing water pollution and habitat degradation due to post–World War II road building, urban growth, and industrial and agricultural pollution, fisheries managers worried about declining trout populations. Their concerns shifted to habitat protection, smaller daily catch limits for trout, and ridding western waters of coarse fish. Fish managers charged coarse fish with competing with trout for valuable food and space. Although some food overlap occurred, biologists assumed that fewer coarse fish would increase trout populations.[48] They embarked on "removal" programs—a euphemism for the widespread carnage—without fully understanding competition between fish or having scientific evidence to prove that decreasing coarse fish populations would increase trout populations.[49] All they needed to know was that anglers desired to fish for trout.

The extent of coarse fish removal programs attests to the popularity and economic importance of trout. The Dingell-Johnson Act (1950) funded many of the projects. The national act taxed fishing gear, giving funds to the states to improve sport fishing opportunities.[50] With Dingell-Johnson money, as well as state funding through fishing licenses, state agencies embarked on massive coarse fish removal campaigns. These operations sought to get rid of various sucker species, chubs, pikeminnow, mountain whitefish, and every other imaginable coarse fish species, as well as introduced carp. Fisheries managers found an assortment of uses for the removed fish, commonly feeding them to hatchery trout, distributing them to the needy, or using them as fertilizer. State agencies used a variety of coarse fish removal techniques. They resorted to seines and gill nets, fish toxicants, dynamite, electroshocking, and dewatering reservoirs in the attempt to control coarse fish populations. For particularly maligned or troublesome species, managers employed multiple techniques. From the 1940s to the 1970s, for instance, they combated northern pikeminnow with gill nets, dynamite, a selective toxicant that targeted only northern pikeminnow, and "drawing down of reservoirs after the spawning season to kill the eggs."[51] Similar coarse fish removal projects took place throughout the twentieth century, but were particularly common midcentury when managers aimed to save trout.

During the midcentury, all western states pursued coarse fish removal programs. The Utah Fish and Game Department chemically treated numerous lakes and reservoirs during the 1950s. They used coarse fish to feed hatchery trout, reportedly taking out "500 tons of trash fish" in 1952 and 1953 alone.[52] Large-scale toxicant or seining operations continued in dozens of lakes per year, as the department attempted to control "undesirable" fish that they wrongly believed competed with trout for food and space.[53] Other states engaged in coarse fish removal to the same extent. The Wyoming Game and Fish Department conducted yearly chemical treatments and seining operations in various lakes, eliminating tons of fish in each locale. The year 1952 was particularly busy for the agency. It put fish toxicants in twenty-six lakes and reservoirs, in addition to seining.[54] Idaho, Montana, and Colorado also killed coarse fish as part of yearly fisheries management techniques.

Fish managers often couched their actions as "rehabilitation" programs and garnered support and free labor from sportsmen's clubs. The Western Montana Fish and Game Association out of Missoula boasted almost three thousand members by 1958. Its members frequently helped in coarse-fish removal efforts in nearby waters during the 1950s.[55] For sporting clubs and state management agencies working in tandem, fish conservation meant saving trout by killing others. State agencies enjoyed the help and found that sometimes their removal work established good rapport with sporting clubs. Star Valley, Wyoming, sportsmen—perhaps descendants of those pioneers who seined mountain whitefish into the 1930s—aided fisheries crews in the 1950s and 1960s, helping managers electroshock the river and seine out the stunned mountain whitefish. The continuous operations took out thousands of fish. Despite the efforts, the mountain whitefish population remained fairly unaffected, but one official reported that it did improve local relations.[56]

On the whole, anglers supported coarse fish removal, even if it meant the use of fish toxicants, a common practice. During the twentieth century, the use of toxicants to control fish populations became ingrained into fisheries management, offering managers a modern method to rid themselves of undesirable fish. For the most effective fish toxicants, fisheries managers turned to indigenous fishing methods. Starting in the late 1930s, the commercially sold insecticide rotenone became a ubiquitous substance for coarse fish removal. Derived from derris and cubé roots of the East Indies and South America, respectively, indigenous fishers first used the plants for subsistence fishing.[57] To them, it represented an effective way to catch fish, with little effect on humans. Like other fish toxicants, when placed in the water, rotenone disrupts fish's respiratory functions, causing them to stop breathing and die.[58] In coarse fish removal projects, fisheries managers usually treated lakes and sometimes rivers, removed the dead fish, waited until the rotenone lost its toxicity, and then planted hatchery trout. Often, lakes had to be sprayed multiple times, otherwise coarse fish reappeared, moving in from lake inlets or outlets.

While the application of fish toxicants was established long before World War II, their use grew exponentially after the war. In the postwar era, state and federal agencies applied rotenone on hundreds of lakes to improve trout fishing. From the beginning of its use to 1959, fisheries managers treated 563 American lakes with rotenone for trout management.[59] From 1952 to 1962, the Dingell-Johnson Act alone funded coarse fish removal projects for "225,000 acres of lakes and 2,500 miles of streams."[60] Many of these projects occurred in Rocky Mountain waters, where fisheries managers used toxicants as just one tool to maintain the trout populations important to the regional economy and culture.

Even after Rachel Carson's *Silent Spring* (1962) alerted Americans to the dangers of insecticides and helped spark the modern environmental movement, fish toxicants continued to be used in coarse fish eradication into the 1970s and beyond. Toxicants remained important to fisheries management despite larger scientific and societal changes in the 1960s and 1970s. The postwar rise of a new ecology largely shifted scientific thought to ecosystems rather than individual species. The survival of species was placed within the larger health of the ecosystem.[61] Additionally, *Silent Spring* connected human health to overall environmental wellbeing when Carson spoke against DDT use. Within this context, predator and pest control started to fade from fish and wildlife management techniques. Within the regional trout culture context, however, fish toxicant use remained prevalent. Scientists created new toxicants for use against coarse fish, illustrating the entrenched sporting values within fisheries management. Since the mid-1960s, fisheries managers used Antimycin, an antibiotic derived from bacteria in the *Streptomyces* genus.[62] In the late 1960s, researchers at the University of Idaho discovered a piscicide selective to pikeminnow, which they later termed "squoxin."[63]

Fisheries managers utilized toxicants extensively in their work, but it did not represent their only response to native coarse fish. State agencies composed of diverse biologists and managers contested the value of native coarse fish just as much as anglers. The large, bureaucratic nature of state fish and game agencies ensured that fisheries managers held different views of native fish. More apt to be trained in ecology in the postwar period, young biologists encountered veterans who continued to see their job as manufacturing trout. Some of the newer biologists promoted native species at the same time their colleagues worked on eradication projects. Working in state fish and game departments, certain biologists began publicity campaigns, attempting to construct new images of coarse fish. For instance, in "Whitefish—The Rainbow's Country Cousin," Montana fisheries biologist J. J. Gaffney sought to alter anglers' opinions of mountain whitefish, laying out the fish's food and sporting benefits. The article included a sketch of mountain whitefish as a "country cousin" traveling to the city, complete with a homely bonnet, freckles, and a worn suitcase.[64] Presumably, Gaffney believed his rural readers could empathize with the fish falsely stereotyped as inferior. Other states' officials also wrote educational tracts in attempts to alter anglers' mindsets about native fish.

These authors noted coarse fish and trout had similar qualities in terms of game, food, and fishing opportunities. If so, why were they so stigmatized among anglers? Coarse fish are unfortunate-looking creatures. The perceptions of the fish have also been shaped by anglers' sensory experiences and reactions. To some extent, anthropomorphism still influences animal protection and many conservation groups concentrate on animals who exhibit human-like features. Many scholars have also debated the central role of charismatic megafauna within wildlife conservation, to the detriment of lesser-valued species. While perhaps not on the hideously ugly level of deep sea creatures or the microscopic level of insects, coarse fish are less attractive than trout species prized for their beauty and game qualities. Scientists David Starr Jordan and Barton Warren Evermann called the Salmonidae family one of the most important among fish groups because of these attributes.[65] Anglers and angling writers also enjoyed the appeal of trout. In 1850, Henry William Herbert described the brook trout as "one of the most beautiful creatures in form, color, and motion, that can be imagined."[66] Coarse fish could not compare to trout in terms of beauty.

Coarse fish, as the name implies, are scaly, lacking the brightly colored, eye-pleasing visual show of trout species. Numerous species have sucker mouths with no teeth, differentiating them from the more well-liked trout that have sharp teeth. Many anglers have discussed the unbecoming qualities of the abundant mountain whitefish, particularly its snout and scaly, brownish-grey body. Even writer and English professor Greg Keeler sings the "White Fish Blues": "Yes, your brook trout look like jewelry / Diamonds and rubies shine like stars / But your white dog look like something sold only on television / That you'd use to vacuum out your car."[67] Other coarse fish were also subject to criticisms. One early Utah resident disliked the food qualities of upper Colorado native fish—two of which have Quasimodo-like deformities—adding, "Of course we didn't think they were pretty either, like rainbow trout or game fish."[68] Fly-fishing humorist John Gierach has observed that Colorado pikeminnow offer game, but not a trophy appearance, to anglers: "Possibly the largest fish most Coloradoans will ever catch in a river, but also probably one you wouldn't stuff and hang over the mantel in the den."[69] As ugly fish, coarser species became trash fish in a trout culture, with few proponents on one hand and fish-wasting anglers and toxicant-wielding managers on the other. Appearance, however, did not play a totalizing role in the fate of coarse fish.

As the focus on wild trout and the development of conservation biology has led to a great emphasis on native fish and preserving biodiversity, fish managers are now forced to confront the past. Has this growing interest in nativeness included the sullied mountain whitefish and other coarse fish? Due to a firmly planted western trout aesthetic, the species remains ignored by managers and anglers. The Idaho Fish and Game biologists who have recently been forced to deal with declining populations in the Big Lost River noted that the species "continue to remain an afterthought for most fisheries research and management programs in western North America."[70] Anglers' mistreatment of mountain whitefish has also continued to the present. Former *Rocky Mountain News* outdoor reporter Ed Dentry once recalled a disturbing sight on the Madison River. He watched a fisherman become more and more irritated by catching numerous mountain whitefish. The fisherman then landed a large whitefish and threw it on the bank. Dentry described the next scene: "He started his next cast, then changed his mind. He rushed up the bank, found the flopping fish and jumped up and down on it." The reporter saw this as "typical" of the species' poor reputation among anglers.[71] Other fish kills still occur, as anglers squeeze to death trash fish or leave them dead on the banks on other western rivers.[72] John Gierach saw this "squeeze-and-release" technique for mountain whitefish on the Henry's Fork River in Idaho, observing that the species "get[s] lumped together with suckers in the 'turd knocker' category."[73] Although discontinued in the early 2000s, the annual whitefish "festival" held on Colorado's Roaring Fork River demonstrated the fish's poor reputation. As if in some type of bizzaro-world, anglers took advantage of the state's lack of regulations and pulled hundreds of whitefish out of the river. Illustrating an entrenched western trout culture, corporate sponsors then replaced the dead fish with hatchery rainbow trout.[74]

The twentieth-century development of a Rocky Mountain trout culture and aesthetic translated into an upsurge of mistreatment or neglect of native coarse fish species by midcentury, indicating how the obsessive focus on trout caused declines for native species. A divided transnational sporting culture influenced anglers' perceptions of these fish, as class, race, and gender defined proper prey. Individual experiences also prompted anglers to champion coarse fish species, fracturing sporting debates. The mainstream fishing culture that disliked coarse fish, however, shaped western fisheries management for much of the twentieth century. State conservation agencies rarely protected coarse fish, refusing to give them "game" fish status. By the midcentury, the new terminology for coarse fish ("trash fish") mirrored the growing economic and cultural importance of nonnative trout in the Rockies. For anglers and fisheries managers, saving these trout often meant killing native coarse fish with toxicants or other methods. Many of these sporting values continue to the present, with few groups lobbying for non-game fishes.[75] Some anglers still stomp on fish. And management agencies remain slow to change. Despite their unprivileged status as ugly creatures, the conservation of so-called trash fish continues to be crucial for preserving biodiversity in western rivers. Genetically pure populations of most coarse fish still exist because, ironically, fisheries managers did not artificially propagate them in the hatchery system, largely ignoring them instead. Therefore, the century-long neglect of western native fish has a bright side, offering anglers and conservationists a chance to address the wrongs of the past before it is too late.

The history of coarse fish shows how anglers and fisheries managers extensively manipulated trout populations at the expense of other species. Coarse fish just got in their way. Tampering with fish species in western waters, they attempted to create an authentic "western" trout fishing experience for regional anglers and tourists. Likewise, the waterways themselves could be manipulated with the same hubristic views that humans could control and shape nature to their liking. By the mid-twentieth century, dams had blocked most western rivers. Many of these dams, ironically, created better trout fishing (known as the tailwater effect). Crowding and conflicts came along with the trout-filled tailwater fisheries. These artificial landscapes offer a different perspective of the Rocky Mountain trout culture, one in which westerners argued over place and region—and even trout. All of this culminated toward the end of the twentieth century with criticisms of the western hatchery system, coarse fish removal projects, tailwater fisheries, and the other ways in which fish managers meddled with nature to maintain good trout fishing.

Lunkers

THE SPRING OF 2011 PROVED TO BE A TRYING TIME FOR STATE politics across the nation. Massive protests erupted as elementary school teachers, labor unionists, and hordes of other private citizens stormed Wisconsin's capital when the Republican-controlled legislature attempted to end collective bargaining rights for state workers. In raging debates, Arizonans disputed continual attempts to make harsh immigration laws even stricter. Other states struggled with serious budget woes or Tea Party–induced challenges to federal and state laws. In Montana, meanwhile, lawmakers debated the definition of an irrigation ditch.

The seemingly unimportant issue attracted an overflowing crowd to the floor, gallery, and halls surrounding one of the chambers in the Montana capitol building that spring. The vast majority opposed a bill that threatened to strip anglers' traditional access to the state's irrigation streams. Ultimately unsuccessful, the bill was a reaction to a 2008 Montana Supreme Court decision over access to public waters. The verdict legitimized angler access to Mitchell Slough along the Bitterroot River after wealthy landowners like Huey Lewis (of 1980s music fame) claimed the slough was manmade, attempting to limit the public access that Montana anglers had enjoyed for decades.[1] The court found that Mitchell Slough followed a historic waterway and rejected the bid to close the slough to anglers. This loss prompted the unsuccessful 2011 bill that raised the ire of the state's powerful angling lobby and filled the capitol with opponents. Few states could garner one of the session's largest crowds over the definition of an irrigation ditch, but as English professor and fly-fishing theorist Ted Leeson reminds us, in Ennis, Montana, and arguably many of the region's towns, "Trout are both a business and an atmospheric condition."[2] The Montana access fights and contemporary political debates illustrate how this rising atmospheric condition and western trout culture dealt with the vast environmental changes and many conflicts arising from irrigation and dams since the nineteenth century, while ironically ignoring all of the region's human-made trout fisheries.

When anglers, fisheries managers, and regional boosters created a Rocky Mountain trout culture and economy during the twentieth century, there were significant environmental consequences for the region's fisheries, especially for coarse fish. Yet sporting culture and fisheries managers debated and contested the values of western native fish, showing that conceptions of place and fish were always contested and selective about who belonged to the region. In the creation of a trout place and the continuous work to sustain Rocky Mountain trout fishing, fisheries managers and anglers also navigated entirely different ideas of place and ways of ordering the landscape within the region's agriculture economy, with its western water law, irrigation infrastructure, and widespread dam building.[3]

Western reliance on irrigation and dam building transformed Rocky Mountain watersheds and their fish starting in the nineteenth century and continuing today. Early western water law and irrigation proved detrimental to an emerging trout culture and its fish populations, revealing the contested nature of water use. At times, irrigation canals pulled fish out of the river or took too much water, creating poor conditions for aquatic life. Early fish culturalists, however, retained their optimism in human control over nature in the arid West. They viewed competing water uses as reconcilable, but over time their actions shifted more toward a grudging acceptance of the havoc the western irrigation system wreaked on trout populations. Anglers, too, took a more realistic approach by using irrigation canals for their sport and food opportunities.

The environmental consequences of early irrigation, however, remained insignificant compared to post–World War II dam building. In this era, federal efforts ensured the construction of dams on almost every major western river. These barriers sometimes paradoxically yielded better trout fishing in the tailwaters flowing out of them. The fun, yet crowded and built environment prompted environmentalist Gary LaFontaine to criticize tailwater fisheries. An obsessive fly fisher and innovator, LaFontaine wrote his master's thesis in behavioral psychology on selective feeding in trout and based his seminal book *Caddisflies* (1989) on years of research and experiments like scuba diving in a river to see how insects and fly patterns looked to fish.[4] He also equated the Bighorn River tailwater trout fishery to Disneyland. Like Disneyland, tailwaters represented a constructed and highly manipulated environment where visitors shared in and benefited from the artificiality of it all, as it took management and control over nature to a new level. While LaFontaine enjoyed catching the large trout, the experience offered a "cheap thrill" in a crowded, unnatural environment.[5] As tailwaters cultivated multitudes of giant trout, they made possible the spread of trout to previously impossible places like the American South. The new environments also transformed fly patterns and fishing, largely standardizing tailwater fishing across the United States as anglers adapted their techniques and fly patterns to changing environmental conditions. This managed landscape and its consequences for native ecosystems and people have been overlooked as the fishing industry and tourists have glorified fly fishing and trout as timeless and natural.

Good trout fishing could be just as contentious as it was revered. At the same time as they enlarged the Rocky Mountain trout culture, tailwaters caused native fish declines, crowding, and user conflicts. Years of environmental change came to a head with the fight over the Bighorn River tailwater in the 1970s and early 1980s. Culminating in a 1981 Supreme Court case, the Crow Tribe ultimately lost its ownership and control over the riverbed to the state of Montana (which represented non-Crow anglers). The case demonstrated that continued environmental transformations within the region's trout culture led to even more struggles over water and fish, eventually creating a backlash against hatchery management and the unnatural aspects of western trout fishing.

The first conflicts stemmed from irrigation and water use. Western water law and the extensive network of headgates, canals, lateral lines, and other irrigation trappings in and along western waterways inflamed problems for Rocky Mountain trout fisheries in the nineteenth and twentieth centuries. Based on the doctrine of prior appropriation, western water law ignored the recreational uses of water, even if these recreational uses supported substantial industries. Irrigation within the prior appropriation water rights doctrine caused low water or no water conditions (now called "dewatering") throughout the West starting in the nineteenth century and continuing to today. Aridity and hydraulic mining prompted western states to adopt the doctrine in the late nineteenth century, as prior appropriation codified individualism and competition within western water use by giving rights to miners, farmers, and ranchers who first used the water ("first in time is first in right") and by ensuring those rights only if irrigators continually used the water for consumption or agriculture ("use it or lose it").[6] The "use it or lose it" mentality offered little incentive for irrigators to regulate their water use under prior appropriation. Irrigation became part of a legacy of extractive western industries that inspired native son Wallace Stegner to remark the region "was not so much settled as raided."[7] This ethos sucked rivers and lakes dry, proving problematic for early fish culturalists who tried to create and maintain good trout fishing.

In the nineteenth and twentieth centuries, dried-up waterways and dying fish were common in some locales, as the hopes of fish culturalists to establish a trout-fishing paradise ran up against agricultural use and prior appropriation. Working for the US Fish Commission, renowned ichthyologist David Starr Jordan, for example, reported this problem in 1889. He observed some Colorado riverbeds "filled with dry clay and dust" because of irrigation use.[8] As the irrigated water provided new life for crops and pastures, its overuse killed many fish. Dewatering occurred frequently in the arid West. Around the turn of the century, an estimated three hundred tons of suckers from Utah Lake died when they ran up Provo River to spawn at the same time that irrigators dried up the riverbed. Upon investigation, the state fish and game commissioner described the scene: "The sight and smell was disgusting, so much so that it was feared that an epidemic would result from the decaying of such a large number of fish and the county commissioners order the water from the canals turned back into the channel of the river for a sufficient time to wash the dead fish down into the lake." As disliked trash fish, the large-scale loss of suckers may or may not have incensed anglers, although the commissioner did qualify the incident by noting they were "considered the best class of suckers."[9] Like the Utah Lake incident, irrigators sometimes dewatered entire rivers, creating problems for state agencies.

Maintaining instream flows for fish did not fall under "use" within prior appropriation water law until the late twentieth century, forcing anglers and state agencies to address dewatering problems throughout the previous century. In 1925, the Idaho state game warden outlined the dilemma that state fish and game agencies faced. Despite Idaho Fish and Game Department efforts to thwart losses through irrigation and dewatering, the warden complained the agency did not control the water and those who held water rights "have the right, if they so desire, to use all the water of such streams for irrigation purposes, regardless of the result."[10] The low water conditions created by irrigation made it harder for state agencies to fulfill their mandates of protecting rivers and fish. Echoing problems from other states and other eras, the Utah fish and game commissioner lamented in 1948 that "the diversion of water for irrigation systems has cut deeply into the amount of fishable water."[11] Dewatering represented just one problem with irrigation for regional fisheries.

Irrigation canals also pulled fish from rivers. As early irrigators diverted and siphoned water for hay or other crops, they unintentionally drew out fish, vexing early fish culturalists and anglers and forcing them to confront agricultural interests. As David Starr Jordan chronicled Colorado and Utah fish species and the problems with dewatering, he observed fish loss in irrigation canals: "Great numbers of trout, in many cases thousands of them, pass into these irrigation ditches and are left to perish in the fields. The destruction of trout by this agency is far greater than that due to all others combined and it is going on in almost every irrigating ditch in Colorado." In Utah, Jordan noticed the same conditions, where irrigation canals siphoned "millions of young trout" from the rivers.[12] Jordan was describing a dilemma generated by the conflicting uses of a scarce western resource: water.

Fish loss through irrigation canals appeared to be widespread in the United States and Canada in the nineteenth and twentieth centuries, but it became particularly pronounced in the arid and semi-arid western sections, where agriculture relied more on irrigation. For instance, in 1900, the Idaho state fish and game warden deplored the "enormous quantities" of fish killed when irrigation stopped each year.[13] Other states dealt with the same problems. Utah officials reported continued loss of trout and other fish through irrigation canals at the turn of the century, listing dynamite, irrigation ditches, and sawdust as the three main factors that harmed fish.[14] Utah county wardens found the problem widespread and one estimated that "one-third" of fish populations died in irrigation ditches yearly.[15] The extensive western irrigation infrastructure pulled fish from rivers and dried up waterways, all of which was legitimized under prior appropriation.

Fish interests did not necessarily view the seemingly opposing water uses (water for fields, water for fish) as incompatible. Like western irrigation, fish culture and the transformation of Rocky Mountain fisheries relied on an optimistic view of western aridity and humans' ability to improve nature. Both failed to consider the natural limits of western water. One federal hatchery superintendent exemplified these beliefs: "Our 'Great American Desert' is being rapidly irrigated out of existence. Where it once stood, we now find prosperous agricultural communities, supporting thriving towns and cities."[16] To him, irrigation and hatcheries represented progress. With proper measures, both could flourish. Other settler societies also held firm in their opinions that environmental realities could be mastered. In Canada, the dominion commissioner of fisheries noted that irrigation and fish was a "grave question" for western states and provinces in the 1920s. Using Australia as an example, he argued that with proper planning, dams and irrigation schemes could benefit fish in western North America.[17] Settlement, as well as state resource planning, represented faith in progress and optimism in science.

Fish culturalists continually promoted better protection of fish under the law and worked to remedy irrigation woes. In the nineteenth and early twentieth centuries, many westerners agreed that, with the right measures, quality trout fisheries could exist alongside dams and irrigation ditches. The earliest attempts to reconcile the two water uses focused on placing screens or barriers in irrigation ditches to prevent trout from being siphoned out with the water. Starting in the territorial period and continuing throughout the twentieth century, both regulations and volunteers worked to save fish from irrigation systems. One of the first territories to act, Wyoming passed territorial laws and later state laws designed to prevent fish loss from small diversion dams and irrigation. Starting in 1879, the territory required fishways for dams and irrigation canals and later directed irrigators to place screens at irrigation diversions.[18] Utah enacted a similar law in 1880, requiring screens for irrigation ditches, but irrigators often disregarded this law, mirroring the enforcement problems surrounding other early state regulations dealing with environmental degradation.[19]

Other states found it difficult to pass legislation despite efforts from fish culturalists and managers. During the early twentieth century, Idaho and Montana did not have irrigation screen laws. In Montana, James A. Henshall failed twice to have the provision included in state laws. With his typical Victorian verbosity, Henshall brought the problem before the American Fisheries Society: "There is a source not generally suspected that is the cause of untold havoc and destruction, whereby millions of fish and fry perish annually. This is all the more lamentable as it could be so easily prevented. I allude to the wholesale destruction of fish life through the operation of irrigation ditches."[20] After being reassigned from Bozeman to a Mississippi station, Henshall continued his work promoting irrigation screens, this time at a national level. Like others, Henshall sought to reconcile irrigation and fish uses of water.

In the region's trout culture, popular sporting clubs backed state and national efforts for fish screen legislation, while working locally alongside irrigators to find solutions and screen canals. Anglers constantly tried to maintain good relations with landowners for fishing access and promoted good relations among ranchers and farmers, some of whom belonged to the same sporting clubs. Based in Missoula, the Western Montana Anglers' Association offered a ten-dollar reward for information leading to the conviction of anglers who committed depredations on lands adjacent to fishing waters in Missoula County.[21] The Western Montana Anglers' Association and other sporting clubs throughout the Rocky Mountains promoted goodwill by helping irrigators install screens on their canals. In Utah, the Cache County Fish and Game Protective Association cooperated with ranchers and the fish and game department, donating both time and money to screen irrigation canals.[22] Such collaboration confirmed the need to maintain strong relationships with irrigators in addition to sustaining good fishing in the region.

The extensive irrigation system, however, made the work never-ending. Despite early laws requiring fish screens and the optimism of fish managers and anglers, fish loss through irrigation ditches continued throughout the twentieth century. In 1914, the Wyoming state game warden lamented that the earlier laws had been unenforced and his department continued to search for an efficient screen.[23] Almost thirty years later, his successor held the same sentiments, stating the department "found it impossible to enforce" the irrigation screen laws, calling for urgency since "the greatest single loss of fish is through irrigation ditches."[24]

Other areas also experienced continual problems, including Indian reservations. On reservations, irrigation ditches took the same form and created similar problems, even though water use fell under the Winters Doctrine, rather than prior appropriation, in which water rights were reserved with the creation of reservations.[25] Wilderness advocate and Bureau of Indian Affairs forester Bob Marshall wrote in the 1930s that fish were "still swimming in the fields" at the Uintah and Ouray reservations. He complained that no action had been taken from the year before and noted that other reservations had similar grievances.[26] Fish continued to die in irrigation ditches into the 1960s on the Flathead Reservation. In response, the tribal council of the Confederated Salish and Kootenai Tribes called for solutions to address the fish loss. The tribal chairman saw the annual losses as a waste: "If the fish are caught for human consumption it is not too bad, however, the many fish that are left to die is something else."[27] Western tribes continued to face problems with fish loss, dewatering, and other irrigation issues in the twentieth century.

The ongoing fish loss throughout the twentieth-century West prompted many anglers and fisheries managers to take a more pragmatic approach in reconciling an emergent trout culture and economy with an entrenched irrigation system. Many westerners used the drawdowns of reservoirs or the fish in irrigation canals as opportunities for food and sport. In the early twentieth century, one Utah official deplored the collection of fish from irrigation canals: "In many localities the farmers get their supplies of trout from the irrigating ditches, and on their land after irrigating, and depend largely on these destructive conditions for fish food."[28] The collection of fish from canals and irrigated fields became a yearly ritual for many westerners. Locals near Mountain Home, Idaho, took advantage; one observer reported that "many are secured by parties who are on the watch for the annual destruction of these fish."[29] Likewise, the late summer drawdown of the Mission Reservoir on the Flathead Reservation furnished the opportunity to easily catch fish. The reservation superintendent noted that before fishing closures, locals took advantage of the low water conditions: "Both Indians and whites were taking these fish by the basket full."[30] Dewatering nourished a festive fishing atmosphere at times. Other anglers turned the irrigation infrastructure into a place for sport. In Idaho, local sporting clubs stocked fish in drainage ditches or farmers themselves fished in the canals.[31]

While some anglers embraced the environmental changes created by the western irrigation system and incorporated them into regional fishing traditions, state agencies pragmatically dealt with fish loss through salvage operations. To save fish from irrigation canals and dewatering, state agencies annually embarked on rescue work during the mid-twentieth century. With prior appropriation ingrained into western water law, state fish agen-

A man fishes Archer Canal near Alameda Avenue in Denver while his dog takes a nap. Photograph taken between 1904 and 1909 by Charles S. Lillybridge. Courtesy of History Colorado (Charles S. Lillybridge Collection, scan #20000002).

cies raced to save fish from irrigation canals and dewatered reservoirs and streams every year in the late summer and fall. For instance Utah officials put back almost 3,500 trout into rivers after the canal waters were shut off in 1908.[32] The numbers grew by midcentury. Wyoming workers saved over 300,000 fish from reservoirs and streams in the low water years of 1939 and 1940.[33] In 1958, the state salvaged almost 10,000 fish from two canals alone.[34] In a similar fashion, Idaho hatchery workers retrieved about 93,000 game fish from Lake Lowell canals in 1951. They used the opportunity to sort out the coarse fish, trucking game fish to nearby ponds, reservoirs, and creeks with more water and feeding the coarse fish to trout in nearby state hatcheries.[35] These managers tried to make the best of the situation by eradicating disliked trash fish and attempting to save trout. By the mid-twentieth century, salvaging fish became a standard part of management operations. While initially optimistic about western irrigation systems, anglers and managers learned hard lessons about low water conditions and combating fish loss through irrigation canals.

In the years following World War II, the increase in western dam building provided a solution. Certain inland dams helped managers in their manipulation of western fisheries by ironically creating ideal trout habitat in many western rivers. Tailwaters, however, represented a continuation of earlier policies in which anglers and fish managers, sometimes catering to tourists, manipulated rivers and fish in a Rocky Mountain trout culture that relied on widespread environmental change. In this case, trout habitat was brought into existence accidentally by postwar dam building.

Although federal involvement in irrigation dated back to the National Reclamation Act in 1902, the large-scale construction of dams started during the New Deal and occurred primarily in the post–World War II era. The Army Corps of Engineers and the Bureau of Reclamation built numerous dams along all of the West's major rivers: the Columbia, the Colorado, and the Missouri.[36] But the dam building did not stop there. The agencies then moved to the major tributary rivers, damming an astounding number of rivers. On the Columbia and its tributaries, the Army Corps of Engineers and various public utility districts erected thirty-six dams, mostly for hydroelectricity and flood control. Likewise, the Bureau of Reclamation constructed hundreds of irrigation dams in western states.[37] The ability of these dams to control water gave rise to the modern West. That is, the sweeping dam system enabled the shift of American economic and political power from the Rust Belt of the northeast toward the Sunbelt of the West and South. Dams allowed urban growth by providing water and electricity for new Sunbelt cities like Phoenix, powered industrial and military manufacturing, and watered extensive agriculture.[38] The water that made it possible—trout water—flowed from headwaters and snow in the Rocky Mountains, filling slack water reservoirs to be pumped onto fields, into growing urban and suburban communities, and through turbines to power the electrical needs of new industrialization and urbanization.

The immense environmental, economic, and social changes wrought by Army Corps of Engineers and Bureau of Reclamation dam building also met resistance from the growing environmental movement in the postwar era. Anglers often contributed, playing key roles in the grassroots opposition to dams. Many anglers believed that dams caused the death of a river, a common analogy employed in the fights against dams. They saw dams as detrimental to both fish and scenery after learning lessons from earlier dam building on eastern coastal rivers as well as other larger rivers around the nation. For example, the Wyoming Division of the Izaak Walton League of America worried about the scenery and fish that would be "destroyed" due to dam building, passing a resolution in 1939 that stated "broad public values" should be considered in the decision-making process.[39] Other opposition employed similar language of death and destruction. When fly-tying innovator, guide, and writer Dave Whitlock spoke out against a revised proposal in the 1970s to dam Montana's Big Hole River, he made a comparison to the nearby Beaverhead River: "In recent years I have had the opportunity to witness the damming and death of the Big Hole's sister river the Beaverhead. I look at the silt filling impoundment and ditch below and I cannot rationalize the worth of such a project and the death of the Beaverhead."[40] Anglers were not just being overly dramatic when they connected dams to the death of rivers.

Dams often killed fish life, especially along coastal rivers and anadromous fish runs. Dams additionally hurt inland fisheries and freshwater fish. After the construction of Clark Canyon Dam on the Beaverhead, one state wildlife official decried the death of fish in almost two river miles below the dam, caused by deadly hydrogen sulfide from decaying plants flooded by the reservoir above. Equally disconcerting, no one knew how long it would occur.[41] Due to the environmental problems created by dam construction, like the fish kills in the Beaverhead, many anglers spoke out against proposed projects on their local waters.

Dams, however, did not necessarily spell the death of rivers. Despite the fears of anglers, over time, inland rivers like the Beaverhead could be remade into arguably better trout fisheries. Fly-fishing environmentalist Gary LaFontaine acknowledged early on this paradox of tailwaters: "Let me admit a bit of hypocrisy: whenever a dam is proposed I try through individual effort and membership in conservation organizations, to stop its construction; but if I had to make a list of my favorite trout fisheries it would include many tail-water rivers—some of them resulting from the very dams I worked hard to prevent."[42] To the dismay and strange approval of LaFontaine and other anglers, dams refashioned many western rivers

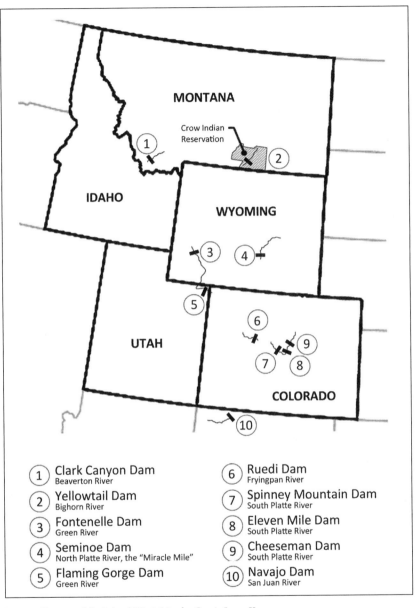

MONTANA

Crow Indian Reservation

IDAHO

WYOMING

UTAH

COLORADO

①	**Clark Canyon Dam** Beaverton River	⑥	**Ruedi Dam** Fryingpan River
②	**Yellowtail Dam** Bighorn River	⑦	**Spinney Mountain Dam** South Platte River
③	**Fontenelle Dam** Green River	⑧	**Eleven Mile Dam** South Platte River
④	**Seminoe Dam** North Platte River, the "Miracle Mile"	⑨	**Cheeseman Dam** South Platte River
⑤	**Flaming Gorge Dam** Green River	⑩	**Navajo Dam** San Juan River

Major tailwaters of the inland West. Map by Carrie Lynn Kyser.

into popular attractions. In these tailwaters, the toxicant use on coarse fish, intensive trout stocking, and other trout management practices forced anglers like LaFontaine to reluctantly come to terms with the unnaturalness of the region's trout culture.

The construction of bottom-release dams, mostly during the 1950s and 1960s, eventually offered some great trout fishing—a benefit entirely unplanned by the Bureau of Reclamation.[43] These tailwaters replaced earlier fisheries with the massive environmental changes. Some of the West's most productive trout fisheries, such as the Bighorn and Beaverhead rivers in Montana, Wyoming's so-called "Miracle Mile" on the North Platte River, the Green River in Utah and Wyoming, and Colorado's South Platte and Fryingpan rivers, occur below dams. All made possible, ironically, by the dams, western tailwater fisheries represent some of the top fishing destinations because of their high populations of large trout. Dammed western rivers may not have died, but they were transformed, integrated into a regional trout culture.

As a manifestation of Rocky Mountain trout culture, these rivers required extensive environmental manipulation to produce trout. Dams transformed the stream flows, water temperatures, and nutrient loads of the rivers below them, which in turn reshaped aquatic life. The best tailwater trout fisheries occur below high, large storage capacity, bottom-release dams. The dams' controlled releases stabilize stream flows, providing more water during the hot, late summer months, as well as mitigating the large spring runoffs. This promotes more streamside and aquatic vegetation, helping trout and insects (trout food) grow. Dams also regulate fluctuations in water temperature throughout the seasons. Lastly, the impoundments trap sediment and nutrients, so the water flowing from the dams is clear, oxygenized, and nutrient-rich, yielding higher growth rates for vegetation, insects, and fish.[44] In essence, these conditions produce abnormal growth rates for trout. Anglers sometimes call large trout "hogs," "footballs," or "lunkers." Unprecedented numbers of football-shaped fish live in tailwaters. At its peak, the Bighorn River boasted 12,000 fish per mile, an unnaturally high population that could not exist without the Yellowtail Dam and Afterbay.[45] Greater numbers of large trout exemplified these new tailwaters, allowing the expansion of a western trout culture and crowds of postwar anglers to escape the growing urban and suburban West to enjoy nature in the Rockies.

Tailwaters replaced earlier environments, creating coldwater fisheries in river sections that historically held warmwater species. Bottom-release dams have produced more trout habitat in places where they could not have previously survived, like the semi-arid, sagebrush- and yucca-filled landscape surrounding the Bighorn River. Before the construction of Yellowtail Dam, the river held warmwater and coolwater fish. Seasoned Jackson Hole fishing guide Jack Dennis remembered catching northern pike from the undammed Bighorn in college with a Crow friend on his baseball team. Dennis recalled: "If someone had told me this was going to be a great trout fishery, I'd have laughed."[46]

Like the Bighorn River in southcentral Montana, trout fisheries now exist in unlikely places, such as in many of the southern states. The South's tailwaters brought both trout and new fishing and management strategies to the region, while many southerners reluctantly embraced trout-fishing methods and ethos. By 1950, dams remade over three hundred miles of southern rivers into trout fisheries in Tennessee, Arkansas, and numerous other states.[47] The White River drainage in Arkansas alone boasts four major trout tailwaters.[48] In these places, the West's trout and fly-fishing traditions and management came up against the South's bass and warmwater fishing culture. When these fishing cultures met, southern anglers often rejected the catch-and-release values so prevalent in the Rocky Mountains.[49] Southern tailwaters enlarged an already vibrant western trout culture and economy.

Dam building transformed insect life as well, which led to standardized fishing techniques and fly patterns along the nation's tailwaters. In constructing the ever-important insect doppelgangers, fly fishers re-create nature at the tying vise. They wrap feathers, fur, and other materials around a hook, trying to match sizes and colors and looks, all in an attempt to tie a perfect little insect doppelganger to catch trout. Fly tiers base this craft on streamside observation and sometimes the collection of insects. Or, through years of fishing the same waters, they have gained an intuitive knowledge of the types of patterns that might work for the season's various hatches. English poet John Gay nicely summed up the whole process centuries ago in *Rural Sports* (1713):

He shakes the boughs that on the margin grow,
Which o'er the stream a waving forest throw,

When, if an insect fall, (his certain guide,)
He gently takes him from the whirling tide,
His gaudy vest, his wings, his horns, his size;
Then round the hook the chosen fur he winds,
And on the back a speckled feather binds;
So just the colors shine in every part,
That nature seems to live again in art.[50]

Dependent on nature's creatures, this art reacts to environmental changes.

Tailwaters, then, altered fly fishing, as fly tiers shifted their art in order to catch lunkers. The varied stream flows, nutrients, and water temperatures downstream from dams created new insect life. Fewer insect species, mainly midges, scuds, sowbugs, aquatic earthworms, and blue-winged olives, inhabited the river sections near the dams, but they existed in high concentrations and tended to be tiny.[51] In the 1970s, one Colorado fly fisher and his fishing partners started to realize their traditional fly patterns did not work so well on the South Platte tailwater. As passionate fly fishers, they attempted to get a copy of entomologist J. V. Ward's 1973 University of Colorado dissertation (imaginatively titled "An Ecological Study of the South Platte River below Cheesman Reservoir, Colorado with Special Reference to Microinvertebrate Populations as a Function of the Distance from the Reservoir Outlet") in order to learn more about what types of fly patterns might work better. Unfortunately, it had "disappeared mysteriously" from the library shelves.[52] He and his friends discovered—albeit a little late, as shown by the stolen dissertation—that tailwaters rendered big trout and different aquatic insects, thereby requiring new fishing methods and flies.

Just as the small changes to gear during the nineteenth-century tackle revolution gave rise to dry fly fishing, new tailwater environments demanded larger changes to the sport. Changes to insect life (Ward's "microinvertebrate populations") happened in all tailwaters, largely standardizing tailwater fly fishing across the country. Fly patterns that work well along Montana's Beaverhead River, such as simple black midges and amber scuds tied on hooks only a few millimeters long, could catch trout in any tailwater, anywhere. These patterns represent the standardization of tailwater fishing, where fly fishers usually dead drift tiny nymphs deep underwater, the fly patterns for which remain remarkably similar across the country. Born on Colorado's South Platte tailwater, the weighted nymph fishing technique (sometimes called the "South Platte technique") became popular in the 1960s.[53] Gary LaFontaine described the later conformity on the Bighorn, as this method spread to Montana and other tailwaters around the nation: "Guides in drift boats continually pass in copy-cat flotillas, every angler in every boat seemingly dangling a nymph pattern below a brightly colored bobber."[54] While insect diversity and more traditional fishing methods return farther downstream from the dams, the surprising lack of variation in fishing methods has been embraced by many anglers searching for gigantic tailwater trout.[55] Tailwaters at once pay homage to the inescapably large dams looming upstream while obscuring the constructed environment of the rivers themselves.

Many bottom-release dams have produced outstanding trout fishing in the last fifty years, but they have also enveloped native fish declines, crowding, and user conflicts due to the allure of fishing for lunker trout. The Army Corps of Engineers and the Bureau of Reclamation built dams for irrigation, flood control, and hydroelectricity, thus water storage and stream flows were not allocated to maintain fisheries below the dams. These uses translated into the "wildly fluctuating flows" that many tailwaters have suffered.[56] Water shutoffs and irregular flows worked against the excellent conditions that produce those gigantic trout. The North Platte's Miracle Mile, for instance, experienced fish kills in the early 1960s due to low water flows and, in some cases, water shutoffs. The populations only returned after the Wyoming Game and Fish Department worked with the Bureau of Reclamation to try to establish minimum flows.[57] One Wyoming angler, after having some nice fall fishing in 1963 below Glendo Dam, arrived at the river one day to find pools of dead and dying fish, as the water had been shut off. He described one scene: "In the one pool there must have been 200 rainbows 17–20 inches long, all dead and many, many more smaller dead rainbows." Upon complaining to Bureau of Reclamation workers, they told him that, by law, they could not "waste water" for the fish.[58] The same arid conditions during the early 1960s caused fish kills in Idaho reservoirs. Officials reported the worst problems below Magic Dam: "Large numbers of trout died due to overcrowding and suffocation after the water was turned off."[59] Similar scenes played out on other tailwaters after dam construction, revealing the problems with conflicting western water uses within the limits of a semi-arid climate.

Even with optimal stream flows, the construction of dams caused difficulties for native ecosystems. As constructed trout fisheries, tailwaters required considerable management. The new trout fisheries throughout the West and the nation did not spring up overnight and in some locales only occurred in close proximity to the dams and their coldwater flows. Fishery agencies had to supplement the new, yet barren, coldwater habitats with trout stocking. Managers described this as "put-grow-and-take" stocking.[60] After the fish-killing hydrogen sulfide subsided from the Beaverhead's Clark Canyon Dam, the Montana Fish and Game Department planted trout with good results.[61] Other agencies similarly introduced trout into tailwaters. On the White River in Arkansas, the cold water temperatures killed most of the warmwater species except suckers below the dams, requiring the planting of trout species.[62]

As stocking gave new life to trout fisheries, warmwater and coolwater fishes declined. Tailwaters spelled the decline of certain native fish species, as cold water temperatures ruined their habitat or fish managers eradicated them with the widespread use of fish toxicants during dam construction. Before being dammed, the Bighorn River did contain some trout, but the dam created the phenomenal trout fishery that amazed Jack Dennis.[63] Downstream from Hardin, the river became warmer and reverted back to its pre-impoundment form. Warmwater species comprised most of the fish population in these lower stretches, with the majority being goldeneye.[64] In the case of the Colorado River, a variety of factors caused the endangerment of the river's endemic fish species. Earlier habitat change, introductions of nonnative species, and water pollution from industrial and urban sources, along with later dam building and toxicant applications, led to native fish declines.[65] While native fish populations started to decline earlier, the closing of the Colorado's upstream dams in the 1960s meant many native fishes could not adapt to or spawn in the new coldwater habitat. The Flaming Gorge Dam on the Green River alone destroyed sixty miles of spawning habitat for native species.[66] Fisheries managers from Utah, Wyoming, and the US Fish and Wildlife Service also used the opportunity to treat the Green River and its tributaries with fish toxicants.[67] They aimed to exterminate maligned trash fish to plant nonnative rainbow trout, a common management move at many western dam sites during construction. In the wake of this manipulation, good trout fishing could reportedly be had by 1964 and 1965.[68] Native fish population declines followed; by the early 1970s, scientists believed four of the Colorado River's endemic fish to be endangered.[69] In order to become excellent trout fisheries, however, native fish had to be removed, naturally or unnaturally, from tailwaters.

Anglers searching for large trout did not necessarily worry about native fish declines in the mid-twentieth century. Instead, they flocked to these trout rivers. Crowding marked the tailwater fishing experience, just as it characterized amusement parks. Fly fishing humorist John Gierach has called this crowding at good fishing spots "hog-hole mob scenes," observing that in most cases they take place at a tailwater fishery: "The local wildlife agency probably describes it in florid terms—'a jewel in the crown of the state's fisheries,' or something like that. It's also public, easily accessible and every fisherman in a three- or four-state area knows about it."[70] Big trout attracted big crowds at most tailwater fisheries. In 1965, anglers fished the Missouri River below Holter Dam more than any other river section in Montana. Montana Fish, Wildlife and Parks reported that the stretch supported "over 40,000 fisherman days per year."[71] By the late 1970s, Wyoming officials likewise observed the popularity of the Miracle Mile, stating that it "supports over 25,000 fisherman days with an average catch rate of .5 trout per hour."[72] The congestion magnified user conflicts. Some agencies have attempted to control overuse through special regulations. On the Beaverhead River, guide trips and out-of-state float fishing on certain stretches one day a week have been prohibited. More recently, the overcrowding on the San Juan River, which brings $20–40 million to the state's economy each year, prompted the New Mexico legislature to propose a user fee specifically for the river.[73] The environmental changes of tailwaters precipitated these and other user disagreements, illustrating the economic importance of large trout in the Rocky Mountains.

Years of environmental change and conflicts culminated in an important case on Montana's Bighorn River that exemplified the new power of the region's outdoor recreation and tourism industry to control both nature and people. The new Bighorn tailwater and the importance of its lunker trout—not the goldeneye, northern pike, or other warmwater fish that once filled the river—triggered conflict. The fights over the Bighorn implicitly involved racial tensions created by the crowds of white anglers drawn to the tailwater trout.

After the creation of Yellowtail Dam, the Crow Tribe sought to prohibit non-member hunting and fishing within the reservation through a tribal resolution passed in 1973.[74] To do so, they claimed ownership of the river-bed and the right to regulate non-Indians on non-Indian land held in fee simple. Dismayed by the ban, Montana Fish and Game Department officials bemoaned that "many miles of good trout waters are located on tribal lands with fishing restricted to Indians."[75] After the official tribal resolution, the state of Montana asserted its authority to regulate the hunting and fishing of non-Indians on the reservation. Acting on the Crows' behalf, the federal government responded by filing an action to seek a judgment over ownership of the riverbed and who held the authority to regulate hunting and fishing within the reservation.

The resulting legal battles took years to decide. The case, *Montana v. United States*, eventually reached the Supreme Court in 1981. In a 6–3 decision, the high court reversed the court of appeals decision and held that earlier treaties with the Crows said nothing of riverbeds and that Montana gained ownership when it was admitted to the union. Justice Stewart's opinion maintained that the treaties failed to define Crow ownership of riverbeds: "The Crow treaties in this case, like the Chippewa treaties in *Holt State Bank*, fail to overcome the established presumption that the beds of navigable waters remain in trust for future States and pass to the new States when they assume sovereignty." The decision agreed that tribes can control hunting and fishing on tribal lands, including the regulation of non-Indians within those lands, but "that power cannot apply to lands held in fee by non-Indians."[76] In addition, the court found two exceptions to this rule, now known as the Montana exceptions. The first stated that if non-Indians held a contractual relationship with a tribe, that tribe had the right to regulate activities in those lands. The second rule declared that a tribe may have authority over non-Indian, fee simple land when the owner's conduct threatens the tribe: "A tribe may also retain inherent power to exercise civil authority over the conduct of non-Indians on fee lands within its reservation when that conduct threatens or has some direct effect on the political integrity, the economic security, or the health or welfare of the tribe."[77] In the decision, Justice Blackmun dissented (joined by Justices Brennan and Marshall), claiming the court must interpret treaties how the tribes would have construed them. In this case, the Crows would have construed the treaty to include ownership of the riverbed. Blackmun argued, "Because I believe that the United States intended, and the Crow Nation understood, that the bed of the Bighorn was to belong to the Crow Indians, I dissent from so much of the Court's opinion as holds otherwise."[78] Despite going against its own principles, the court took away Crow rights to regulate one of the nation's most famous and most crowded tailwaters.

The case was an example of how seemingly beneficial environmental change could lack social justice in the 1970s and 1980s. After the verdict, many tribal members lamented the loss of the river. In response to the decision and the opening of the river, Crow activists immediately launched a protest. Using American Indian Movement actions of the 1970s as examples, they briefly occupied a bridge. At one point, a tense confrontation broke out between a BIA policeman protecting protestors with his gun drawn and a sheriff from a neighboring county (far from his jurisdiction) ready to sic dogs on the Crow protestors that included children and tribal elders.[79] The alarming standoff quickly died down, but the resentment lasted for years. Since the opening, the Bighorn River has become a top destination for non-Indian anglers and tourists seeking those monstrous tailwater trout. The whole affair showed the controversial and unsettling aspects in manufacturing place and trout in the Rocky Mountains. The state officials, outfitters, anglers, tourists, and boosters who made a regional trout culture held the power and political sway to control fisheries in a way only imagined by earlier government officials and fish culturalists in the rise of state conservation.

Dam construction and the consequences of building a massive irrigation infrastructure revealed a complicated history of environmental change, proving both problematic and beneficial to the region's fisheries and people. In the nineteenth and twentieth centuries, anglers and fisheries managers first rallied against, and then became somewhat reconciled to, irrigation canals draining water and fish from streams and lakes. The construction of bottom-release dams throughout the arid West created remarkable tailwater trout fisheries by the 1960s. These dams forced fly fishers to tie new fly patterns adapted to the remade river environs, creating a new type of interchangeability within fly fishing techniques. Tailwaters produced assorted ecological and social problems as much as they cranked out lunkers. The new environments turned out deadly for many native fish species. Additionally, the crowding and popularity brought forth user conflicts like those surrounding Crow rights to the Bighorn River. In the postwar era, control over those outside of this trout culture became more pronounced with the rising importance of conservation to the western tourist economy. Yet the sobering realities of troubles along tailwaters failed to diminish the cultural and economic importance of western trout in the twentieth century. In some ways, tailwaters epitomized all the historical changes and environmental manipulations ignored in the mythology of fly fishing and trout.

At the very height of carnival fisheries management, however, many western anglers and some state agencies started to reject the artificiality of tailwaters and the modern world to celebrate the wild qualities of Rocky Mountain rivers and trout. Within a growing environmental movement, they stood up against water pollution, habitat degradation, and the well-established western hatchery system. This shift to "wild trout" marked the enduring effects of the West's entrenched trout culture.

Wild Trout

I N THE EARLY 1970S, A DENTIST AND A PLASTICS SALESMAN with hobbies in entomology revolutionized American fly patterns with their book *Selective Trout.* Authors Doug Swisher and Carl Richards conducted not-so-amateurish scientific studies on Michigan's Au Sable River that formed the basis of the book, which reads as part fly-tying manual, part entomology textbook. After meticulously collecting, categorizing, and photographing insects, they developed new fly patterns designed to more accurately imitate mayflies and other insects. The book transformed dry fly fishing with the simple, no-hackle (no feathers wrapped around the hook) patterns, quickly gaining popularity across the United States. In the Rocky Mountains, the dressed-down flies became especially prevalent on waters like the Henry's Fork of the Snake River and Armstrong Spring Creek along the Yellowstone.[1] As *Selective Trout* refashioned fly fishing on certain waters, it exemplified the wild trout era of the 1960s and 1970s. Swisher and Richards argued that fly fishers needed better patterns to trick trout, believing trout had become more and more selective with the rise of catch-and-release fishing as well as the growth of fly fishing.[2]

In the wild trout era, many anglers rejected the plasticity of the put-and-take fishing experience on western rivers, especially on tailwaters. For all the new and unintended trout-fishing fabulousness birthed by postwar dam building, not all anglers and fisheries managers embraced the manipulation of natural systems, even if it had created rivers filled with lunker trout. In illustrating the shift in values that privileged wild trout (self-sustaining native and nonnative populations) over hatchery varieties, this chapter serves as the logical, if unnatural, end to the history of Rocky Mountain trout. Nonnative trout held a central position in these new conceptions of place that privileged "wild," while obscuring the environmental costs of the Rocky Mountain trout culture and economy and creating a lasting blind spot in western river and fish conservation.

While western anglers had a history of advocating for wild trout under a larger American celebration of untamed nature, during the 1960s and 1970s, they started the slow dismantling of the western hatchery system that had made trout fishing so popular and accessible, along with some willing biologists and fish managers. Preference for wild trout, then, defined both the shifting values of many anglers and the changing management techniques. Responding to scientific studies and demands from anglers, fisheries managers realized widespread hatchery upkeep of Rocky Mountain trout was detrimental to trout populations as well as expensive. Angler-conservationist support, however, made possible the more restrictive regulations for trout (but not coarse fish species) and decline from planting millions of catchable-sized trout yearly. *Selective Trout* reflected these significant changes. Swisher and Richards pragmatically created their more realistic fly patterns amidst both a fly fishing boom and the growing popularity of catch-and-release. Like Swisher and Richards, many anglers saw wild trout as harder to catch than hatchery copies and they enjoyed the challenge. Anglers' concerns over catching wild trout also translated into better environmental protections, strengthened by the mainstream environmental concern of the 1960s and 1970s.[3] Wild trout meant wild rivers as the shift away from reliance on hatcheries made healthy habitat all the more important in sustaining regional trout fisheries.

During the wild trout era, the region's trout culture reached its apex. Over a century of environmental change led to self-sustaining (defined as "wild" by fish managers) populations of trout throughout western waters. The central irony, however, was that they focused mostly on nonnative species. During the 1970s, anglers and state agencies naturalized this history of trout introductions and fish stocking as they looked beyond hatcheries to save local and state fisheries. The wild trout era solidified the continued economic and cultural importance of western trout, creating the Rocky Mountain fisheries that exist today. Many westerners and tourists still enjoy—or confront—trout fishing in the Rocky Mountains while grassroots constituencies of anglers, guides, outfitters, local business owners, and conservationists have worked to address continued and significant environmental problems surrounding regional rivers and trout. Yet new scientific and ethical ideals of nativeness and the preservation of biodiversity have recently offered new challenges to this western trout aesthetic. For instance, the use of fish toxicants to kill nonnative trout in native fish restoration projects suggests an urgent need to revisit western trout conservation.

Long before the wild trout era, some anglers valued native fish and wild trout, in a strand of angling culture that has always been present in the Rocky Mountains, even if just a small minority. During the nineteenth century, many Americans began to see the wild qualities of nature in a more positive light. Influenced by Romanticism, evangelical revivalism, and nationalism, they connected nature to God, redefining the sublime to appreciate the awe of wild landscapes.[4] Holding a sort of collective amnesia for dispossession, western industrialization, urbanization, and environmental change, the conception of wild nature shaped angling and recreational experiences.

This aspect of angling culture proved central to the later shift to "wild" trout. Influenced by a reverence for the wild, some anglers criticized the western hatchery system in the late nineteenth and early twentieth centuries because they disliked catching fish that had become accustomed to humans. In a nineteenth-century fish culture handbook, Livingston Stone pondered the consequences of artificial propagation to the character and temperament of fish themselves, wondering if trout would become domesticated like horses and farm animals.[5] Future generations noticed these changes to trout; hatchery trout acted tamer than wild trout. "This is the last generation of trout fishers. The children will not be able to find any," Denver angler and socialist preacher Myron W. Reed lamented in the late nineteenth century, "Already there are well-trodden paths by every stream in Maine, New York, and in Michigan. I know of but one river in North America by the side of which you will find no paper collar or other evidence of civilization. It is the Nameless River. Not that trout will cease to be. They will be hatched by machinery and raised in ponds, and fattened on chopped liver, and grow flabby and lose their spots."[6] Other anglers echoed these criticisms of hatchery trout. Adapted to human feeding and artificial environments, hatchery trout often approached humans, the creatures they associated with food. Anglers found the willing prey a little too easy to catch. After easily hooking fish, anglers complained hatchery fish did not fight as hard. Anglers detested the characteristics that made fishing into more of a catching activity. In addition, the altered appearances and comparatively dull colors of hatchery fish did not exactly please the senses of anglers who valued the beauty of trout. Anglers had developed these substantial critiques of hatchery fish by the start of the wild trout era.

Only during the 1960s and 1970s did fish agencies start to scale back their hatchery work. Before then, fisheries managers often brushed off critics and continued their heavy reliance on hatcheries to maintain regional trout fisheries. Hatchery stocking represented an ingrained part of twentieth-century fish management. Managers focused on regulations and some habitat improvement, but only slowly overturned their confidence in controlling nature. Federal and state agencies often touted public demand and support from conservation organizations in validating their hatchery policies.[7] The political aspects of fisheries management guaranteed that federal and state agencies would only change slowly, as the hatchery system juggernaut remained hard to criticize.

Due to growing pressure in the 1920s and 1930s, however, some fish managers felt they needed to respond to angler criticisms, justifying the expensive and widespread hatchery activities. In 1929, one federal manager observed that parasites "only rarely" attacked wild trout, whereas hatcheries constantly dealt with disease and parasites due to the unnatural environment and crowding. Yet solutions centered on the continued manipulation of hatcheries and fish, demonstrating the ingrained optimism placed on human supremacy over nature within modern fisheries management.[8] In the 1930s, one US Bureau of Fisheries scientist conducted experiments with hatchery brook and rainbow trout to prove anglers wrong about their poor opinions of hatchery fish. He addressed numerous concerns, arguing that hatchery trout were "about as pretty as any fish had a right to be," and that they tasted better than wild trout, fought well, ate natural insects, provided sport, and were difficult to catch. After finishing the angling experiments, the fish culturalist concluded that hatcheries did not change trout behavior. His almost absurdly reactionary response revealed the entrenched hatchery use in the era's fisheries management practices. Accordingly, the scientist thought that trout would act wild just by being stocked in natural waters: "When trout that look like real trout are put out in trout waters for trout fishermen to catch, I firmly believe they will act like trout."[9] Despite problems with hatchery trout, fish culturalists continued to search for better management solutions within hatcheries themselves.

By the mid-twentieth century, these ideas started to change. The quiet rise of ecology profoundly altered the western world's ideas of nature, bringing with it criticisms of modern scientific management. In speaking of the sea change needed for a more ethical and ecological concern for nature, Aldo Leopold once said, "Perhaps such a shift of values can be achieved by reappraising things unnatural, tame, and confined in terms of natural, wild, and free."[10] Leopold knew that the concept of "wild" could only exist as a dichotomy that compared wild to domesticated, or civilized, or hatchery, or tailwater. No wonder then, in the midst of postwar put-and-take stocking that planted millions of catchable-sized trout in western waters, ecologists and anglers started to denounce hatchery trout and modern fisheries management techniques.

The ecological viewpoint conceptualized the environment as a biotic community that included humans as both a member of the community and its moral protector. By the mid-twentieth century, "natural resources" became ecosystems, as this frame of reference abandoned the optimistic and controlling attitudes of modern fish culturalists.[11] The focus on ecosystems rather than single species did not entirely transform scientific thinking and management, as the continued trash fish eradication programs revealed, but it did erect a framework for criticisms of hatcheries. Central to the conversion, Aldo Leopold's and others' early concerns for native fish criticized the often haphazard nature of western trout introductions and hatchery management. In his seminal *A Sand County Almanac* (1949), Leopold wrote eloquently about a land ethic, developed in the years since his defense of native western fish in 1918. Leopold's placement of humans in a community of life—expressed so simply and profoundly—marked the rise of ecology and the biocentric ethics it championed.[12]

Modern resource management did not fit in this community and land ethic. At the height of put-and-take fishing and catchable-sized trout stocking, Leopold and others began to question the unnaturalness of it all. He promoted sporting values that brought people closer to nature and wildlife and that prevented overharvesting through "self-imposed limitations."[13] Leopold believed the manipulation of natural systems created second-rate aesthetics and poor management practices that ignored environmental degradation:

> Consider, for example, a trout raised in a hatchery and newly liberated in an over-fished stream. The stream is no longer capable of natural trout

production. Pollution has fouled its waters, or deforestation and tram-pling have warmed or silted them. No one would claim that this trout has the same value as a wholly wild one caught out of some unmanaged stream in the high Rockies. Its esthetic connotations are inferior, even though its capture may require skill . . . several over-fished states now depend almost entirely on such manmade trout. All intergrades of artifi-ciality exist, but as mass-use increases it tends to push the whole gamut of conservation techniques toward the artificial end, and the whole scale of trophy-values downward.[14]

From Leopold's viewpoint, hatcheries could never provide quality fishing experiences, in large part, because they failed to address important con-servation issues.

Leopold voiced a growing concern from anglers and new generations of fisheries biologists. Other writers likewise began to rethink the hatch-ery system around the same time. In *Fishing in the West* (1950), Arthur Carhart addressed conservation issues in a fishing manual that capitalized on the growing numbers of Rocky Mountain anglers in the postwar era. After chronicling the history of the degeneration of western waters from gold mining, poor forestry practices, overgrazing, and dam building, Car-hart observed the problems with contemporary hatchery work. Western states continued stocking catchable-sized trout, despite earlier studies that found the practice expensive and not necessarily a good fix for declining fish populations. He then called for more habitat protection rather than the hatcheries so prevalent in the time period: "The fundamental salva-tion of trout fishing in the West, or anywhere, lies in the maintenance of environment."[15] Optimistically ending with the hope of anglers working together on habitat problems, Carhart foretold the later shift to wild trout ethics and management in the 1960s and 1970s.

State and federal agencies, however, had also sporadically managed for wild trout before the wild trout era, as the influence of anglers' apprecia-tions of wild trout and nature helped shape changing management prac-tices. Even in the early and mid-twentieth century, at the western hatchery system's height, fish managers still governed some wild trout streams. First, despite the millions of fish poured into regional lakes and rivers each year, state and federal agencies still did not have the resources to annually stock every single body of water. These neglected waters inadvertently became wild trout rivers. Conversely, fish managers intentionally left some rivers alone. In the 1940s, Wyoming officials shifted stocking practices to reflect anglers' dislike of hatchery trout, observing that anglers favored "wild fish to the hatchery-reared variety."[16] A decade later, the agency sought to preserve cutthroat trout fishing in the Snake River, one of the few places the native fish still existed. It opposed a proposed federal hatchery in Jackson Hole, worried that the nonnative rainbow trout from it would threaten the holdout position of the Snake River cutthroat. One official noted a divide between locals who liked wild fish and tourists who wanted the easier, catchable-sized hatchery fish: "The idea that large fish should be stocked in the Snake River as a tourist attraction is not well taken since most people that fish that area are looking for wild trout rather than the hatchery-reared variety and unfortunately, unless hatchery-reared fish of this size are caught within a week or two of their planting they do not survive any better than small fish. On the other hand, the cost of their production is significantly greater."[17] Like certain employees of the Wyoming Game and Fish Department, locals contested the monetary and environmental costs of the largely unchecked trout stocking that was widespread in the mid-twentieth century.

The National Park Service increasingly managed for wild trout at the same time other western agencies were ramping up their hatchery stocking programs. The National Park Service had already curtailed nonnative trout stocking in the 1930s and began to focus on maintaining native fish within park borders. The agency diverged from other management units due to its mandate to preserve the unique flora and fauna of the parks. In trying to promote the unique fish life of national parks, the park service represented the only federal or state agency that refused to stock catchable-sized trout in the Rocky Mountains. Instead, it became more concerned with native fish. Consequently, it continued with some native fish "maintenance stocking," mostly under the erroneous belief that it could help sustain native fish populations. But even native fish stocking declined within various park boundaries by the mid-twentieth century. The National Park Service, for instance, ended maintenance stocking of cutthroat in Yellowstone Lake during the 1950s.[18] By 1960, the Park Service entirely shifted its focus to the restoration of native fisheries by regulating catches with more restrictive creel limits.[19] Unique among western fish management agencies, the Park Service did not cater solely to anglers and included non-game fish (a.k.a. trash fish) in their management plans. One official observed non-game fish held other values besides that of game: "Species which are of little interest to the angler may be of greater significance ecologically and biologically than sport fishes."[20] With a progressive policy, the Park Service helped usher in a widespread critique of hatcheries and the hubris of many management practices.

Wild trout ethics and management gained ground in the midst of the 1960s and 1970s modern environmental movement, made possible by catch-and-release fishing, a conservation- and sport-oriented technique. While catch-and-release has an extended history, it became an ethos to growing numbers of anglers, particularly fly fishers, by the 1970s, as they rallied against postwar environmental degradation and tried to embrace a more natural fishing experience. Purposefully releasing fish dates back centuries, reflecting both the sporting ideals of the English leisure class and the more practical consideration of all anglers that small fish were often not worth the effort to clean or were too small to eat (and became illegal to keep during the rise of state conservation). Above all, ethics defined sporting values over time and place. When British angler Humphry Davy warned in the early nineteenth century of "an end to the sport in the river" if fellow anglers kept too many fish, he extolled the virtues that have remained surprisingly static over the years.[21] Master fly fisher Lee Wulff (who else could tie a size 28 fly, smaller than a pencil tip, with no vise?) helped popularize the concept of catch-and-release fishing among mid-twentieth-century Americans in his *Handbook of Freshwater Fishing* (1939) as well as his other writings. In the book, Wulff observed a blossoming catch-and-release sentiment: "There is a growing tendency among anglers to release their fish, returning them to the water in order that they may furnish sport again for a brother angler. Game fish are too valuable to be caught only once."[22] In that last sentence, the oft-repeated words of the value of game fish defined the fly fishing ethos for many of its twentieth-century practitioners.

While catch-and-release fishing was not unique to the Rocky Mountains, it did have numerous homegrown advocates. For instance, Ted Trueblood frequently promoted catch-and-release in his column by the 1950s.[23] The values, however, appeared much earlier in his fishing journal. In 1930, just short of his seventeenth birthday, Trueblood talked about putting back numerous smaller fish. Several weeks later, he related some problems with barbed hooks and releasing fish, writing, "I think from now on I will use barbless hooks altogether."[24] These early instances became more refined over the years, while Trueblood's writing influenced anglers on a national level. During the 1960s and 1970s, the cultural and economic power of western fisheries combined with these ethics to create a growing concern for wild trout and river conservation. Of course, more pragmatic concerns guided catch-and-release in the West. A century of mining poisoned numerous western rivers, as new concerns over human health and mercury, lead, and other heavy metal poisoning marked the age of ecology and motivated anglers to release more fish. For a variety of reasons, then, catch-and-release fishing became more popular on Rocky Mountain rivers. A late 1970s study on Montana's Big Hole River illustrated these changes. Despite a ten-pound limit for trout, over 60 percent of anglers released all their fish and less than 1 percent kept the entire limit.[25] (Incidentally, Norman Maclean once complained that "The Big Hole used to be home, sweet home for every son-of-a-bitch from Butte."[26])

These profound shifts within the growing popularity of fly fishing in the 1970s mirrored the environmental consciousness of the era and ushered in the shift to wild trout management. In this era, the modern environmental movement coalesced, centering on health and the human environment, in part thanks to the science of ecology. The movement connected humans and nature, focusing on quality of life issues and standards of living.[27] It renounced the artificialness of the modern world, or at least its resulting environmental degradation.

With the publication of Rachel Carson's *Silent Spring* (1962), environmental activists found a powerful and growing voice. Rachel Carson's thoughtful criticisms of DDT and modern pesticide use in *Silent Spring* helped launch the modern environmental movement in the United States. Carson started the book dramatically by warning of a "spring without voices," that is, sickness among humans and birds and nature in an imaginary town with all-too-real health and environmental maladies.[28] She then cataloged the numerous consequences of DDT use, from birds and fish to humans. Carson's narrative ebbed and flowed with lyrical descriptions of a pastoral nature alongside disturbing premonitions of the future. The results? A bestseller, the *Common Sense* pamphlet that sparked an American environmental revolution.[29] *Silent Spring* had immeasurable influence, not only on postwar chemical use, but also on the environmental movement as a whole.

Western trout and river conservationists joined a varied group of environmental activists responding to numerous postwar changes such as suburbanization, nuclear testing, and toxics. Their work became mainstream by the first Earth Day on April 22, 1970; legislation and consensus marked the 1970s, the so-called "environmental decade" or the "age of ecology." A series of improved endangered species acts in 1966, 1969, and 1972 sought to protect species in danger of extinction and became particularly important for western native fish.[30] These environmental concerns prompted catch-and-release fishing and wild trout ethics.

During the age of ecology, anglers promoted, and sometimes disagreed over, the value of wild trout. Butte conservationist George Grant fished the nearby Big Hole for over fifty years, cherishing the experience of pursuing wild trout: "The fascination or allure of this unusual river was not merely in the pursuit or killing of its wild trout, or later in the taking and releasing of them, but equally so in the appreciation of nature's contribution to the pleasures of man's existence. . . . Few men have ever been so rich."[31] Grant recalled fondly the prime rainbow trout fishing of the midcentury Big Hole River. Many other anglers enjoyed both native and nonnative varieties of wild trout, as one conservationist observed: "There is a significant number of anglers who not only delight in 'wild trout' but also in that species, and if possible, that strain, which is indigenous to a particular body of water."[32] Appreciation for relict populations of native trout revealed the era's increasing concern for nativeness and naturalness, yet nonnative wild trout still overshadowed native fish in the 1970s.

Western anglers often revered wild trout and despised hatchery trout. Always concerned about the artificiality of fishing experiences, environmentalist Gary LaFontaine described hatchery trout as "super-market rainbows" in 1976.[33] David Quammen likewise derided fish planting as "an Easter egg hunt for tourists with fishing rods."[34] Many of the same anglers who championed wild trout ethics formed new conservation groups like Trout Unlimited (TU) and the Federation of Fly Fishers (FFF) in the 1960s, institutionalizing catch-and-release and wild trout ethics throughout the Rocky Mountains and the nation.

Wild trout management proved successful because of the ideals imparted by TU, FFF, and other sporting organizations that grew out of the modern environmental movement. Both organizations had a western focus and promoted sport fishing, conservation, and catch-and-release.[35] They worked

The crowds and carnival atmosphere of fish stocking has often annoyed anglers in search of wild nature. Here, a fish truck stocks Joe's Valley Reservoir in Utah while onlookers gather. Used by permission, Utah State Historical Society, all rights reserved.

closely with management agencies and pressed for wild trout, a dramatic shift in policies compared to previous generations of conservationists who promoted fish culture. Ennis, Montana, fly fisherman Dick McGuire, for instance, complained in 1960 to the Montana Fish and Game Department about the declining fishing on the upper Madison River. McGuire blamed the stocking of catchable-sized rainbows, stating there was "only one reason for the poor fishing[:] . . . the planting program."[36] His concern for wild trout and wild rivers prompted McGuire and others to later found the Southwestern Montana Fly Fishers, a club affiliated with the Federation of Fly Fishers.[37] By the decade's end, scientific studies proved McGuire right.

Anglers' advocacy lent itself well to an already vibrant Rocky Mountain trout culture, yet not all anglers wholly supported wild trout ethics. Sporting culture has always remained contentious; some anglers saw little aesthetic difference between hatchery and wild trout. In *The Sportsman's Notebook* (1964), outdoor writer H. G. Tapply noted a disdain for hatchery trout: "Many fishermen still hold man-reared trout in contempt. Stocked fish are too easy to catch. They can't fight. They taste like liver. They are but pale copies of the real thing." Tapply, however, pragmatically defended hatchery fish, seeing no alternative: "Trout are trout. And since today it's pretty much a choice of fishing for hatchery-produced trout or not fishing for trout at all, the tolerant fisherman will be grateful for what he has and not care whether the trout he catches was born in the rubble of the stream bottom or in an egg tray under electric lights."[38] Like Tapply, some anglers continued to demand hatchery stocking, although this viewpoint became less prevalent over time.

Even if incomplete, the acceptance of catch-and-release fishing and wild trout among many fly fishers created some interesting consequences for fishing and fish, such as changing fly patterns and meeting the same individual fish on a regular basis. Wild trout ethics partially transformed fly fishing starting in the 1970s. First, fly patterns changed to reflect that fish became more selective after being released again and again. Doug Swisher and Carl Richard's book *Selective Trout* pioneered this new fishing philosophy. On the water, their no-hackle patterns looked remarkably real. Returning to that old fly fishing debate of imitators v. attractors, however, attractor patterns still proved effective. Fly fishers continued to use older patterns and methods with frequent success while adding the new patterns to their fly boxes. And some anglers refused to even accept the premise behind selective trout. "We like to think of the idea of selective trout," writer Tom McGuane later observed, "it serves our anthropocentricity to believe that we are in a duel of wits with a fish, a sporting proposition."[39] Wild trout also changed this sporting proposition. In attempts to keep fish alive when released, the fly fisher began to value the fight less than the ability to quickly land and release the fish. Additionally, catch-and-release fishing has given anglers an added familiarity with individual fish, an unsettling intimacy, according to fly fishing philosopher and historian Paul Schullery. Schullery discerned that the continued release of fish has made wild trout fishing not so wild: "I'm not sure

I'm interested in fishing for a fish I know I've caught three times before, named Orville, who resides just under that bush, and who demands a 5X tippet. That's too tame a *situation*, whether the *trout* is wild or not."[40] The Orvilles of the trout world have reminded many anglers that wild trout can be boring too.

Despite the sometimes unintended consequences of catch-and-release and wild trout ethics, anglers continually pressured state agencies for more wild trout opportunities throughout the 1960s and 1970s. In response to this growing ethos, many state agencies offered more wild trout fishing opportunities. Many fisheries managers scaled down their hatchery work by the 1970s, influenced by anglers' criticisms of hatcheries as well as the growing emphasis on ecology and the modern environmental movement. During the age of ecology, Rocky Mountain states still concentrated mostly on game species and trout, but some states shifted more and more to wild trout management.

Montana Fish, Wildlife and Parks led wild trout management during the 1960s and 1970s. In 1967, one agency official observed that many anglers believed wild trout to be "an essential part of a 'quality' fishing trip." In response to angler demands as well as the prohibitive expenses of stocking catchable-sized trout, the agency set aside certain waters as wild trout streams. The official noted that good fishing existed in sections of streams, like the lower Madison River, that had not been planted in years, a sort of default wild trout management that justified current actions.[41] Throughout this time period, the agency promoted the importance of water quality, water quantity, and healthy habitat. Wild trout management, then, came as a natural extension of these policies.

The most important factor in Montana's shift to wild trout management, however, was a pathbreaking study on the Madison River near Ennis. From 1967 to 1971, Montana Fish, Wildlife and Parks biologist Dick Vincent conducted his now-infamous study on the Madison River that led to a wholesale shift to wild trout management on all Montana rivers starting in 1972. Now known as the "godfather" in some department circles, Vincent initially started his study in an entirely different direction. Worried about wild trout populations in the Madison and its tributary O'Dell Creek due to Hebgen Reservoir flows, Vincent realized that in good water years, the fishing still suffered. He then shifted the study to look at the impacts of stocking catchable-sized rainbow trout on the Madison's populations of wild rainbow and brown trout.[42] Local anglers, including Dick McGuire's Southwestern Montana Fly Fishers, supported the study.[43]

The study concluded that catchable-sized fish adversely affected wild trout populations, making hatchery stocking an expensive way to yield even worse fishing. While earlier studies only showed the inefficiency and high costs of stocking catchables, Vincent's study definitively demonstrated the environmental tolls of the reliance on hatcheries.[44] After stocking of catchable rainbows ended in 1969, the wild trout population in the popular Varney section exploded. In two years, the wild trout population grew by 180 percent.[45] By 1975, wild brown and rainbow trout populations in the Varney section had grown tremendously, as Vincent later reported: "By September, 1975, the number of two-year-old and older brown trout had increased 159% from the 1967–69 stocking years and the total pounds increased 103%. Wild rainbow trout have shown even more significant increases, as the number of two-year-old and older rainbows increased 1087% and the total pounds increased 828%."[46] In short, Montana Fish, Wildlife and Parks quickly learned that the absence of hatchery activity produced more and larger fish. With Vincent's Madison River study, the department had the definitive evidence needed to start wild trout management. Starting in 1972 and completed by 1975, the agency ended hatchery stocking in all the state's rivers. Wild trout proved wildly successful in Montana, creating better fishing opportunities and strengthening the state's tourist economy.

Other Rocky Mountain states incorporated some wild trout management, but not on a statewide scale, showing the entrenched use of hatcheries within fisheries management. The shift to wholly wild trout management remained incomplete among western state agencies that continued to partially rely on hatcheries for fisheries management. Some criticisms of the wild trout idea rested on class. Two fisheries biologists attacked wild trout management at the first semiannual Wild Trout Symposium in 1974, arguing that ending catchable-sized trout stocking entirely was the idea of "some elitist trout fishermen and a few fishery biologists." These biologists saw a need for continued tailwater stocking, where natural reproduction in certain rivers was impossible. They also contended that wild trout management could not sustain the demand for good trout fishing.[47] While the paper might not have gone over so well at a conference comprising wild trout anglers, ecologists and biologists, fisheries managers, and conservationists, no state ever entirely abandoned its hatchery work. Other appraisals rested not on class, but on place, portraying wild trout ethics as increasingly popular, at least among locals. Sometimes, local anglers and agency employees aimed their critiques at tourists who demanded hatchery stocking, like the opposition to new hatchery construction at Jackson Hole that threatened Snake River cutthroat. The reproval of "dudes" (which also had a certain class element) implied that tourists could not fish very well and had to rely on easy-to-catch hatchery fish.

Even with criticisms and only partial acceptance, wild trout still represented an important shift in management. Wild trout defenders believed that fisheries management should center on habitat protection. At that first Wild Trout Symposium, for instance, one zoology professor spoke about the restoration of streams or protection of those with healthy habitats. In doing so, he emphasized the importance of habitat and ecology within wild trout management:

> [M]any anglers and biologists feel that fish stocked from hatcheries, no matter how laudable as a recreational supplement if properly handled, cannot fully substitute for wild trout. Owing to appearance, flavor and behavior, hatchery fish may be unsatisfactory. Moreover, any stocked hatchery fish may represent an injection of artificiality into the natural streamscape which is out of keeping with the spirit of angling practiced by some.[48]

The growing significance of wild trout in ethics and management made the protection of habitat all the more important during the age of ecology.

Wild trout ethics and management translated into more concerns for wild rivers and habitat protection during the 1960s and 1970s. Anglers and fish managers increasingly privileged healthy ecosystems over hatchery fish. They rallied against habitat degradation in its many postwar forms, from industrial and urban pollution to highway and dam building. The grassroots political and environmental involvement showcased the regional importance of nonnative trout fishing and its democratic nature.

Much of the conservationist focus on habitat started in the 1950s with concerns over increasing water pollution. In the post–World War II era, western anglers frequently discovered fish kills from water pollution due to a variety of industrial, mining, and urban sources. Throughout the 1950s,

Montana anglers came across various fish kills, including ones along Rattlesnake Creek and the Clark Fork River near Missoula.[49] Instances such as these all too frequently occurred in the time period. In 1961 alone, the US Department of Health, Education, and Welfare reported fifteen million fish killed across the nation from a variety of industrial, mining, agriculture, and residential sources.[50] Fish kills indicated poor water quality and threats to human health, ensuring that diverse political constituencies like anglers and the League of Women Voters took up the cause of water pollution. Before the Clean Water Act of 1972, states institutionalized these growing water pollution concerns by charging state agencies or creating entirely new sectors of government to oversee and regulate water pollution. Utah, for example, created a State Water Pollution Control Board in 1953, a move welcomed by the Utah Fish and Game Commission.[51]

Anglers' and fish managers' fights against pollution reflected the swelling consideration for habitat protection in an era of widespread environmental problems. Environmental degradation plagued inland waters in the postwar period. In *Wildlife in America* (1959), writer and activist Peter Matthiessen chronicled the richness of the nation's fish, birds, and wildlife as well as their declining populations. Matthiessen endorsed both wild trout and wild rivers. He admonished the wastefulness of the hatchery system, in what became a critique of Cold War consumerism: "A few upland game birds excepted, the fishes include the only game species which lend themselves readily to the indignities of mass culture, and incredible sums have been poured away in the form of ill-fated fingerlings and fry."[52] Documenting native freshwater fish declines, he blamed humans for habitat damage: "Pollution, siltation, dredging, drainage, damming, irrigation, stream-straightening, and other practices, have been extremely harmful to our native species."[53] Matthiessen voiced the frequent concerns of anglers and fish managers who were becoming increasingly bothered by a variety of habitat changes in the postwar world.

Highway building destroyed all types of western trout habitat in the 1950s and 1960s, triggering protests and political action from anglers and managers. The passage of the Interstate Highway Defense Act (1956) remade the American landscape, contributing to suburban sprawl, increased oil use, and, among other environmental problems, damaged trout habitat.[54] In Montana and other Rocky Mountain states, highway building and resulting trout declines raised the ire of anglers and fish managers. In the early 1960s, Utah officials lamented the losses on numerous rivers, including the Logan, Sevier, and Weber rivers.[55]

Other western rivers experienced the same loss of habitat during highway building. During the early 1960s, members of the Montana Junior Chamber of Commerce (Jaycees), a civic organization with separate men's and women's branches, began to notice the deterioration of trout fishing around the state due to highway building and launched a state crusade to fix the problem. At the 1962 state convention, the Jaycees adopted a legislative bill to regulate river damage from road construction.[56] Harry B. Mitchell led the campaign while continuing to run the family dairy in Great Falls and serving as a captain in the Montana Air National Guard.[57] During the drive, Mitchell and other Jaycees relied on the value of Montana trout streams. "The crux of the problem is," Mitchell wrote in early 1963, "our trout streams are expendable, have no legal protection, and their economic and recreational value is not considered in any stream alteration project."[58] Due to their political work, the Montana legislature passed Substitute Senate Bill 45 in March 1963 to address trout habitat protection during highway building, enacting a more thorough version in the 1965 Streambed Preservation Act.

Many western state fish and game agencies and national politicians also supported improved legislation to regulate the environmental problems created by road construction. Wild trout represented a guiding factor in new concerns over environmental protection. Longtime Montana Senator Lee Metcalf promoted the economic value of good hunting and fishing. In his first of three terms before his death, the Democrat observed tourism had become the third-largest industry in the state, and he used its economic value to promote better conservation measures on a national level, including wilderness and wetlands protection, public access to rivers, and water pollution.[59] Metcalf extended his conservation work to concerns over highway building in the pre-NEPA days, introducing a bill that would have required highway planners to cooperate with the Department of the Interior.[60]

Rocky Mountain state fish and game agencies additionally advanced environmental concerns. In the 1960s and 1970s, state agencies frequently used their publications to promote habitat protection. During the Jaycees' political work over streambed protection, the Montana Fish and Game Department published an article to support the movement. In "Montana

Trout Streams: Will We Have Tomorrow What We Have Today?" (1962), the author regretted the loss of trout fishing due to stream rechanneling near places like Philipsburg and Red Lodge. He then noted that road and railroad building caused half of these damages and that no legislation existed to control the problem. The sport and economic values of trout proved central to the argument: "[A]lmost half of the eligible residents buy a fishing license. Two-thirds of them fish for trout in streams. Anglers also drop a sizable chunk of money into the state's economy."[61] Other states printed similar tracts. In one Idaho Fish and Game pamphlet, the department provided disturbing numbers of fish losses and habitat alterations, noting that over 1,100 miles on forty-five of the state's rivers had been altered in the 1960s. Fish kills followed. The author stated that during the previous nine years, water pollution and habitat degradation had killed over 1.5 million fish in Idaho, lamenting that in many streams "only trash fish can survive."[62]

In combating environmental devastation, fisheries managers and anglers often worked together, as in the case of opposition to dam building. Despite the fact that dams could remake rivers into phenomenal tailwater fisheries, they still represented unwanted development for many anglers who contributed to the growing environmental movement. Dam building became a rallying point for new environmental consciousness in the postwar era.[63] In the Rocky Mountains, anglers played an important role in dam opposition, especially in some of the lesser-known battles. One example should suffice. In the 1960s, the proposed Reichle Dam on Montana's Big Hole River worried fish managers and anglers alike. The Montana Fish and Game Department opposed the project, believing that the new types of recreation created by reservoirs, such as waterskiing, could hardly replace quality trout fishing and the ten miles of the blue-ribbon Big Hole that would be destroyed.[64] In the fight against Reichle Dam, Butte fly fisherman and working-class conservationist George Grant spearheaded a successful coalition of sport fishers and ranchers.[65] The large Western Montana Fish and Game Association joined the campaign, worried about Big Hole trout.[66] Concerns about trout fishing and Big Hole's wild qualities drove many anglers and fish managers to reject proposals for new dams. Like the Reichle Dam opposition, sometimes they won.

During the wild trout era, wild rivers and healthy habitats became important in the partial abandonment of the western hatchery system.

Anglers and fish managers joined the growing environmental movement to speak out against the vast postwar changes to rivers and the natural world. They criticized water pollution, stream alterations due to road construction, and dam building—and the resulting trout declines caused by all of this. The wild trout era solidified a broad constituency of western anglers that advocated for environmental protection, ironically by naturalizing nonnative fish within the region's trout culture and illustrating the importance of locals in conservation work.

When writer David Quammen moved to Montana in the 1970s for the trout, he explained to friends that trout represented a synecdoche for lifestyle: "Trout were the indicator species for a place and a life I was seeking."[67] Trout also serve as a synecdoche for changes to the Rocky Mountain region in the twentieth century. By the 1970s, trout symbolized more than just popular nonnative game fish; they indicated clean waters, healthy habitats, outdoor lifestyles, and a quality of life cherished by many residents and visitors in the New Rocky Mountains.

As much as wild trout perpetuated a deep-seated Rocky Mountain trout culture, wild trout principles proved central to the growing importance of native fish ethics since the 1970s. Native fish management and habitat protection sprouted in the midst of the wild trout era, transitioning some anglers and managers to contemporary native fish preservation.[68] Opposition to hatcheries has characterized these new values. Writer David James Duncan has observed that hatcheries and native fish are irreconcilable for many western fly fishers: "For the 'Average American'—those bland creatures Gallup and Harris always manage to locate before conducting their opinion polls—the opposite of *native* is probably a word such as *foreigner, alien,* or *immigrant.* If Gallup interviewed a bunch of Western fly-fishing freaks, though, they'd learn to their amazement that the opposite of the word *native* is a hatchery trout!"[69] While some contemporary fly fishers and anglers have upheld the values of native fish, it remains unknown whether other western anglers, tourists, state fish agencies, and those who benefit from the region's outdoor recreation and tourism economy will embrace native fish management and ethics within the Rocky Mountain's persistent trout culture.

Epilogue

A map of the world without Utopia is not worth glancing at.
— OSCAR WILDE

. . . if the trout are lost, smash the state.
— TOM MCGUANE, *THE LONGEST SILENCE*[1]

THE ENVIRONMENTAL HISTORY OF THE ROCKY MOUNTAIN trout culture and its vast and unintended consequences reminds me of the time I finally discovered my late grandpa's favorite fishing spot. A few years ago while visiting family in Bozeman, some of my cousins and an uncle offered to take my twin sister and me there. We jumped at the opportunity and hopped in my car. Would it be a hidden place on the Gallatin River or some out-of-the-way mountain lake? My imagination went wild trying to imagine the type of secret fishing Eden that my grandpa frequented. My grandparents, wheat farmers on Montana's Hi-Line, bought a house in Bozeman near the university during the 1960s, presumably so the eight kids (including my mom) could attend college there and they could retire somewhere with milder winters, mountain views, and good fishing.

We had barely left town when my relatives told me to pull over on a busy one-lane highway. A trickle of an irrigation ditch ran beneath it, so small I probably could have jumped across it. Although overgrown with foliage, it still had the trappings of its human creation, with headgates and lateral lines. Above it loomed a billboard. Perhaps this was just a little family mischief on our way to the real location, but on my uncle's first cast up beneath the bridge, he pulled out a rainbow trout. And, upon a closer look, I noticed some nice trout swimming around in the tiny canal. After a few laughs, we spent the rest of the afternoon at the American Legion bar, which apparently also was Grandpa's style—and one of the benefits of having a favorite fishing spot so close to town.

Rarely does the history of environmental change, however, become this obvious to the many anglers conditioned by mythology and their own ostensibly natural experiences catching wild trout from flowing rivers. As historian Paul Schullery has put it, most fly fishers "wouldn't know history if it came up and bit us on our breathables, but we love to think it's on our side."[2] Over a century of environmental change birthed new trout fisheries while destroying native fish and ecosystems. And not everyone benefited from the new cultural and economic importance of nonnative trout, as the fishing industry produced new avenues of power and control.

The history of Rocky Mountain trout began with nineteenth-century westward expansion and industrialization, as white leisure-class anglers defined sport, spreading trout and leisure throughout empires. They strove to distinguish their fish catches from those of market and subsistence fishers who came from lower classes, immigrant communities, and other races. To do so, they used constructions of race, gender, and national identity as well as their new consumer gear, produced by the era's world trade and industrialization in attempts to legitimize angling as a sport. These anglers contributed to the transatlantic conservation movement by limiting their own catches and promoting hatcheries to repopulate depleted waters. While this sporting culture influenced conservation, local people and environmental realities also transformed it at a local level. A variety of westerners helped state and federal fish culturalists introduce trout to the region. Westerners also wrestled with the role of the government in conservation and defining regulations.

By the early twentieth century, the western hatchery system was churning out millions of rainbow, brown, and brook trout, while westerners and tourists alike promoted the region's nonnative trout fisheries. In this evolution of place, the economic and cultural importance of swimming creatures melded together the material realities and social constructions of the Rocky Mountain trout culture and economy. The emergence of regional fly fishing traditions marked the significance of the outdoor recreation industry in the early twentieth century. This popular pastime and growing economy, however, rested on environmental change and massive amounts of trout stocking. These conceptions of place and region and their accompanying hatchery activities caused the devastation of western native fish, both trout and trash varieties.

The codification and amplification of Euroamerican prejudices against coarse fish mirrored the growth of the Rocky Mountain trout culture and the continued assault on native ecosystems and creatures. In the glorification of the region's charismatic and beautiful trout, anglers and fish managers overlooked—or eradicated—the less magnetic and attractive coarse fish species. The trout-based conception of place sometimes had devastating impacts, but remained only one way of knowing the West.

The region's outdoor recreation and tourism economy often ran up against the region's extractive economies like mining, timber, and agriculture. In the arid West, anglers and fish managers were forced to reconcile with irrigation use and dewatering in an utterly transformed landscape. Following World War II, the construction of irrigation and hydroelectricity dams sometimes unintentionally manufactured extraordinary tailwater trout fisheries. Tailwaters also caused major conflicts, like the fight over Montana's Bighorn River. Simultaneously, many anglers started to reject the artificial aspects of western trout fishing like tailwaters and put-and-take stocking.

During the wild trout era of the 1960s and 1970s, these environmental changes became naturalized as local anglers and fish managers started to tear down the western hatchery system and focus on preserving wild trout and wild rivers. Wild trout likewise obscured a century of environmental change as well as the obsession with nonnative trout of Rocky Mountain anglers, tourists, fish managers, businesses, and boosters. This legacy has extended to the present. In reality, Rocky Mountain fisheries continue to be heavily manipulated. Despite substantial scientific and ethical criticisms of hatcheries starting in the mid-twentieth century, they remain a part of fisheries management in many places. Montana has maintained wild trout management on its rivers, but other Rocky Mountain states still rely on hatcheries and trout stocking to varying extents. Sometimes the unnatural, manipulative aspects of the hatchery system continued. Idaho officials, for instance, recently had to train hatchery rainbow trout how to eat worms because they were used to eating food pellets.[3] Hatcheries and wild trout management exist simultaneously in this present conception of region that also now includes more concern for native fish.

Instead of addressing the long history of western trout in the continued fights to protect regional rivers and fish, conservationists perpetuate a fly fishing mythology. Many fly fishers might know every eddy, rock, and riffle in their favorite stretch of river, but they have overlooked the historical transformations of nature. They invoke Norman Maclean, not James A. Henshall. They celebrate mythical fish and rivers, not the polluted stream running through town (or that the film adaptation for *A River Runs Through It* had to be filmed on the Gallatin and other area rivers because of pollution and development on the Big Blackfoot River). They often write about destinations, fish sizes, or fishing contests, not the costs and consequences of the sport itself. In some ways, the historical illiteracy and superficial writing does little to inform fly fishers' concerns for many of the environmental issues and problems of Rocky Mountain fisheries.

Take, for instance, the recent controversies surrounding native fish restoration in the American West. Rainbow, brown, and brook trout have overrun the vast majority of Rocky Mountain waters. Nonnative trout are permanent, barring pollution, habitat degradation, and things like whirling disease.[4] Dozens of recent native trout restoration projects, however, provide notable exceptions. Privileging nativeness over biodiversity, these efforts all involve the heavy use of fish toxicants to remove nonnative trout (and anything else that swims in the river), then the planting of native cutthroat trout, in most cases, taken from brood stocks maintained by state agencies.

The use of fish toxicants to save native species has become increasingly popular within the last fifteen years. In one case, not too far from Grandpa's fishing hole, Montana Fish, Wildlife and Parks, in conjunction with Ted Turner Enterprises, sought to bring back westslope cutthroat in Cherry Creek, a tributary to the world-famous Madison River that begins in the Lee Metcalf Wilderness Area and runs through one of Turner's many ranches. They spent over five years applying toxicants to eradicate the nonnative fish in the creek.[5] The project drew extensive public criticism from the beginning due to the use of Antimycin A, then rotenone, as well as the perceived threats to the Madison fishery. (The project's continued failures have also lent support to its critics.) In contrast, a similar venture on the Comanche Creek in northeastern New Mexico aimed at bringing back Rio Grande cutthroat trout garnered widespread support from a grassroots group of fly fishers, ranchers, and others.[6] These attempts to restore native fish point to a need for more anglers to consider native fish values in the Rocky Mountains, which have become known for nonnative trout over time. The restoration projects themselves ironically illustrate a continued regional trout aesthetic and collective amnesia.

Despite the recent shift to more scientific and ecological interest in native fish, the restoration projects themselves have all sought to restore native trout and not native suckers, chubs, or other endangered coarse fish. The toxicants themselves do not distinguish between nonnative trout and all of the native coarse fish and minnows present in these rivers. The mountain whitefish and other species in Cherry Creek were also native. (Did Montana FWP and Turner bother to conduct DNA studies to see if these species represented genetic uniqueness?) Should the goal be native-ness or biodiversity? Fisheries managers have extremely hard jobs in which they are constantly faced with tough decisions, along with the small budgets and incessant demands of any state agency. Yet the history of trash fish reveals that fish managers are often quick to the draw with fish toxicant use, viewing it as a panacea for native fish ills. Their quests to preserve native fish are valiant, even if the means need to be reexamined. And although anglers have ignored native concerns in their Rocky Mountains with the big trout, their continued romanticization of western fly fishing has been beneficial for other environmental issues.

Despite the drawbacks of romanticism, the Rocky Mountain troutopia, with its nostalgic and simplified past, has also had real and tangible advantages for river and fish protection. In a recent *New York Times* article, writer Rick Bass attributed the success of Montana's 1998 voter initiative banning cyanide heap-leach gold mining to *A River Runs Through It*: "We never would have won if it hadn't been for Norman Maclean's novel and Robert Redford's movie."[7] While fly-fishing mythology has been recently evoked to campaign for healthy watersheds, it remains myopic in its focus on well-known rivers and their nonnative trout.

When Norman Maclean ended *A River* with "the hope that a fish will rise," he taught readers that trout waters created hope anew. In a similar fashion, this book concludes with optimism that western anglers, fisheries managers, conservationists, guides, outfitters, local businesses, regional boosters, and tourists will address the history and legacies of Rocky Mountain trout. The willingness to grapple with the complexity of the past and look beyond the romanticized Rocky Mountain trout culture essentially comes down to local anglers whose favorite fishing spots may be in unlikely and seemingly unnatural locations—like an irrigation ditch under a billboard adjacent to a busy highway—that still hold rising trout.

NOTES

INTRODUCTION

1   Norman Maclean, *A River Runs Through It, and Other Stories* (1976; repr., Chicago: University of Chicago Press, 2001), 56.

2   For concise overviews of fly fishing and western culture see Paul Schullery, "Frontier Fly-Fishing in the New West," *Montana: The Magazine of Western History* 52, no. 2 (Summer 2002): 2–9, and Ken Owens, "Fishing the Hatch: New West Romanticism and Fly-Fishing in the High Country," *Montana: The Magazine of Western History* 52, no. 2 (Summer 2002): 10–19. For more on western sport fishing and trout, see Paul Schullery, *Cowboy Trout: Western Fly Fishing As If It Matters* (Helena: Montana Historical Society Press, 2006); Anders Halverson, *An Entirely Synthetic Fish: How Rainbow Trout Beguiled America and Overran the World* (New Haven, CT: Yale University Press, 2010); "The History of Fly-Fishing in the West," special issue, *Montana: The Magazine of Western History* 52, no. 2 (Summer 2002); Adrian A. Bantjes, ed., special issue, *Annals of Wyoming: The Wyoming History Journal* 76, no. 2 (Spring 2004); and John H. Monnett, *Cutthroat and Campfire Tales: The Fly-Fishing Heritage of the West* (Boulder: University Press of Colorado, 2001). For studies outside of the inland West, see Malcolm Draper, "Going Native? Trout and Settling Identity in a Rainbow Nation," *Historia* 48, no. 1 (May 2003): 55–94; Neil S. Forkey, "Anglers, Fishers, and the St. Croix River: Conflict in a Canadian-American Borderland, 1867–1900," *Forest and Conservation History* 37, no. 4 (Oct. 1993): 179–87; Scott E. Giltner, *Hunting and Fishing in the New South: Black Labor and White Leisure after the Civil War* (Baltimore, MD: Johns Hopkins University Press, 2008); and William Knight, "Samuel Wilmot, Fish Culture, and Recreational Fisheries in Late 19th Century Ontario," *Scientia Canadensis: Canadian Journal of the History of Science, Technology and Medicine* 30, no. 1 (2007): 75–90. Scholarship on salmon includes Joseph E. Taylor III, *Making Salmon: An Environmental History of the Northwest Fisheries Crisis* (Seattle: University of Washington Press, 1999); Richard White, *The Organic Machine: The Remaking of the Columbia River* (New York: Hill and Wang, 1995); and Arthur F.

McEvoy, *The Fisherman's Problem: Ecology and Law in the California Fisheries, 1850–1980* (New York: Cambridge University Press, 1986).

3   David James Duncan, writer and narrator, *Trout Grass*, DVD, directed by Ed George (Vashon, WA: Volcano Motion Pictures, 2007).

4   Wallace Stegner, *The Sound of Mountain Water: The Changing American West* (1969; repr., New York: Penguin Books, 1997), 32.

5   For imperialism and nature, see Paul S. Sutter, "When Environmental Traditions Collide: Ramachandra Guha's *The Unquiet Woods* and U.S. Environmental History," *Environmental History* 14, no. 3 (July 2009): 543–50; John M. MacKenzie, ed., *Imperialism and the Natural World* (Manchester: Manchester University Press, 1990); Harriet Ritvo, *The Animal Estate: The English and Other Creatures in the Victorian Age* (Cambridge, MA: Harvard University Press, 1987); and John M. MacKenzie, *The Empire of Nature: Hunting, Conservation and British Imperialism* (Manchester: Manchester University Press, 1988). For more on settler societies and the environment, see Tom Griffiths and Libby Robin, eds., *Ecology and Empire: Environmental History of Settler Societies* (Seattle: University of Washington Press, 1998), and Thomas R. Dunlap, *Nature and the English Diaspora: Environment and History in the United States, Canada, Australia, and New Zealand* (New York: Cambridge University Press, 1999). For introductions of nonnative species within the context of immigration, see Peter Coates, *American Perceptions of Immigrant and Invasive Species: Strangers on the Land* (Berkeley: University of California Press, 2006). For transatlantic exchanges of ideas and species, see Daniel T. Rodgers, *Atlantic Crossings: Social Politics in a Progressive Age* (Cambridge, MA: Harvard University Press, 1998); Char Miller, *Ground Work: Conservation in American Culture* (Durham, NC: Forest History Society, 2007), 11–33; Darin Kinsey, "'Seeding the water as the earth': The Epicenter and Peripheries of a Western Aquacultural Revolution," *Environmental History* 11, no. 3 (July 2006): 527–66; Cindy Ott, *Pumpkin: The Curious History of an American Icon* (Seattle: University of Washington Press, 2012); and Matthew Taylor, ed., special issue, *Journal of Global History* 8, no. 2 (July 2013). For the West and the world, see Margaret Jacobs, *White Mother to a Dark Race: Settler Colonialism, Maternalism, and the Removal of Indigenous Children in the American West and Australia, 1880–1940* (Lincoln: University of Nebraska Press, 2009), and David M. Wrobel, *Global West, American Frontier: Travel, Empire, and Exceptionalism from Manifest Destiny to the Great Depression* (Albuquerque: University of New Mexico Press, 2013).

6   The work on imperialism and nature helped redefine scholarship on American conservation. With the notable exception of Richard W. Judd's examination

of early conservation ethics in New England and Sarah Mittlefehldt's work on the Appalachian Trail, recent historiography has focused on the consequences of establishing new laws based upon elite ideals of nature. Richard W. Judd, *Common Lands, Common People: The Origins of Conservation in Northern New England* (Cambridge, MA: Harvard University Press, 1997) and Sarah Mittlefehldt, *Tangled Roots: The Appalachian Trail and American Environmental Politics* (Seattle: University of Washington Press, 2013). For examples of conservation history that criticizes elite involvement, see Karl Jacoby, *Crimes against Nature: Squatters, Poachers, Thieves, and the Hidden History of American Conservation* (Berkeley: University of California Press, 2001) and Louis S. Warren, *The Hunter's Game: Poachers and Conservationists in Twentieth-Century America* (New Haven, CT: Yale University Press, 1997).

7   Andrew Herd, *The Fly* (Ellesmere, UK: Medlar Press, 2003), 24–31.

8   Western fish culturalists and anglers introduced rainbow trout, *Oncorhynchus mykiss*, native to the American Pacific Coast and the Kamchatka peninsula in Russia (Idaho and a small section of northwestern Montana are the exceptions, as rainbow trout are native to those areas); brown trout, *Salmo trutta*, from Europe and central Asia; brook trout, *Salvelinus fontinalis*, which lived in eastern North America; golden trout, *O. mykiss* spp., from the Sierra Nevada range; and lake trout, *Salvelinus namaycush*, native to northern and northeastern North America; along with various other species. Fish culturalists also reared many of the native western species of cutthroat trout, *Oncorhynchus clarkii* spp., as well as Arctic grayling, *Thymallus arcticus*, in hatcheries, creating a sort of standardized hatchery version of each to be planted yearly outside of their smaller home ranges within the region. For more on trout, see Robert J. Behnke, *Trout and Salmon of North America* (New York: Free Press, 2002).

9   For other histories that define a region or place by its animals, see Jon T. Coleman, *Vicious: Wolves and Men in America* (New Haven, CT: Yale University Press, 2004); Alice Wondrak Biel, *Do (Not) Feed the Bears: The Fitful History of Wildlife and Tourists in Yellowstone* (Lawrence: University Press of Kansas, 2006); Matthew Klingle, *Emerald City: An Environmental History of Seattle* (New Haven, CT: Yale University Press, 2009); and Taylor, *Making Salmon*. For political constructions of region, see Eve Vogel, "Defining One Pacific Northwest among Many Possibilities: The Political Construction of a Region and Its River during the New Deal," *Western Historical Quarterly* 42, no. 1 (Spring 2011): 29–53. For regionalism in general, see Robert L. Dorman, *Hell of a Vision: Regionalism and the Modern American West* (Tucson: University of Arizona Press, 2012).

10   For tourism and outdoor recreation in the West, see Hal K. Rothman, *Devil's Bargains: Tourism in the Twentieth-Century American West* (Lawrence: University Press of Kansas, 1998); William Philpott, *Vacationland: Tourism and Environment in the Colorado High Country* (Seattle: University of Washington Press, 2013); Michael W. Childers, *Colorado Powder Keg: Ski Resorts and the Environmental Movement* (Lawrence: University Press of Kansas, 2012); Melanie Shellenbarger, *High Country Summers: The Early Second Homes of Colorado, 1880–1940* (Tucson: University of Arizona Press, 2012); Annie Gilbert Coleman, *Ski Style: Sport and Culture in the Rockies* (Lawrence: University Press of Kansas, 2004); Liza Nicholas, Elaine M. Bapis, and Thomas J. Harvey, eds., *Imagining the Big Open: Nature, Identity, and Play in the New West* (Salt Lake City: University of Utah Press, 2003); Paul S. Sutter, *Driven Wild: How the Fight against Automobiles Launched the Modern Wilderness Movement* (Seattle: University of Washington Press, 2002); David M. Wrobel and Patrick T. Long, eds., *Seeing and Being Seen: Tourism in the American West* (Lawrence: University Press of Kansas, 2001); Susan Rhoades Neel, ed., "Tourism and the American West," special issue, *Pacific Historical Review* 65, no. 4 (Nov. 1996); and Earl Pomeroy, *In Search of the Golden West: The Tourist in Western America* (New York: Alfred A. Knopf, 1957).

11   S. Lowe et al., *100 of the World's Worst Invasive Alien Species: A Selection from the Global Invasive Species Database* (Auckland, New Zealand: IUCN/SSC Invasive Species Specialist Group, November 2004), http://www.issg.org/pdf/publications/worst_100/English_100_worst.pdf (accessed September 26, 2011).

12   J. A. Cambray, "Impact on Indigenous Species Biodiversity Caused by the Globalisation of Alien Recreational Freshwater Fisheries," *Hydrobiologia* 500, nos. 1–3 (June 2003): 217–18.

13   Howard L. Jelks et al., "Conservation Status of Imperiled North American Freshwater and Diadromous Fishes," *Fisheries* 33, no. 8 (Aug. 2008): 395–98. For more information on cutthroat trout, see Behnke, *Trout and Salmon of North America*, 137–234, and Patrick Trotter, *Cutthroat: Native Trout of the West*, 2nd ed. (Berkeley: University of California Press, 2008). For cutthroat subspecies and problems with conservation, see Amy L. Haak et al., "Conserving Peripheral Trout Populations: The Values and Risks of Life on the Edge," *Fisheries* 35, no. 11 (Nov. 2010): 530–49.

14   Jelks et al., "Conservation Status," 397. For more information, see Behnke, *Trout and Salmon of North America*, 293–99.

15   The US Fish and Wildlife Service is currently reconsidering the status of fluvial Arctic grayling, after refusing to list the species previously. See http://www.fws.gov/endangered/improving_ESA/listing_workplan.html (accessed

September 5, 2011). A December 2008 Department of Justice report found that a USFWS deputy assistant secretary, Julie MacDonald, pressured scientists within the agency to alter scientific findings, among other abuses of the Endangered Species Act. The fluvial Arctic grayling was one of the species listed in the report. "Bush's Interior Department Interfered with Scientific Work to Limit Endangered Species Protections," *Huffington Post*, December 15, 2008, http://www.huffingtonpost.com/2008/12/16/bushs-interior-department_n_151307.html (accessed December 15, 2008). For the inspector general's report, see http://www.doi.gov/oig/reports/upload/EndangeredSpeciesFINAL.pdf (accessed July 15, 2014).

16   Stegner, *Sound of Mountain Water*, 38.

17   Roderick L. Haig-Brown, *A River Never Sleeps* (1946; repr., New York: Skyhorse Publishing, 2010), 352.

CHAPTER 1: HEADWATERS

1   Paul Schullery, *American Fly Fishing: A History* (New York: Lyons Press, 1987), 80. Wilson's pseudonym was Christopher North.

2   Mary Orvis Marbury, *Favorite Flies and Their Histories* (1892; repr., Guilford, CT: Lyons Press, 2001), 350.

3   For the Professor as a stone fly imitation, see Paul Schullery, *Cowboy Trout: Western Fly Fishing As If It Matters* (Helena: Montana Historical Society Press, 2006), 135.

4   Works on imperialism in the American West and elsewhere include Margaret Jacobs, *White Mother to a Dark Race: Settler Colonialism, Maternalism, and the Removal of Indigenous Children in the American West and Australia, 1880–1940* (Lincoln: University of Nebraska Press, 2009) and David M. Wrobel, *Global West, American Frontier: Travel, Empire, and Exceptionalism from Manifest Destiny to the Great Depression* (Albuquerque: University of New Mexico Press, 2013).

5   Norman Vance, "Imperial Rome and Britain's Language of Empire 1600–1837," *History of European Ideas* 26, nos. 3–4 (2000): 213n3.

6   Richard White, *The Organic Machine: The Remaking of the Columbia River* (New York: Hill and Wang, 1995), 38–39; 33–34.

7   Schullery, *Cowboy Trout*, 19–20.

8   Paul Schullery has importantly argued that fishing cannot be separated into clear categories of sport, subsistence, or science. Schullery uses the example of the Washburn Expedition to Yellowstone in 1870. For the group of Montana territorial officials accompanied by a military detachment, angling held

multiple meanings: "Fishing was, for this or that subset of the party, a means of acquiring food, of testing one's angling skill, of engaging in friendly competition with other sportsmen, and of studying the natural world." Schullery, *Cowboy Trout*, 57–96; quote from p. 86.

9   Sue O'Connor, Rintaro Ono, and Chris Clarkson, "Pelagic Fishing at 42,000 Years before the Present and the Maritime Skills of Modern Humans," *Science* 334, no. 6059 (Nov. 25, 2011): 1117–21.

10 See Schullery, *Cowboy Trout*, 57–86.

11 Andrew Herd, *The Fly* (Ellesmere, UK: Medlar Press, 2003), 33–34.

12 Humphry Davy, *Salmonia: Or Days of Fly Fishing in a Series of Conversations with Some Account of the Habit of Fishes Belonging to the Genus Salmo*, 3rd ed. (London: John Murray, 1832), 299, http://www.archive.org/details/salmoniaordaysofi832davy (accessed December 27, 2010).

13 Herd, *Fly*, 35.

14 William Radcliffe, *Fishing from the Earliest Times* (London: John Murray, 1921), 451, http://www.archive.org/details/fishingfromearliooradc (accessed March 20, 2011).

15 Herd, *Fly*, 67.

16 Ephemera [Edward Fitzgibbon], *A Handbook of Angling: Teaching Fly-Fishing, Trolling, Bottom-Fishing, and Salmon-Fishing: With the Natural History of River Fish, and the Best Modes of Catching Them*, 3rd ed. (London: Longman, Brown, Green, and Longmans, 1853), 1.

17 C. M. Mundahl, *Line Fishing*, Papers of the Conferences Held in Connection with the Great International Fisheries Exhibition, London, 1883 (London: William Clowes and Sons, 1883), 5, http://www.archive.org/details/linefishingoomund (accessed May 16, 2011).

18 John J. Brown, *The American Angler's Guide. Being a Compilation from the Works of Popular English Authors, from Walton to the Present Time; Together with the Opinions of Practices of the Best American Anglers: Containing Every Variety of Mode Adopted in Ocean, River, Lake and Pond Fishing; the Necessary Tackle and Baits Required; Manner of Making Artificial Flies, &c. &c. &c.; with Engravings on Wood*, 2nd ed. (New York: Burgess, Stringer, 1846), 13–19.

19 Works on the Gilded Age include Alan Trachtenberg, *The Incorporation of America: Culture and Society in the Gilded Age* (New York: Hill and Wang, 1982) and Nell Irvin Painter, *Standing at Armageddon: The United States, 1877–1919* (New York: W. W. Norton, 1989). For whiteness and national identity, see Nell Irvin Painter, *The History of White People* (New York: W. W. Norton, 2010); Edward J. Blum, *Reforging the White Republic: Race, Religion, and American Nationalism 1865–1898* (Baton Rouge: Louisiana State University

Press, 2005); David Roediger, *The Wages of Whiteness: Race and the Making of the American Working Class*, rev. ed. (London: Verso, 1999); Matthew Frye Jacobson, *Whiteness of a Different Color: European Immigrants and the Alchemy of Race* (Cambridge, MA: Harvard University Press, 1998); and Gail Bederman, *Manliness and Civilization: A Cultural History of Gender and Race in the United States, 1880–1917* (Chicago: University of Chicago Press, 1995). For the middle class, see Stuart M. Blumin, *The Emergence of the Middle Class: Social Experience in the American City, 1760–1900* (New York: Cambridge University Press, 1989).

20 Genio C. Scott, *Fishing in American Waters* (New York: Harper & Brothers, 1869), 143.

21 Bederman, *Manliness*, 12–17.

22 J. J. Manley, *Notes on Fish and Fishing* (London: Sampson Low, Marston, Searle, and Rivington, 1877), 93.

23 R. Barnwell Roosevelt and Seth Green, *Fish Hatching and Fish Catching* (Rochester, NY: Union and Advertiser Co.'s Book and Job Print, 1879), 124–25.

24 David McMurray, "Rivaling the Gentleman in the Gentle Art: The Authority of the Victorian Woman Angler," *Sport History Review* 39, no. 2 (Nov. 2008): 99–102. See also McMurray, "'The Charm of Being Loose and Free': Nineteenth-Century Fisherwomen in the North American Wilderness," *International Journal of the History of Sport* 30, no. 8 (2013): 826–52.

25 Marbury, *Favorite Flies*, 3.

26 Ibid., 447–49.

27 Letter to the editor from Chs. Bendire, *Forest and Stream* 12, no. 8 (Mar. 27, 1879): 154. For more on Bendire, see his obituary in *Forest and Stream* 48, no. 7 (Feb. 13, 1897): 122. For the officer-sportsman "type," see Schullery, *American Fly Fishing*, 21.

28 Monmouth [Major E. August Egbert], "The Land of the Pointed Heart, Number One," *Forest and Stream* 12, no. 7 (Mar. 20, 1879): 123. The second part of the article is found in *Forest and Stream* 12, no. 8 (Mar. 27, 1879): 143–44.

29 John H. Monnett, "Mystery of the Bighorns: Did a Fishing Trip Seal Custer's Fate?" *American Fly Fisher* 19, no. 4 (Fall 1993): 2.

30 Quoted in Ken Owens, "While Custer Was Making His Last Stand: George Crook's 1876 War on Trout in the Bighorn Country," *Montana: The Magazine of Western History* 52, no. 2 (Summer 2002): 59.

31 Ibid., 59.

32 Richard Lessner, "How Meriwether Lewis's Cutthroat Trout Sealed Custer's Fate at the Little Bighorn," *American Fly Fisher* 36, no. 4 (Fall 2010): 17.

33 Henry William Herbert, *Frank Forester's Fish and Fishing of the United States*

and British Provinces of North America (New York: Stringer and Townsend, 1850), 111, http://www.archive.org/details/frankforestersfiooherb (accessed December 27, 2010).

34   Thaddeus Norris, The American Angler's Book: Embracing the Natural History of Sporting Fish, and the Art of Taking Them. With Instructions in Fly-Fishing, Fly-Making, and Rod-Making; and Directions for Fish-Breeding (Philadelphia: E. H. Butler, 1864), 203.

35   Ibid., 194–95.

36   Robert Barnwell Roosevelt, Game Fish of the Northern States of America, and British Provinces (New York: Carleton, 1862), 28–29, http://archive.org/details/ gamefishofnortheooroos (accessed August 12, 2013).

37   The Complete Fly Fisherman: The Notes and Letters of Theodore Gordon, ed. John McDonald (New York: Charles Scribner's Sons, 1947), 186–87.

38   One of the earliest, and perhaps the most well-known, descriptions of Native American use of artificial flies comes from naturalist William Bartram. Bartram chronicled this bass fishing technique during his southern travels in 1774: "They are taken with hook and line, but without any bait . . . having a rod ten or twelve feet in length, to one end of which is tied a strong line, about twenty inches in length, to which is fastened three large hooks, back to back. These are fixed very securely, and covered with the white hair of a deer's tail, shreds of red garter, and some particoloured feathers, all which form a tuft, or tassel, nearly as large as one's fist, and entirely cover and conceal the hooks; this is called a bob." Quoted in Schullery, American Fly Fishing, 20. While cultural syncretism and the influence of colonists' fishing techniques remains unclear in this particular example, using hook and line represented just one of the many indigenous fishing methods. Interestingly, Joe Brooks once related a story about fishing in Tierra del Fuego in Argentina in which his host gave him a sort of bucktail fly made out of guanaco fur (an undomesticated relative of the llama) dating back to the mid-nineteenth century and tied by an Ona Indian. Joe Brooks, Trout Fishing (New York: Outdoor Life, 1972), 239.

39   Herd, Fly, 340; Schullery, American Fly Fishing, 20.

40   Quoted in Schullery, Cowboy Trout, 66.

41   Montana v. United States, 450 US 544, 101 S.Ct. 1245, 67 L.Ed.2d 493 (1981).

42   Deward E. Walker, Jr., Lemhi Shoshone-Bannock Reliance on Anadromous and Other Fish Resources, Idaho Bureau of Land Management Technical Bulletin No. 94–4 (Boise: Bureau of Land Management, April 1994), 218–32.

43   Clifford Duncan, "The Northern Utes of Utah," in A History of Utah's American Indians, ed. Forrest S. Cuch (Salt Lake City: Utah State Division of Indian Affairs and the Utah State Division of History, 2000), 174. See also Jared

Farmer, *On Zion's Mount: Mormons, Indians, and the American Landscape* (Cambridge, MA: Harvard University Press, 2008), ch. 1.

44 William F. Sigler and John W. Sigler, *Fishes of the Great Basin: A Natural History* (Reno: University of Nevada Press, 1987), 19.

45 Ibid., 19; Farmer, *Zion's Mount*, 26. For guddling or tickling, see Sheridan Anderson, *The Curtis Creek Manifesto: A Fully Illustrated Guide to the Strategy, Finesse, Tactics and Paraphernalia of Fly Fishing* (Portland, OR: Frank Amato, 1978), 41. Guddling and tickling are not to be confused with noodling, a technique used for catfish, where your hand is used as bait and when the fish grabs it, you pull it out of the water, hoping not to lose a finger or get dragged underwater in the process.

46 William C. Harris, *The Angler's Guide Book and Tourists' Gazetteer of the Fishing Waters of the United States and Canada* (New York: American Angler, 1885), 56, 114. For guiding, see Tina Loo, *States of Nature: Conserving Canada's Wildlife in the Twentieth Century* (Seattle: University of Washington Press, 2006), ch. 2, and Annie Gilbert Coleman, "The Rise of the House of Leisure: Outdoor Guides, Practical Knowledge, and Industrialization," *Western Historical Quarterly* 42, no. 4 (Winter 2011): 437–57.

47 "Colorado Fish Commission," *Forest and Stream* 32, no. 4 (Feb. 14, 1889): 67.

48 "Wyoming Should Act," *Forest and Stream* 36, no. 7 (March 5, 1891): 121.

49 John Sharp, *Fourth Biennial Report of the State Fish and Game Commissioner, to the Governor and the Fifth Session of the State Legislature of Utah, for the Years 1901 and 1902* (Salt Lake City, UT: Star Printing Company, 1903), 29–30.

50 John H. Monnett, *Cutthroat and Campfire Tales: The Fly-Fishing Heritage of the West* (Boulder: University Press of Colorado, 2001), 24.

51 J. E. Curtis, "Fish in the National Park and Tributaries of Snake River—Propagation of Whitefish," *Fishery Bulletin* 4, no. 1 (1884): 335–36, http://fisherybulletin.nmfs.noaa.gov/4-1/curtis.pdf (accessed November 14, 2010).

52 Monnett, *Cutthroat*, 24.

53 Ibid., 111–16.

54 Lewis B. France, *With Rod and Line in Colorado Waters* (Denver, CO: Chain, Hardy, 1884), 37.

55 Works on consumption of nature include Ramachandra Guha, "Movement Scholarship," *Environmental History* 10, no. 1 (Jan. 2005): 40–41; Guha, *How Much Should a Person Consume? Environmentalism in India and the United States* (Berkeley: University of California Press, 2006); Jennifer Price, *Flight Maps: Adventures with Nature in Modern America* (New York: Basic Books, 1999); Matthew W. Klingle, "Spaces of Consumption in Environmental History," *History and Theory* 42, no. 4 (Dec. 2003): 94–110; and William Philpott,

Vacationland: Tourism and Environment in the Colorado High Country (Seattle: University of Washington Press, 2013).

56   See Trachtenberg, *Incorporation of America*, ch. 2.

57   Herd, *Fly*, 244.

58   Schullery, *American Fly Fishing*, 82.

59   By definition, fancy flies were not necessarily gaudy and colorful, but they became more so in the mid-nineteenth century. Ibid., 77.

60   Geo. M. Kelson, *The Salmon Fly: How to Dress It and How to Use It* (London: privately printed, 1895), 171–72; 54–55, http://www.archive.org/details/salmon-flyhowtodookelsgoog (accessed February 28, 2011).

61   William Blacker, *Blacker's Art of Fly Making, &c, Comprising Angling, and Dyeing of Colours, with Engravings of Salmon and Trout Flies Shewing [sic] the Process of the Gentle Craft as Taught in the Pages. With Descriptions of Flies for the Season of the Year as They Come Out on the Water. Rewritten and Revised by the Author Blacker, Himself, Fishing Tackle Maker of 54, Dean St, Soho, London. 1855* (London, 1855), 256–58.

62   Marbury, *Favorite Flies*, 5.

63   Alan Trachtenberg has called this Gilded Age transformation the "incorporation of America," defining the post–Civil War development of a truly national economy and society. Trachtenberg, *Incorporation of America*, 3.

64   Price, *Flight Maps*, 58–59.

65   Herd, *Fly*, 114.

66   Price, *Flight Maps*, 57–58.

67   Herd, *Fly*, 241, 276–77; Schullery, *American Fly Fishing*, ch. 7.

68   Norman Maclean, *A River Runs Through It, and Other Stories* (Chicago: University of Chicago Press, 1976), 1.

69   Paul Schullery, "Fly Fishing's Three-Century Saga of Silkworm Gut," *American Fly Fisher* 32, no. 2 (Spring 2006): 3.

70   Ibid., 5–6.

71   Herbert, *Fish and Fishing*, 254.

72   Quoted in Schullery, "Silkworm Gut," 4. For the introduction of silkworms for clothing manufacturing to the United States, see Kim Todd, *Tinkering with Eden: A Natural History of Exotics in America* (New York: W. W. Norton, 2001), ch. 6.

73   Herd, *Fly*, 241–47. Lines made from silkworm gut also had drawbacks: after fishing, they had to be strung, dried, and carefully dressed with oil again to ensure their longevity. Herd, 245. The lines tended to rot or grow fungus easily and only after DuPont's 1938 patent of nylon did anglers start using less time-consuming lines and leaders. Ernest Schwiebert, *Trout* (New York: E. P.

Dutton, 1978), 1:762–63; Schullery, "Silkworm Gut," 8.

74 Schullery, *American Fly Fishing*, 62.

75 Herd, *Fly*, 217–26.

76 Schullery, *American Fly Fishing*, 65.

77 Quoted in Trachtenberg, *Incorporation of America*, 41.

78 Herd, *Fly*, 236–37.

79 Frederic M. Halford, *Floating Flies and How to Dress Them: A Treatise on the Most Modern Methods of Dressing Artificial Flies for Trout and Grayling with Fully Illustrated Directions and Containing Ninety Hand-Coloured Engravings of the Most Killing Patterns Together with a Few Hints to Dry-Fly Fishermen* (London: Sampson Low, Marston, Searle, and Rivington, 1886), 2.

80 Schullery, *American Fly Fishing*, 69–70.

81 Herd, *Fly*, 249–54.

82 White, *Organic Machine*, 35.

83 Herd, *Fly*, 283–89.

84 Halford, *Floating Flies*, 117.

85 Ibid., 7–29.

86 Herd, *Fly*, 304.

87 Gordon, *Complete Fly Fisherman*, 356.

88 John F. Reiger, *American Sportsmen and the Origins of Conservation*, 3rd ed. (Corvallis: Oregon State University Press, 2001), 16–17, 64. For fish conservation in New England, see Richard W. Judd, *Common Lands, Common People: The Origins of Conservation in Northern New England* (Cambridge, MA: Harvard University Press, 1997).

89 Herd, *Fly*, 122, 215–16.

90 Some clubs, for instance, now allow members to fish upstream only with a dry fly. Robert Arlinghaus et al., "Understanding the Complexity of Catch-and-Release in Recreational Fishing: An Integrative Synthesis of Global Knowledge from Historical, Ethical, Social, and Biological Perspectives," *Reviews in Fisheries Science* 15, nos. 1–2 (Jan.–June 2007): 84.

91 W. H. Spackman, *Trout in New Zealand: Where to Go and How to Catch Them* (Wellington, NZ: George Didsbury, 1892), 92. For the connections between Anglo settlement cultures, see Thomas R. Dunlap, *Nature and the English Diaspora: Environment and History in the United States, Canada, Australia, and New Zealand* (New York: Cambridge University Press, 1999). Works on European acclimatization societies include Christopher Lever, *They Dined on Eland: The Story of Acclimatisation Societies* (London: Quiller Press, 1992) and Michael A. Osborne, *Nature, the Exotic, and the Science of French Colonialism* (Indianapolis: Indiana University Press, 1994).

92 Francis Day, *Report of the Fresh Water Fish and Fisheries of India and Burma* (Calcutta: Office of the Superintendent of Government Printing, 1873), 53, http://www.archive.org/details/reportonfreshwatooday (accessed March 20, 2011).

93 Peter Reeves, "Inland Waters and Freshwater Fisheries: Issues of Control, Access and Conservation in Colonial India," in *Nature, Culture, Imperialism: Essays on the Environmental History of South Asia*, ed. David Arnold and Ramachandra Guha (New York: Oxford University Press, 1998), 287–89. For Thomas's ideas of sport and conservation in India, see Henry Sullivan Thomas, *The Rod in India: Being Hints How to Obtain Sport, with Remarks on the Natural History of Fish, Their Culture, and Value; and Illustrations of Fish and Tackle*, 2nd ed. (London: Hamilton, Adams, 1881). For more on the British impacts on the Indian environment, see David Arnold, *The Problem of Nature: Environment, Culture and European Expansion* (Oxford: Blackwell, 1996), ch. 9.

94 Elliott West, *The Contested Plains: Indians, Goldseekers, and the Rush to Colorado* (Lawrence: University Press of Kansas, 1998), 145; William J. Wiltzius, *Fish Culture and Stocking in Colorado, 1872–1978*, Division Report no. 12, DOW-R-D-12–85 (Denver: Colorado Division of Wildlife, June 1985), 4–5.

95 Monnett, *Cutthroat*, 113.

96 Photocopy of the Laws of Wyoming, 1869, chapter 12, "An Act for the Protection of Game and Fish in the Territory of Wyoming," box 16, folder 9, collection #10483: Neal L. Blair Papers, AHC.

97 Edwin V. Rawley, *A Review of Utah Fish and Game Licensing and Financing, 1876–1972*, publication no. 72–12 ([Salt Lake City?]: State of Utah Division of Natural Resources, October 1972), 1.

98 Quoted in William Alvord, *A History of Montana's Fisheries Division from 1890–1958* (Helena: Montana Fish, Wildlife and Parks, 1991), 1.

99 See Clyde A. Milner II and Carol A. O'Connor, *As Big as the West: The Pioneer Life of Granville Stuart* (New York: Oxford University Press, 2009). Granville Stuart's published diary and reminiscences mention nothing about fish conservation, but rather read as pioneer history writ large.

100 *Forty Years on the Frontier As Seen in the Journals and Reminiscences of Granville Stuart, Gold-Miner, Trader, Merchant, Rancher and Politician*, ed. Paul C. Phillips (Cleveland, OH: Arthur H. Clark, 1925), 1:248.

101 Ibid., 1:249.

102 See West, *Contested Plains*, 185–91. Both Stuart brothers married and later left native women; Granville had a long-lasting marriage and eleven children with a Shoshone woman, and James had numerous relationships and children with native and métis women. Milner and O'Connor, *Granville Stuart*, 65–68.

103 Milner and O'Connor, *Granville Stuart*, 153, 173. For Hauser and his business dealings, see William G. Robbins, *Colony and Empire: The Capitalist Transformation of the American West* (Lawrence: University Press of Kansas, 1994), ch. 6.

104 Pat Munday, *Montana's Last Best River: The Big Hole and Its People* (Guilford, CT: Lyons Press, 2001), 100.

105 H. C. Yarrow, "On the Speckled Trout of Utah Lake," in US Commission of Fish and Fisheries, *Report of the Commissioner for 1872 and 1873* (Washington, DC: GPO, 1874), 366, http://docs.lib.noaa.gov/rescue/cof/COF_1872–1873.PDF (accessed December 29, 2010). For more on the common support of fisheries regulations in New England, see Judd, *Common Lands*, 53–56.

106 Yarrow, "Speckled Trout," 366.

CHAPTER 2: TROUT EMPIRE

1 Darwin Payne, *Owen Wister: Chronicler of the West, Gentleman of the East* (Dallas, TX: Southern Methodist University Press, 1985), xi–xiii, 77–90.

2 Transcript of Owen Wister's July–August 1885 diary, p. 8, box 1, folder 1, collection #290: Owen Wister Papers, American Heritage Center, University of Wyoming, Laramie [hereafter AHC].

3 For conceptions of masculinity and the West, see Gail Bederman, *Manliness and Civilization: A Cultural History of Gender and Race in the United States, 1880–1917* (Chicago: University of Chicago Press, 1995) and G. Edward White, *The Eastern Establishment and the Western Experience: The West of Frederic Remington, Theodore Roosevelt, and Owen Wister* (New Haven, CT: Yale University Press, 1968).

4 Scholarship on conservation includes Karl Jacoby, *Crimes against Nature: Squatters, Poachers, Thieves, and the Hidden History of American Conservation* (Berkeley: University of California Press, 2001); Louis S. Warren, *The Hunter's Game: Poachers and Conservationists in Twentieth-Century America* (New Haven, CT: Yale University Press, 1997); Tina Loo, *States of Nature: Conserving Canada's Wildlife in the Twentieth Century* (Seattle: University of Washington Press, 2006); Richard W. Judd, *Common Lands, Common People: The Origins of Conservation in Northern New England* (Cambridge, MA: Harvard University Press, 1997); Richard W. Judd, *The Untilled Garden: Natural History and the Spirit of Conservation in America, 1740–1840* (New York: Cambridge University Press, 2009); Samuel P. Hays, *Conservation and The Gospel of Efficiency: The Progressive Conservation Movement, 1890–1920* (Cambridge, MA: Harvard University Press, 1959); Stephen Fox, *The American Conservation Movement:*

John Muir and His Legacy (1981; repr., Madison: University of Wisconsin Press, 1985); Thomas R. Dunlap, Saving America's Wildlife (Princeton, NJ: Princeton University Press, 1988); John F. Reiger, American Sportsmen and the Origins of Conservation, 3rd ed. (Corvallis: Oregon State University Press, 2001); Benjamin Heber Johnson, "Conservation, Subsistence, and Class at the Birth of Superior National Forest," Environmental History 4, no. 1 (Jan. 1999): 80–99; and Sarah Mittlefehldt, Tangled Roots: The Appalachian Trail and American Environmental Politics (Seattle: University of Washington Press, 2013).

5   Works on women and conservation have expanded the familiar narrative of conservation, masculinity, and the "strenuous life." See Jennifer Price, Flight Maps: Adventures with Nature in Modern America (New York: Basic Books, 1999); Cameron Binkley, "'No Better Heritage than Living Trees': Women's Clubs and Early Conservation in Humboldt County," Western Historical Quarterly 33, no. 2 (Summer 2002): 179–203; and Glenda Riley, Women and Nature: Saving the "Wild" West (Lincoln: University of Nebraska Press, 1999). For gender, class, and race in conservation, see Andrea L. Smalley, "'Our Lady Sportsmen': Gender, Class, and Conservation in Sport Hunting Magazines, 1873–1920," Journal of the Gilded Age and Progressive Era 4, no. 4 (Oct. 2005): 355–80, and David McMurray, "Rivaling the Gentleman in the Gentle Art: The Authority of the Victorian Woman Angler," Sport History Review 39, no. 2 (Nov. 2008): 99–126. More recently, Carolyn Merchant has sought to connect gender and conservation through George Bird Grinnell's work, but she did not dwell on his ideas of angling and fish conservation. Carolyn Merchant, "George Bird Grinnell's Audubon Society: Bridging the Gender Divide in Conservation," Environmental History 15, no. 1 (Jan. 2010): 3–30.

6   For more information on conceptions of class and masculinity in Owen Wister's The Virginian, see Richard Slotkin, Gunfighter Nation: The Myth of the Frontier in Twentieth-Century America (New York: Atheneum, 1992), 169–83, and Christine Bold, The Frontier Club: Popular Westerns and Cultural Power, 1880–1924 (New York: Oxford University Press, 2013), xvii–xx, 6–12.

7   For more on local people shaping state conservation, see Judd, Common Lands, Common People.

8   The loose enforcement as well as treaty fishing rights made fishing in its various forms less controlled than hunting. In the complexity of federal Indian law, the Supreme Court prohibited off-reservation hunting in Ward v. Race Horse (1896) while upholding certain fishing rights in United States v. Winans (1905). The Winans ruling upheld the Yakamas' reserved treaty rights for salmon fishing and, by extension, all tribes under treaties with the now-famous "usual and accustomed places" clause, including inland tribes like the Nez Perce, Ute,

and Montana Salish. *Ward v. Race Horse*, 183 US 504, 16 S.Ct. 1076, 41 L.Ed. 244 (1896); *United States v. Winans*, 198 US 371, 25 S.Ct. 662, 49 L.Ed. 1089 (1905); David E. Wilkins and K. Tsianina Lomawaima, *Uneven Ground: American Indian Sovereignty and Federal Law* (Norman: University of Oklahoma Press, 2001), 125–30, 208. The *Winans* decision upheld fishing rights for only some tribes, and federal control over fisheries and the reservation system certainly posed new hardships for subsistence fishers. The complicated picture of dispossession and fish conservation that emerges in the inland West begs for more substantial research. Works on dispossession and conservation in general include Mark David Spence, *Dispossessing the Wilderness: Indian Removal and the Making of the National Parks* (New York: Oxford University Press, 1999) and Mark Dowie, *Conservation Refugees: The Hundred-Year Conflict between Global Conservation and Native Peoples* (Cambridge, MA: MIT Press, 2009).

9   William Cronon, foreword to *Man and Nature*, by George Perkins Marsh (1864; repr., Seattle: University of Washington Press, 2003), xx. See also David Lowenthal's introduction in the same edition.

10 For an in-depth description of one of the earliest US hatchery experiments, along with a description of French methods and early experiments in other European nations, see Theodatus Garlick, *A Treatise on the Artificial Propagation of Certain Kinds of Fish with the Description and Habits of Such Kinds as Are the Most Suitable for Pisciculture* (Cleveland, OH: Tho. Brown, 1857), 5–64.

11 Darin Kinsey, "'Seeding the Water as the Earth': The Epicenter and Peripheries of a Western Aquacultural Revolution," *Environmental History* 11, no. 3 (July 2006): 535.

12 Livingston Stone, *Domesticated Trout: How to Breed and Grow Them* (Boston: James R. Osgood, 1873), 4. For more on Stone, see Anders Halverson, *An Entirely Synthetic Fish: How Rainbow Trout Beguiled America and Overran the World* (New Haven, CT: Yale University Press, 2010), chs. 3 and 4.

13 R. Barnwell Roosevelt and Seth Green, *Fish Hatching and Fish Catching* (Rochester, NY: Union and Advertiser Co.'s Book and Job Print, 1879), 9–10.

14 Robert R. Stickney, *Aquaculture in the United States: A Historical Survey* (New York: John Wiley and Sons, 1996), 9.

15 Al Lucke to William Alvord, February 14, 1969, box 1, folder 3, RS 261: Montana Fisheries Division Records, Montana Historical Society, Helena [hereafter MHS].

16 David Starr Jordan, "A Reconnaissance of the Streams and Lakes of the Yellowstone National Park, Wyoming, in the Interest of the United States Fish Commission," *Fishery Bulletin* 9, no. 1 (1889): 41, http://fisherybulletin.nmfs.noaa.gov/9-1/jordan1.pdf (accessed November 15, 2010). In August and September

1889, federal officials introduced brook, rainbow, and brown trout into the park as well as transplanted mountain whitefish and Yellowstone cutthroat trout from neighboring streams to barren waters. Ibid., 46–61.

17 Patrick Trotter, *Cutthroat: Native Trout of the West*, 2nd ed. (Berkeley: University of California Press, 2008), 254.

18 Payne, *Owen Wister*, 82–83; White, *Eastern Establishment*, 127–28. For more on Wolcott and his involvement in the Johnson County War, see John W. Davis, *Wyoming Range War: The Infamous Invasion of Johnson County* (Norman: University of Oklahoma Press, 2010).

19 Kinsey, "'Seeding the Water,'" 529–45.

20 Roosevelt and Green, *Fish Hatching*, 13.

21 David Lowenthal, introduction to *Man and Nature*, by Marsh, xx; US Commission of Fish and Fisheries, *Report of the Commissioner for 1872 and 1873* (Washington, DC: GPO, 1874), xxxiii, http://docs.lib.noaa.gov/rescue/cof/COF_1872–1873.PDF (accessed December 29, 2010).

22 US Commission of Fish and Fisheries, *Report of the Commissioner for the Year Ending June 30, 1900* (Washington, DC: GPO, 1901), 82, http://docs.lib.noaa.gov/rescue/cof/COF_1900.PDF (accessed January 24, 2011).

23 William J. Wiltzius, *Fish Culture and Stocking in Colorado, 1872–1978*, Division Report no. 12, DOW-R-D-12-85 (Denver: Colorado Division of Wildlife, June 1985), 11.

24 T. S. Palmer, "Licenses for Hook and Line Fishing," *Transactions of the American Fisheries Society* [hereafter *TAFS*] 41, no. 1 (Jan. 1912): 92.

25 John Sharp, *Report of the State Fish and Game Warden, to the Governor and Third Session of the State Legislature of Utah, for the Years 1897 and 1898* (Salt Lake City, UT: Deseret News, 1899), 17.

26 Ibid., 17–19.

27 Wiltzius, *Fish Culture*, 1.

28 John R. Leonard, *The Fish Car Era*, US Fish and Wildlife Service (Washington, DC: GPO, 1979), no pagination.

29 Walter Nugent, *Crossings: The Great Transatlantic Migrations, 1870–1914* (Indianapolis: Indiana University Press, 1992), 29–30.

30 See, for example, Stone's discussion on the use of a Russian dry method of fertilizing eggs. *Domesticated Trout*, 87–96.

31 Leon J. Cole, "The German Carp in the United States," in US Bureau of Fisheries, *Report of the Bureau of Fisheries 1904* (Washington, DC: GPO, 1905), 544–47, http://docs.lib.noaa.gov/rescue/cof/COF_1904.PDF (accessed January 24, 2011).

32 E. A. Tulian, "Acclimatization of American Fishes in Argentina," *Fishery Bul-*

letin 28, no. 2 (1908): 955, http://fisherybulletin.nmfs.noaa.gov/28-2/tulian.pdf (accessed November 17, 2010).

33 For Henshall's autobiography (and the portraits), see *Forest and Stream* 89–91 (May 1919–July 1921).

34 US Bureau of Fisheries, *Report 1904*, 29.

35 Francis Francis, *A Book on Angling: Being a Complete Treatise on the Art of Angling in Every Branch with Explanatory Plates, Etc.*, 3rd ed. (London: Longmans, Green, 1872), 133.

36 Stone, *Domesticated Trout*, 200. Under Stone's leadership, the US Fish Commission also disseminated rainbow trout from their California hatchery. See Halverson, *Synthetic Fish*, 21–47.

37 David Starr Jordan and Barton Warren Evermann, *American Food and Game Fishes: A Popular Account of All the Species Found in America North of the Equator, with Keys for Ready Identification, Life Histories and Methods of Capture* (New York: Doubleday, Page, 1902), 196, 177.

38 Eminent trout biologist Robert Behnke has observed that hatchery managers "generally assumed that all members of a species are essentially the same, like so many standardized interchangeable parts." Robert J. Behnke, "Wild Trout and Native Trout: Is There a Difference?" In *In Praise of Wild Trout: On the Pleasure, Biology, and Preservation of Wild Trout*, ed. Nick Lyons (New York: Lyons Press, 1998), 83.

39 Halverson, *Synthetic Fish*, 59.

40 US Commission of Fish and Fisheries, *Report of the Commissioner for the Year Ending June 30, 1897* (Washington, DC: GPO, 1898), 72, http://docs.lib.noaa.gov/rescue/cof/COF_1897.PDF (accessed January 23, 2011).

41 US Commission of Fish and Fisheries, *Report of the Commissioner for the Year Ending June 30, 1893* (Washington, DC: GPO, 1895), 115, http://docs.lib.noaa.gov/rescue/cof/COF_1893.PDF (accessed January 22, 2011).

42 For more on the transatlantic interchanges, see Daniel T. Rodgers, *Atlantic Crossings: Social Politics in a Progressive Age* (Cambridge, MA: Harvard University Press, 1998); Char Miller, *Ground Work: Conservation in American Culture* (Durham, NC: Forest History Society, 2007), 11–33; and Kinsey, "'Seeding the Water,'" 527–66.

43 Humphry Davy, *Salmonia: or, Days of Fly Fishing in a Series of Conversations with Some Account of the Habit of Fishes Belonging to the Genus Salmo*, 3rd ed. (London: John Murray, 1832), 25, http://www.archive.org/details/salmoniaordaysof1832davy (accessed December 27, 2010).

44 Henry William Herbert, *Frank Forester's Fish and Fishing of the United States and British Provinces of North America* (New York: Stringer and Townsend,

1850), 17, http://www.archive.org/details/frankforestersfiooherb (accessed December 27, 2010).

45 Lewis B. France, *With Rod and Line in Colorado Waters* (Denver, CO: Chain, Hardy, 1884), 37.

46 Roosevelt and Green, *Fish Hatching*, 9–10.

47 Reiger, *American Sportsmen*, 80.

48 Millard [pseud.], *Forest and Stream* 39, no. 21 (Nov. 24, 1892): 450.

49 Shoshone [pseud.], "Rod and Gun in Nevada," *Forest and Stream* 29, no. 8 (Sept. 15, 1887): 143.

50 Letter to the editor from Coahama [pseud.], *Forest and Stream* 29, no. 11 (Oct. 6, 1887): 209.

51 *Owyhee Avalanche*, July 18, 1868.

52 Photocopy of the Session Laws of Wyoming, 1899, chapter 19, "Game and Fish," box 16, folder 9, Neal L. Blair Papers, AHC.

53 Clipping, Don Rabe, "Wyoming's First Game Warden," and clipping, "Albert Nelson: Wyoming's First State Game Warden," *Wyoming Wild Life* (May 1948), box 20, folder 8, Neal L. Blair Papers, AHC.

54 D. C. Nowlin, *Report of the State Game Warden to the Governor of Wyoming* (Laramie, WY: Republic Book and Job Print, 1903), 7.

55 William Alvord, *A History of Montana's Fisheries Division from 1890–1958* (Helena: Montana Fish, Wildlife and Parks, 1991), 1–7.

56 Charles H. Arbuckle, *First Biennial Report of the State Fish and Game Warden of the State of Idaho, 1900* (Boise, ID: State Fish and Game Warden, December 20, 1900), 1–6.

57 Ibid., 1.

58 Sharp, *1897 and 1898*, 38.

59 John Sharp to Fred Wilson, August 12, 1896, box 1, letter book A, series 1068: Fish and Game Commissioner, Correspondence Sent, Utah State Archives and Research Center, Salt Lake City [hereafter USARC].

60 For more on nativism and conservation, see Warren, *Hunter's Game*, ch. 1.

61 H. B. Cromar, *Biennial Report of the State Game and Fish Commissioner and the Commissioner of Hatcheries of Utah* (Ogden, UT: State Industrial School, 1908), 24.

62 Labor union involvement in game warden appointments illustrates some working-class involvement in conservation, but more research remains to be done. With the exception of Lawrence M. Lipin, *Workers and the Wild: Conservation, Consumerism, and Labor in Oregon, 1910–30* (Chicago: University of Illinois Press, 2007), few historians have focused on working-class conservation before World War I.

63   Fred W. Chambers to George Van Wagoner, July 26, 1911, box 2, letter book 7/17/1911–1/20/1912, Fish and Game Commissioner, Correspondence Sent, USARC.

64   Fred W. Chambers to H. H. Peterson, April 22, 1912, box 2, letter book 1/23/1912–7/6/1912, Fish and Game Commissioner, Correspondence Sent, USARC.

65   H. J. Miller to Edwin L. Norris, November 27, 1908, box 210, folder 13, MC 35: Montana Governors Records, MHS.

66   James P. Blaisdell, "A History of the Conservation Effort in Wyoming and the Wyoming Game and Fish Commission to 1950" (MA thesis, University of Wyoming, 1964), 38.

67   Alvord, *History*, 14.

68   Fred W. Chambers to Jos. Wignall, February 6, 1912, box 2, letter book 1/23/1912–7/6/1912, Fish and Game Commissioner, Correspondence Sent, USARC.

69   Photocopy of the Session Laws of Wyoming, 1921, chapter 83, "Game and Fish," box 16, folder 12, Neal L. Blair Papers, AHC.

70   John F. Sharp, *Third Biennial Report of the State Fish and Game Commissioner, to the Governor and the Fourth Session of the State Legislature of Utah, for the Years 1899 and 1900* (Salt Lake City, UT: Deseret News, 1901), 28.

71   Photocopy of the Laws of Wyoming, 1884, chapter 45, "An Act for the Propagation and Culture of Fish throughout the Territory of Wyoming," box 16, folder 9, Neal L. Blair Papers, AHC.

72   Will M. Grove to Moses Alexander, March 30, 1915, box 4, folder 14, AR2/11: Governor Moses Alexander Records, Idaho State Historical Society, Boise [hereafter ISHS].

73   Petition to Moses Alexander from undersigned citizens of Blaine County [1915], box 4, folder 14, Governor Moses Alexander Records, ISHS.

74   Wm. Parsons to Moses Alexander, July 8, 1916, box 4, folder 15, Governor Moses Alexander Records, ISHS.

75   William T. Judkins, *Biennial Report of the State Game Warden of the State of Wyoming 1919–1920* (Laramie, WY: Laramie Printing Company, 1921), 5–6.

76   Arbuckle, *History*, 5.

77   Sharp, *1897 and 1898*, 30.

78   J. S. Swan, *Biennial Report of the State Forest, Game and Fish Commissioner of the State of Colorado, for the Years 1897 and 1898* (Denver, CO: Smith-Brooks Printing, 1898), 9, http://www.biodiversitylibrary.org/item/80520 (accessed November 8, 2010).

79   W. N. Stevens, *Annual Report of the [Idaho] Fish and Game Department, for*

the Year 1906 (Boise: [Idaho Fish and Game Department?], January 1, 1907), no pagination.

80 Swan, *1897 and 1898*, 11.

81 David Starr Jordan, "Report of Explorations in Colorado and Utah during the Summer of 1889, with an Account of the Fishes Found in Each of the River Basins Examined," *Fishery Bulletin* 9, no. 1 (1889): 4, http://fisherybulletin. nmfs.noaa.gov/9–1/jordan.pdf (accessed November 15, 2010).

82 Barton W. Evermann, "A Reconnaissance of the Streams and Lakes of Western Montana and Northwestern Wyoming," *Fishery Bulletin* 11, no. 1 (1891): 15, http://fisherybulletin.nmfs.noaa.gov/11–1/evermann.pdf (accessed November 15, 2010). When the first state fish commissioner corroborated that the pollution also destroyed Deer Lodge Valley crops and livestock, he was fired from his position as professor at the University of Montana. See Laurie Mercier, *Anaconda: Labor, Community, and Culture in Montana's Smelter City* (Chicago: University of Illinois Press, 2001), 18. For more on the first Montana fish commission, see Alvord, *History*, 4.

83 See Donald J. Pisani, "Fish Culture and the Dawn of Concern over Water Pollution in the United States," *Environmental Review* 8, no. 2 (Summer 1984): 117–31. Some fish culturalists were concerned about both fish and human health; one Philadelphia fish culturalist complained about the lack of conformity to pollution laws, stating, "Instead of regarding the water-courses as sources of health to human beings as well as to fish, they are deemed fit places of deposit for noisome and noxious materials of whatever kind that can be most conveniently disposed of through their agency." A. M. Spangler, "The Decrease of Food-Fishes in American Waters, and Some of the Causes," *Fishery Bulletin* 13, no. 1 (1893): 23, http://fisherybulletin.nmfs.noaa.gov/13–1/spangler.pdf (accessed November 15, 2010).

84 James A. Henshall, "Fish Protection," *TAFS* 19, no. 1 (Jan. 1890): 80, 82. Emphasis in original.

85 Many states still allowed it in some locales, like the commercial fishery that sprung up at Utah Lake, allowing fishermen to sell trout, suckers, chubs, and later carp, from the lake. William F. Sigler and John W. Sigler, *Fishes of the Great Basin: A Natural History* (Reno: University of Nevada Press, 1987), 20.

86 Quoted in Jacoby, *Crimes*, 137.

87 Pisani noted that nineteenth-century pollution laws were "ambitious but very weak." Pisani, "Fish Culture," 123.

88 Solon B. Clark to Moses Alexander, September 14, 1916, box 4, folder 17, Governor Moses Alexander Records, ISHS.

89 L. S. Niece to Leroy C. Jones, August 3, 1916, box 4, folder 15, Governor Moses

Alexander Records, ISHS.

90   Department of Fish and Game Receipts and Disbursements, April 1, 1934, to December 31, 1934, *Report of Audit and Examination of the Department of Fish and Game for the Period April 1, 1934 to February 29, 1936* ([Boise: Idaho Department of Fish and Game?], September 14, 1936), 1–6, box 40, folder 4, Governor C. Ben Ross Records, ISHS.

91   W. E. Wheeler to Moses Alexander, April 20, 1915, box 4, folder 14, Governor Moses Alexander Records, ISHS.

92   John H. Monnett, *Cutthroat and Campfire Tales: The Fly-Fishing Heritage of the West* (Boulder: University Press of Colorado, 2001), 24–25.

93   US Bureau of Fisheries, *Report of the Commissioner of Fisheries for the Fiscal Year 1912 and Special Papers* (Washington, DC: GPO, 1914), 50, http://docs.lib. noaa.gov/rescue/cof/COF_1912.PDF (accessed January 25, 2011).

94   US Commission of Fish and Fisheries, *Report of the Commissioner for the Year Ending June 30, 1898* (Washington, DC: GPO, 1899), 90, http://docs.lib.noaa. gov/rescue/cof/COF_1898.PDF (accessed January 23, 2011).

95   Robert J. Behnke, *Trout and Salmon of North America* (New York: Free Press, 2002), 201–205.

96   W. T. Thompson, "Is Irrigation Detrimental to Trout Culture?" *TAFS* 41, no. 1 (Jan. 1912): 105.

CHAPTER 3: TROUT CULTURE

1   *Field & Stream* pamphlet, "Is There Really a Ted Trueblood," series II, box 8, folder 12, MSS 89: Ted Trueblood Collection, Boise State University, Boise, Idaho.

2   Ken Owens, "Fishing the Hatch: New West Romanticism and Fly-fishing in the High Country," *Montana: The Magazine of Western History* 52, no. 2 (Summer 2002): 16.

3   For instance, in 1952, over 36 percent of Wyoming residents bought a fishing license, a per capita high for the nation. Wyoming Game and Fish Commission, *Annual Report 1952* (Cheyenne, [1953?]), 26.

4   Fred W. Chambers, *Eighth Biennial Report of the Fish and Game Commissioner of the State of Utah, to the Governor and Members of the Ninth Legislature of the State of Utah, for the Years 1909–1910* (Salt Lake City, UT: Tribune-Reporter Printing, 1910), 16.

5   Red Collar Steam Ship Line, *Lake and River Excursions via Red Collar S. S. Line in the Panhandle of Idaho* (n.p.: Red Collar Steam Ship Line, 1910), 8.

6   Will M. Grove to Moses Alexander, March 30, 1915, box 4, folder 14, AR2/11:

Governor Moses Alexander Records, Idaho State Historical Society, Boise [hereafter ISHS].

7   Thornton Waite, *Union Pacific: Montana Division, Route of the Butte Special* (Idaho Falls, ID: Brueggenjohann/Reese and Thornton Waite, 1998), 151.

8   Colorado and Southern Railway, *Trouting in Colorado's Waters* (Denver, CO: Smith-Brooks Press, 1907), no pagination.

9   Great Northern Railway, *Shooting and Fishing along the Line of the Great Northern Railway*, 4th ed. (Chicago: Poole Bros., 1901), 12.

10   Union Pacific Railroad, *Union Pacific Outings: Fishing in Colorado and Wyoming* (n.p.: Union Pacific Railroad, 1909), 19.

11   Ibid., 5.

12   Ibid., 28–29.

13   Ibid., 5.

14   John M. Haines to J. B. Gowen, July 15, 1914, box 28, folder "Official Correspondence—Game Warden" [folders unnumbered], AR2/10: Governor John M. Haines Records, ISHS.

15   John Sharp, *Fifth Biennial Report of the State Fish and Game Commissioner and the Commissioner of State Hatcheries, to the Governor and the Sixth Session of the State Legislature of Utah, for the Years 1903 and 1904* (Salt Lake City, UT: Star Printing, 1905), 7.

16   Aldo Leopold, "Mixing Trout in Western Waters," *Transactions of the American Fisheries Society* [hereafter *TAFS*] 47, no. 3 (June 1918): 101–102.

17   Ibid., 102, emphasis mine. For more on Leopold's early writings, see Julianne Lutz Warren, "Weaving a Wider Net for Conservation: Aldo Leopold's Water Ethic," *Organization and Environment* 23, no. 2 (2010): 220, 228.

18   Quoted in Warren, "Wider Net," 229.

19   James A. Henshall, "Indiscriminate and Inconsiderate Planting of Fish," *TAFS* 48, no. 3 (June 1919): 168.

20   Henshall, "Planting of Fish," 169, 167.

21   Ibid., 167.

22   Russell F. Lord, "Rearing a Brood Stock of Blackspotted Trout," *TAFS* 60, no. 1 (Jan. 1930): 164.

23   David H. Madsen, "Protection of Native Fishes in the National Parks," *TAFS* 66, no. 1 (Jan. 1937): 395–97.

24   Paul Schullery, *Searching for Yellowstone: Ecology and Wonder in the Last Wilderness* (Helena: Montana Historical Society Press, 2004), 167. For more on Yellowstone's changing management policies, see Alice Wondrak Biel, *Do (Not) Feed the Bears: The Fitful History of Wildlife and Tourists in Yellowstone* (Lawrence: University Press of Kansas, 2006).

25 For consumerism, see William Leach, *Land of Desire: Merchants, Power, and the Rise of a New American Culture* (New York: Vintage Books, 1993) and Jackson Lears, *Fables of Abundance: A Cultural History of Advertising in America* (New York: Basic Books, 1994).

26 Earl Pomeroy, *In Search of the Golden West: The Tourist in Western America* (New York: Alfred A. Knopf, 1957), 127–30.

27 US Bureau of Fisheries, *Report of the United States Commissioner of Fisheries for the Fiscal Year 1919 with Appendixes* (Washington, DC: GPO, 1921), 56, http://docs.lib.noaa.gov/rescue/cof/COF_1919.PDF (accessed January 27, 2011).

28 For an overview of the history of fly fishing, see Andrew Herd, *The Fly* (Ellesmere, UK: Medlar Press, 2003), 122, 215. For more on the western traditions of fly tying, see Paul Schullery, *Cowboy Trout: Western Fly Fishing As If It Matters* (Helena: Montana Historical Society Press, 2006), 125–64; John H. Monnett, *Cutthroat and Campfire Tales: The Fly-Fishing Heritage of the West* (Boulder: University Press of Colorado, 2001), 56–66; George F. Grant, *Montana Trout Flies* ([Butte, MT?]: privately printed, 1972); and Jack H. Dennis, Jr., *Western Trout Fly Tying Manual* (Jackson Hole, WY: Snake River Books, 1974). While the Maclean family clearly held disdain for bait fishers, from Izaak Walton to Norman's brother-in-law Neal, fly fishing and spin fishing cannot be easily delineated in western angling. Not until the post–World War II technological improvements did western anglers take up spin fishing in large numbers, and it was not until the 1970s that fly fishing again grew in popularity. Despite the fluctuating numbers and the many westerners who used both techniques, fly fishing outfitters and guides catering to wealthy tourists formed the mainstay of the regional fishing industry during the twentieth century. Fly fishers also played a central role in shaping conservation and management practices. For more on spin fishing history, see Schullery, *If Fish Could Scream: An Angler's Search for the Future of Fly Fishing* (Mechanicsburg, PA: Stackpole Books, 2008), 31–50.

29 Pamphlet, "The Pott Trout Flies," series I, box 3, folder 1, MSS 89: Ted Trueblood Collection, Special Collections, Boise State University.

30 Schullery, *Cowboy Trout*, 149–54.

31 *Her Majesty Montana Has a "Come-Hither" Look* (Butte: Montana Standard Printers, 1940), no pagination.

32 Wyoming Travel Commission, *This Is BIG Wyoming* (Cheyenne: Wyoming Travel Commission, [1963–1967?]), 24.

33 Idaho-Golden Gate International Exposition Commission, *It's a Privilege to Live in Idaho: A Balanced State* (n.p.: [1939?]), no pagination.

34 W. W. Crosby, *Some Western Fishing* (Baltimore, MD: Waverly Press, 1926), 13, 43.

35　Bertram D. Lackey, *Outwitting Trout with a Fly: Letters of a Western Angler* (Los Angeles: Phillips Printing, 1929).

36　Glen C. Leach, "Appendix IX: Propagation and Distribution of Food Fishes, 1921," in US Bureau of Fisheries, *Report of the United States Commissioner of Fisheries for the Fiscal Year 1921 with Appendixes* (Washington, DC: GPO, 1922), 3, http://docs.lib.noaa.gov/rescue/cof/COF_1921.PDF (accessed January 27, 2011).

37　D. H. Madsen, *Fourteenth Biennial Report of the Fish and Game Commissioner of the State of Utah, for the Years 1921 and 1922* (Salt Lake City, UT: Arrow Press, [1923?]), 5.

38　S. B. Locke, "The National Forests of the West and the Fish Supply," *TAFS* 58, no. 1 (Jan. 1928): 202.

39　John H. Hatton, "Trout Fishing in the National Forests," *TAFS* 55, no. 1 (Jan. 1925): 154–55.

40　D. C. Booth, "Some Observations on Fish Culture," *TAFS* 55, no. 1 (Jan. 1925): 165.

41　For more on this new consumerist view of nature and planting larger fish because of it, see Lawrence M. Lipin, *Workers and the Wild: Conservation, Consumerism, and Labor in Oregon, 1910–30* (Chicago: University of Illinois Press, 2007).

42　Frank N. Clark, "Disadvantage of Planting Small Fish," *Fishery Bulletin* 6, no. 1 (1886): 421, http://fisherybulletin.nmfs.noaa.gov/6-1/clark1.pdf (accessed November 15, 2010).

43　Glen C. Leach, "Co-operative Fish Culture," *TAFS* 55, no. 1 (Jan. 1925): 102.

44　J. Arthur Mecham, *Biennial Report of the [Utah] State Fish and Game Commissioner, 1927 and 1928* (Salt Lake City, UT: Arrow Press, [1929?]), 22.

45　A. A. Sanders, *Biennial Report of the State Game and Fish Commissioner of the State of Wyoming 1925–1926* (Cheyenne, WY: Labor Journal, [1927?]), 27.

46　Bruce Nowlin, *Biennial Report of the State Game and Fish Commissioner of the State of Wyoming 1927–1928* (Casper, WY: S. E. Boyer, [1929?]), 31–35.

47　Herbert Clark Hoover, *A Remedy for Disappearing Game Fishes* (New York: Huntington Press, 1930), 3.

48　Ibid., 4–6.

49　H. S. Davis, "The Purpose and Value of Stream Improvement," *TAFS* 64, no. 1 (Jan. 1934): 63–66.

50　Clarence R. Lucas, "Game Fish Management," *TAFS* 68, no. 1 (Jan. 1939): 67.

51　Pat Munday, "'A Millionaire Couldn't Buy a Piece of Water as Good': George Grant and the Conservation of the Big Hole River Watershed," *Montana: The Magazine of Western History* 52, no. 2 (Summer 2002): 24.

52 Mrs. J. W. Shumate to C. Ben Ross, July 31, 1934, box 5, folder 6, AR2/15: Governor C. Ben Ross Records, ISHS.

53 Owens, "Fishing the Hatch," 14–15.

54 Grant, *Montana Trout Flies.*

55 Ibid.

56 In *Montana Trout Flies*, George Grant noted that one of the most popular flies, the Dr. Mummy, lost popularity in the postwar years due to spin fishing: "The Dr. Mummy was a most popular fly until the advent of the spinning reel about 1950 when flyfishing [sic] went into a decline in Montana, and many of these old patterns were lost because they were unknown to a new generation of fly-tyers [sic] and fly fishermen when the fly resurgence occurred" (Ibid., no pagination).

57 Dennis, *Fly Tying Manual*, 2–3.

58 Ibid., 71.

59 US Bureau of Fisheries, *Report of the United States Commissioner of Fisheries for the Fiscal Year 1929 with Appendixes* (Washington, DC: GPO, 1929), 768–69, http://docs.lib.noaa.gov/rescue/cof/COF_1929.PDF (accessed January 30, 2011).

60 Andrew J. Martin, *Biennial Report, State Game and Fish Department Wyoming, January 1, 1935–January 1, 1937* (Cheyenne, WY: Game and Fish Department, [1937?]), 15.

61 Halverson, *Synthetic Fish*, 78–80.

62 US Bureau of Fisheries, *Report of the United States Commissioner of Fisheries for the Fiscal Year 1935 with Appendixes* (Washington, DC: GPO, 1936), 410–15, http://docs.lib.noaa.gov/rescue/cof/COF_1935.PDF (accessed January 30, 2011).

63 US Bureau of Fisheries, *Report of the United States Commissioner of Fisheries for the Fiscal Year 1931 with Appendixes* (Washington, DC: GPO, 1932), 669, http://docs.lib.noaa.gov/rescue/cof/COF_1932.PDF (accessed January 30, 2011).

64 See Paul S. Sutter, *Driven Wild: How the Fight against Automobiles Launched the Modern Wilderness Movement* (Seattle: University of Washington Press, 2002).

65 Susan B. Adams, Christopher A. Frissell, and Bruce E. Rieman, "Geography of Invasion in Mountain Streams: Consequences of Headwater Lake Fish Introductions," *Ecosystems* 4, no. 4 (June 2001): 297.

66 Roland A. Knapp, Paul Stephen Corn, and Daniel E. Schindler, "The Introduction of Nonnative Fish into Wilderness Lakes: Good Intentions, Conflicting Mandates, and Unintended Consequences," *Ecosystems* 4, no. 4 (June 2001): 275.

67 Clipping, "Pioneer Conservationist Receives Degree," box 1, folder Biographical Information [no folder number], collection #3190: Finis Mitchell Papers,

American Heritage Center, University of Wyoming, Laramie [hereafter AHC].

68   Finis Mitchell, *Wind River Trails: A Hiking and Fishing Guide to the Many Trails and Lakes of the Wind River Range in Wyoming* (Salt Lake City, UT: Wasatch Publishers, 1975), 6.

69   Jeffrey Nichols, "'These Waters Were All Virgin': Finis Mitchell and Wind River," *Annals of Wyoming: The Wyoming History Journal* 76, no. 2 (Spring 2004): 29. See also John H. Monnett, *Cutthroat and Campfire Tales: The Fly-Fishing Heritage of the West* (Boulder: University Press of Colorado, 2001), 103–108.

70   Mitchell, *Wind River Trails*, 12.

71   Nichols, "'Waters,'" 26–30.

72   James P. Brooks, "Introduction of Trout and the Planting of Eyed Eggs in Remote and Isolated Waters of Glacier National Park," *TAFS* 55, no. 1 (Jan. 1925): 149–50.

73   Clipping [1925?], series I, box 6, folder 14, collection #400008: Grace Raymond Hebard Papers, AHC.

74   Mitchell, *Wind River Trails*, 8; Nichols, "'Waters,'" 26.

75   Utah State Fish and Game Commission, *Twenty-sixth Biennial Report of the State Fish and Game Commission of the State of Utah, July 1, 1944 to June 30, 1946* (n.p.: [1946?]), 40.

76   Schullery, *If Fish Could Scream*, 37–39.

77   Pomeroy, *Golden West*, 225.

78   For more on Cold War westerns, see Richard Slotkin, *Gunfighter Nation: The Myth of the Frontier in Twentieth-Century America* (New York: Atheneum, 1992), chs. 11 and 12.

79   Wyoming Travel Commission, *Wyoming Historical Handbook* (Cheyenne: Wyoming Travel Commission, 1950), 6–16.

80   Ibid., 24.

81   Syl MacDowell, *Western Trout* (New York: Alfred A. Knopf, 1948), 166.

82   Arthur H. Carhart, *Fishing in the West* (New York: Macmillan, 1950), 123. For more on Carhart's views, see William Philpott, *Vacationland: Tourism and Environment in the Colorado High Country* (Seattle: University of Washington Press, 2013), ch. 4.

83   Robert Grieve, *Biennial Report of the Wyoming Game and Fish Commission 1941–1942* (Cheyenne: Wyoming Game and Fish Department, [1943?]), 43.

84   N. B. Cook, *Biennial Report of the State Fish and Game Commission, July 1, 1938 to June 30, 1940* (n.p.: [1940?]), 34. Federal officials also noted the failures of stream improvement projects. See Lucas, "Game Fish Management," 71–72.

85   Edwin P. Pister, "Wilderness Fish Stocking: History and Perspective," *Ecosys-*

tems 4, no. 4 (June 2001): 281.

86   Wesley C. Nelson, *High Lake Research and Management in Colorado,* special report no. 64, R-S-64–88 (n.p.: Colorado Division of Wildlife, June 1988), 1, 25.

87   Knapp, Corn, and Schindler, "Nonnative Fish," 275. For wilderness stocking in general, see the special issue of *Ecosystems* 4, no. 4 (June 2001) on "Fish Stocking Impacts to Mountain Lake Ecosystems."

88   For postwar consumerism, see Lizabeth Cohen, *A Consumers' Republic: The Politics of Mass Consumption in Postwar America* (New York: Vintage Books, 2003). For leisure, tourism, and consumer landscapes generally, see Philpott, *Vacationland.*

89   See for example, Utah Fish and Game Commission, *Twenty-sixth Biennial Report,* 16.

90   Utah State Fish and Game Commission, *Twenty-ninth Biennial Report of the State Fish and Game Commissioner of the State of Utah, July 1, 1948 to June 30, 1950* (n.p.: [1950?]), 41.

CHAPTER 4: TRASH FISH

1   Norman Maclean, *A River Runs Through It, and Other Stories* (Chicago: University of Chicago Press, 1976), 38. Now known as pikeminnow, squawfish became a derogatory common name for fish in the *Ptychocheilus* genus during the late nineteenth and early twentieth century. A lengthier discussion of the changing terminology follows later in this chapter.

2   Under the banner of conservation, people have exterminated a lot of critters (predators and pests) to save the environment or to protect favored animals. In their work on animals and the West, historians have stressed both culture and economics in shaping the treatment of animals. See, among others, Jon T. Coleman, *Vicious: Wolves and Men in America* (New Haven, CT: Yale University Press, 2004); Thomas R. Dunlap, *Saving America's Wildlife* (Princeton, NJ: Princeton University Press, 1988); and Donald Worster, *Nature's Economy: A History of Ecological Ideas,* 2nd ed. (New York: Cambridge University Press, 1994), ch. 13.

3   Howard L. Jelks, et al., "Conservation Status of Imperiled North American Freshwater and Diadromous Fishes," *Fisheries* 33, no. 8 (Aug. 2008): 387–403.

4   In certain western trout waters, mountain whitefish serve an important role as an indicator species, alerting biologists to ecological problems like pollution or low water temperatures that may endanger other fish populations or drinking water sources. Kevin A. Meyer, F. Steven Elle, and James A. Lamansky, Jr., "Environmental Factors Related to the Distribution, Abundance, and Life His-

tory Characteristics of Mountain Whitefish in Idaho," *North American Journal of Fisheries Management* 29, no. 3 (June 2009): 753.

5 Idaho Department of Fish and Game, *Mountain Whitefish Conservation and Management Plan for the Big Lost River Drainage, Idaho* (May 2007), 3–23, 15–16, https://fishandgame.idaho.gov/public/wildlife/planFishBigLostRiver-Whitefish.pdf (accessed July 15, 2014). Scientists have noted a lack of scientific studies on mountain whitefish available to managers. See Meyer, Elle, and Lamansky, "Environmental Factors," 753; J. D. McPhail and P. Troffe, "The Mountain Whitefish (*Prosopium williamsoni*): A Brief Review of the Distribution, Biology, and Life History of a Neglected Recreational Species," in *Bull Trout II*, ed. M. K. Brewin, A. J. Paul, and M. Monita (Calgary: Trout Unlimited Canada, 2001), 17–20; and T. G. Northcote and G. L. Ennis, "Mountain Whitefish Biology and Habitat Use in Relation to Compensation and Improvement Possibilities," *Reviews in Fisheries Science* 2, no. 4 (1994): 348.

6 Cooke et al. have observed: "Generally, non-game fishes lack comprehensive management strategies, and those species are often pushed to extinction without the declines being noticed." "Threats, Conservation Strategies, and Prognosis for Suckers (*Catostomidae*) in North America: Insights from Regional Case Studies of a Diverse Family of Non-game Fishes," *Biological Conservation* 121, no. 3 (Feb. 2005): 318.

7 Andrew Herd, *The Fly* (Ellesmere, UK: Medlar Press, 2003), 122, 215.

8 Francis Francis, *Fish-Culture: A Practical Guide to the Modern System of Breeding and Rearing Fish* (London: Routledge, Warne, and Routledge, 1863), 122–33. Francis also briefly served as the piscicultural director for the English Acclimatization Society, an organization that introduced new species of plants and animals throughout Great Britain.

9 John Lowerson, "Brothers of the Angle: Coarse Fishing and English Working-Class Culture, 1850–1914," in *Pleasure, Profit, Proselytism: British Culture and Sport at Home and Abroad, 1700–1914*, ed. J. A. Mangan (London: Frank Cass, 1988), 105–107. In the years following enclosures and the divide between British game and coarse fishing, a vibrant coarse and roach fishing culture sprung up among the skilled artisans and working-class fishermen, admired so greatly by Roderick Haig-Brown. The English emigrant and noted Canadian conservationist believed that these coarse fishermen were "more truly representative of British angling than all the trout and salmon fishermen about whom the books are written." Roderick L. Haig-Brown, *A River Never Sleeps* (1946; repr., New York: Skyhorse Publishing, 2010), 53.

10 John Lowerson, *Sport and the English Middle Classes, 1870–1914* (Manchester, UK: Manchester University Press, 1993), 43.

11 Andrew Herd, *Angling Giants* (Ellesmere, UK: Medlar Press, 2010), 265.

12 Henry William Herbert, *Frank Forester's Fish and Fishing of the United States and British Provinces of North America* (New York: Stringer and Townsend, 1850), 165, 173, http://www.archive.org/details/frankforestersfiooherb (accessed December 27, 2010).

13 Quoted in Anders Halverson, *An Entirely Synthetic Fish: How Rainbow Trout Beguiled America and Overran the World* (New Haven, CT: Yale University Press, 2010), 72.

14 Genio C. Scott, *Fishing in American Waters* (New York: Harper and Brothers, 1869), 149, 35.

15 John F. Sharp, *Third Biennial Report of the State Fish and Game Commissioner, to the Governor and the Fourth Session of the State Legislature of Utah, for the Years 1899 and 1900* (Salt Lake City, UT: Deseret News, 1901), 28.

16 Fred W. Chambers to Jos. Wignall, February 6, 1912, box 2, letter book 1/23/1912–7/6/1912: Fish and Game Commissioner, Correspondence Sent, Utah State Archives and Research Center, Salt Lake City.

17 Mountain whitefish, *Prosopium williamsoni*, inhabit rivers and lakes throughout the West, from the headwaters of the Mackenzie River in British Columbia, south to the Sierra Nevada's east slope in California, west to rivers in northwestern Colorado, and north to Montana's upper Missouri River basin and Yellowstone River, and the North Saskatchewan River in Alberta. Whitefish and grayling are progenitors of trout and other salmonids. Robert J. Behnke, *Trout and Salmon of North America* (New York: Free Press, 2002), 3, 335–40. Historical common names include Rocky Mountain whitefish, mountain herring, Williamson's whitefish, or grayling (a mistaken identity).

18 Peter N. Jones, "Identity through Fishing: A Preliminary Analysis of Impacts to the Nez Perce as a Result of the Damming of the Clearwater and Snake Rivers," *Cultural Dynamics* 17, no. 2 (July 2005): 166.

19 Deward E. Walker, Jr., *Lemhi Shoshone-Bannock Reliance on Anadromous and Other Fish Resources*, Idaho Bureau of Land Management Technical Bulletin no. 94–4 (Boise, ID: Bureau of Land Management, April 1994), 232.

20 David Starr Jordan and Barton Warren Evermann, *American Food and Game Fishes: A Popular Account of All the Species Found in America North of the Equator, with Keys for Ready Identification, Life Histories and Methods of Capture* (New York: Doubleday, Page, 1902), 50.

21 Jared Farmer, *On Zion's Mount: Mormons, Indians, and the American Landscape* (Cambridge, MA: Harvard University Press, 2008), ch. 2.

22 Jon Erickson, *Summarization of Life History and Management Studies on the Rocky Mountain Whitefish in the Snake River Drainage*, project 0166–23–5501

([Cheyenne?]: Wyoming Game and Fish Department, July 13, 1966), 11.

23   William F. Sigler and Robert Rush Miller, *Fishes of Utah* (Salt Lake City: Utah State Department of Fish and Game, 1963), 59.

24   Barton W. Evermann, "A Report upon Salmon Investigations in the Headwaters of the Columbia River, in the State of Idaho, in 1895, Together with Notes upon the Fishes Observed in That State in 1894 and 1895," *Fishery Bulletin* 16, no. 1 (1896): 178–79, http://fisherybulletin.nmfs.noaa.gov/16-1/evermann.pdf (accessed November 17, 2010).

25   Louis S. Warren, *The Hunter's Game: Poachers and Conservationists in Twentieth-Century America* (New Haven, CT: Yale University Press, 1997), 157.

26   Jordan and Evermann, *American Food and Game Fishes*, 70. They qualified this statement by adding that in the Colorado basin "where species of food-fishes are not numerous, it is a fish of considerable importance."

27   Fred Quartarone, *Historical Accounts of Upper Colorado River Basin Endangered Fish* (n.p.: Recovery Program for Endangered Fish of the Upper Colorado River Basin, September 1995), 1–5, 19–21.

28   Ibid., 7, 21–22.

29   Ibid., 7, 21–22, 50.

30   Ibid., 7. Throughout the twentieth century, habitat change, introductions of nonnative species, and water pollution from industrial and urban sources, along with later dam building and toxicant applications, led to pikeminnow and other native fish declines. Ibid., 37–42.

31   Jordan and Evermann, *American Food and Game Fishes*, 36–37.

32   Chancey Juday, "A Study of Twin Lakes, Colorado, with Special Consideration of the Food of the Trouts," *Fishery Bulletin* 26, no. 1 (1906): 161, http://fisherybulletin.nmfs.noaa.gov/26-1/juday1.pdf (accessed November 17, 2010).

33   Jordan and Evermann, *American Food and Game Fishes*, 71.

34   Big Horn [pseud.], "Rocky Mountain Grayling," *Forest and Stream* 36, no. 26 (July 16, 1891): 519. See also Livingston [pseud.], "Grayling or Whitefish?" *Forest and Stream* 36, no. 3 (Aug. 6, 1891): 48. These debates in *Forest and Stream* in the late 1880s and early 1890s also revolved around correctly identifying mountain whitefish compared to arctic grayling, its native cousin in the upper Missouri River basin of Montana. Their identification became confusing to some because mountain whitefish were sometimes mistakenly called grayling, especially in Wyoming and Colorado, and other places where grayling were not introduced until later.

35   Quoted in John Gay, "Colorado Trout and Whitefish," *Forest and Stream* 37, no. 15 (Oct. 29, 1891): 293. Due to his appreciation, France reportedly tried to

get mountain whitefish reared in hatcheries and distributed beyond Colorado's western slope to rivers closer to Denver. Ibid.

36 Joseph S. Nelson et al., "Recommended Changes in Common Fish Names: Pikeminnow to Replace Squawfish (*Ptychocheilus* spp.)," *Fisheries* 23, no. 9 (Sept. 1998): 37.

37 John Richardson, *Fauna Boreali-Americana; or, The Zoology of the Northern Parts of British America: Containing Descriptions of the Objects of Natural History Collected on the Late Northern Land Expeditions under Command of Captain Sir John Franklin, R. N., Part Third. The Fish* (London: Richard Bentley, 1836), 305–6, http://www.archive.org/details/faunaborealiamero3rich (accessed December 30, 2010).

38 Barton W. Evermann, "A Reconnaissance of the Streams and Lakes of Western Montana and Northwestern Wyoming." *Fishery Bulletin* 11, no. 1 (1891): 12. http://fisherybulletin.nmfs.noaa.gov/11–1/evermann.pdf (accessed November 15, 2010).

39 Evermann, "Report," 175.

40 Barton W. Evermann and Cloud. Rutter, "The Fishes of the Colorado Basin," *Fishery Bulletin* 14, no. 1 (1894): 482, http://fisherybulletin.nmfs.noaa.gov/14–1/evermann1.pdf (accessed November 15, 2010).

41 Jordan and Evermann, *American Food and Game Fishes*, 68–70.

42 Evermann, "Reconnaissance," 12.

43 Evermann, "Report," 175, 176.

44 Quartarone, *Historical Accounts*, 49.

45 William A. Dill and Leo Shapovalov, "An Unappreciated California Game Fish, the Rocky Mountain Whitefish, *Prosopium williamsoni* (Girard)," *California Fish and Game* 25, no. 3 (July 1939): 226.

46 James R. Simon, "The Whitefish—A Neglected Resource," *Wyoming Wild Life* 6, no. 9 (1941): 1–2.

47 Harriet Wheatley, *Lady Angler: Fishing, Hunting, and Camping in Wilderness Areas of North America* (San Antonio, TX: Naylor, 1952), 50. Wheatley did not elaborate on whether they previously threw their catches of mountain whitefish on the bank or just released the fish back into the river.

48 See, for example, William F. Sigler, "The Life History and Management of the Mountain Whitefish *Prosopium williamsoni* (Girard) in Logan River Utah," bulletin 347 (Logan: Utah State Agricultural College, May 1951), 3.

49 Meyer, Elle, and Lamansky observed that that even though some agencies engaged in mountain whitefish removal between the 1950s and 1970s, the idea that the species compete with trout "has not been substantiated." "Environmental Factors," 753. Likewise, Larry R. Brown and Peter B. Moyle argued,

"There is little evidence to indicate that squawfish compete strongly with salmonids." "The Impact of Squawfish on Salmonid Populations: A Review," *North American Journal of Fisheries Management* 1, no. 2 (April 1981): 104. Scientists came to the same conclusions on sucker species: "An extensive literature review by Holey et al. (1979) summarized available research on the topic and concluded that although suckers do consume the offspring of other organisms, there was no evidence of any negative effects on prey populations. Further, although there can be substantial overlap in habitat use and food consumption between suckers and other fishes, there is little evidence that either is limiting, such that competition would be detrimental. Holey et al. (1979) determined that there was evidence that both supported and refuted the notion that sucker removal resulted in positive benefits to game fish." Cooke et al., "Threats," 326.

50   Halverson, *Synthetic Fish*, 97.

51   B. G. Patten and D. T. Rodman, "Reproductive Behavior of the Northern Squawfish, *Ptychocheilus oregonensis*," *Transactions of the American Fisheries Society* [hereafter *TAFS*] 98, no. 1 (Jan. 1969): 108.

52   Utah State Fish Commission, *Thirty-first Biennial Report of the State Fish and Game Commission of the State of Utah, July 1, 1952 to June 30, 1954* (n.p.: [1954?]), 59.

53   The State of Utah Department of Fish and Game, *Thirty-third Biennial Report, July 1, 1956 to June 30, 1958* (n.p.: [1958?]), 53.

54   Wyoming Game and Fish Commission, *Annual Report 1952* (Cheyenne, WY: Pioneer Printing, [1953?]), 39.

55   Wm. H. Bush to Albert M. Orr, February 16, 1957, series IV, box 4, folder 2, MSS 213: Western Montana Fish and Game Association Records, Archives and Special Collections, Maureen and Mike Mansfield Library, University of Montana-Missoula.

56   Erickson, *Summarization*, 15–19.

57   M. W. Smith, "Copper Sulphate and Rotenone as Fish Poisons," *TAFS* 69, no. 1 (Jan. 1940): 148.

58   Mark R. Vinson, Eric C. Dinger, and Deanna K. Vinson, "Piscicides and Invertebrates: After 70 Years, Does Anyone Really Know?" *Fisheries* 35, no. 2 (Feb. 2010): 62. Rotenone kills only fish, although its effects on invertebrates and amphibians are still debated. Ibid., 61–71.

59   R. W. Kiser, John R. Donaldson, and Paul R. Olson, "The Effect of Rotenone on Zooplankton Populations in Freshwater Lakes," *TAFS* 92, no. 1 (Jan. 1963): 17.

60   Robert R. Miller, "Is Our Native Underwater Life Worth Saving?" *National Parks Magazine* 37, no. 188 (May 1963): 4.

61   Worster, *Nature's Economy*, ch. 13.

62   F. Herr, E. Greselin, and C. Chappel, "Toxicology Studies of Antimycin, a Fish Eradicant," *TAFS* 96, no. 3 (July 1967): 320.

63   Craig MacPhee and Richard Ruelle, "A Chemical Selectively Lethal to Squaw-fish (*Ptychocheilus oregonensis* and *P. umpquae*)," *TAFS* 98, no. 4 (Oct. 1969): 676.

64   J. J. Gaffney, "Whitefish—The Rainbow's Country Cousin," *Montana Wildlife* 5, no. 1 (Winter 1955): 24.

65   Jordan and Evermann, *American Food and Game Fishes*, 116.

66   Herbert, *Fish and Fishing*, 101.

67   Greg Keeler, lyrics to "White Fish Blues," Troutball, http://www.troutball.com/songs/lyrics/all_you_can_eat/White_Fish_Blues.htm (accessed February 16, 2010).

68   Quartarone, *Historical Accounts*, 50.

69   John Gierach, *Sex, Death, and Fly-fishing* (New York: Fireside Books, 1990), 84.

70   Meyer, Elle, and Lamansky, *Environmental Factors*, 765.

71   Ed Dentry, "Lowly Whitefish Deserves Respect—and Research," *Rocky Mountain News*, February 7, 2007.

72   See Nick Gevock, "A Matter of Respect: Much-Maligned Montana Native Rarely Treated as Well as Its More Attractive Cousins," *Bozeman Daily Chronicle*, August 12, 2004, http://bozemandailychronicle.com/articles/2004/08/12/features/outdoors/whitefish.txt (accessed September 9, 2008).

73   Gierach, *Sex, Death*, 84.

74   Ed Dentry, "Not-So-Great Whitefish Still Offers a Little Hope," *Rocky Mountain News*, October 6, 1999.

75   Cooke et al., "Threats," 328.

CHAPTER 5: LUNKERS

1   Charles S. Johnson, "Debate Centers on Definition of 'Ditch,'" *Montana Standard*, March 9, 2011. More recently, the Montana Supreme Court again upheld the state's stream access law from disputes along the Ruby River involving a wealthy out-of-state landowner. See Charles S. Johnson, "High Court Upholds Public Access Right to Montana Streams," *Montana Standard*, January 16, 2014, http://mtstandard.com/news/local/high-court-sides-with-montana-stream-access-law-in-madison/article_c062a544-7eda-11e3-8c8c-0019bb2963f4.html?fb_action_ids=10203035905963430&fb_action_types=og.recommends&fb_ref=.Uti1yBjfCcA.like (accessed January 20, 2014).

2   Ted Leeson, *Inventing Montana: Dispatches from the Madison Valley* (New York: Skyhorse Publishing, 2009), 70.

3   For western dam building, see Donald Worster, *Rivers of Empire: Water, Aridity, and the Growth of the American West* (New York: Oxford University Press, 1985); Richard White, *The Organic Machine: The Remaking of the Columbia River* (New York: Hill and Wang, 1995); Donald J. Pisani, *Water and the American Government: The Reclamation Bureau, National Water Policy, and the West, 1902–1935* (Berkeley: University of California Press, 2002); Pisani, *Water, Land, and Law in the West: The Limits of Public Policy, 1850–1920* (Lawrence: University Press of Kansas, 1996); Mark Fiege, *Irrigated Eden: The Making of an Agricultural Landscape in the American West* (Seattle: University of Washington Press, 1999); Marc Reisner, *Cadillac Desert: The American West and Its Disappearing Water*, rev. ed. (New York: Penguin, 1993); and Wallace Stegner, *Beyond the Hundredth Meridian: John Wesley Powell and the Second Opening of the West* (1954; repr., New York: Penguin, 1992). Works on tailwaters include Joel William Helmer, "Float Trips, Dams, and Tailwater Trout: An Environmental History of the White River of Northern Arkansas, 1870–2004" (PhD diss., Oklahoma State University, 2005) and Ken Owens, "Blue-Ribbon Tailwaters: The Unplanned Role of the U.S. Bureau of Reclamation in Western Fly Fishing," *American Fly Fisher* 33, no. 2 (Spring 2007): 2–10.

4   Gary LaFontaine, *Caddisflies* (Guilford, CT: Lyons Press, 1981).

5   Gary LaFontaine, "The Bighorn River: As You Like It," *Trout* (Spring 1998): 59.

6   Fiege, *Irrigated Eden*, 87.

7   Wallace Stegner, *The Sound of Mountain Water: The Changing American West* (1969; repr., New York: Penguin Books, 1997), 20.

8   David Starr Jordan, "Report of Explorations in Colorado and Utah during the Summer of 1889, with an Account of the Fishes Found in Each of the River Basins Examined," *Fishery Bulletin* 9, no. 1 (1889): 5, http://fisherybulletin.nmfs.noaa.gov/9-1/jordan.pdf (accessed November 15, 2010).

9   John F. Sharp, *Sixth Biennial Report of the State Fish and Game Commissioner and the Commissioner of State Hatcheries, to the Governor and the Seventh Session of the State Legislature of Utah, for the Years 1905 and 1906* (Salt Lake City, UT: Deseret News, 1907), 10. For more on irrigation problems at Utah Lake, see Jared Farmer, *On Zion's Mount: Mormons, Indians, and the American Landscape* (Cambridge, MA: Harvard University Press, 2008), 121–23.

10   R. E. Thomas, *[Idaho] Department of Fish and Game, Biennial Report for 1923–4* ([Boise: Idaho Fish and Game Department?], January 1, 1925), 25.

11   Utah Fish and Game Commission, *Twenty-eighth Biennial Report of the State Fish and Game Commission of the State of Utah, July 1, 1946 to June 30, 1948* (n.p.: [1948?]), 72.

12   Jordan, "Report," 5, 30.

13   Photocopy of Charles H. Arbuckle, *First Biennial Report of the State Fish and Game Warden of the State of Idaho, 1900* (n.p.: December 20, 1900), 9, box 3, folder Fish and Game Department [folders unnumbered], AR 2/17: Governor C. A. Bottolfsen Records, Idaho State Historical Society, Boise [hereafter ISHS].

14   John F. Sharp, *Fourth Biennial Report of the State Fish and Game Commissioner, to the Governor and the Fifth Session of the State Legislature of Utah, for the Years 1901 and 1902* (Salt Lake City, UT: Star Printing, 1903), 30.

15   Sharp, *Sixth Biennial Report*, 23–25.

16   W. T. Thompson, "Is Irrigation Detrimental to Trout Culture?" *Transactions of the American Fisheries Society* [hereafter *TAFS*] 41, no. 1 (Jan. 1912): 103.

17   E. E. Prince, "Irrigation Canals as an Aid to Fisheries Development in the West," *TAFS* 52, no. 1 (Jan. 1923): 157.

18   Photocopy of the Laws of Wyoming, 1879, chapter 42, "An Act to Provide for the Propagation and Culture of Fish throughout the Territory of Wyoming," and photocopy of the Laws of Wyoming, 1884, chapter 44, "An Act to Protect Fish," box 16, folder 9, collection #10483: Neal L. Blair Papers, American Heritage Center, University of Wyoming, Laramie [hereafter AHC].

19   William F. Sigler and John W. Sigler, *Fishes of the Great Basin: A Natural History* (Reno: University of Nevada Press, 1987), 21.

20   James A. Henshall, "On the Protection of Fish in Inland Waters," *TAFS* 34, no. 1 (Jan. 1905): 141.

21   Western Montana Anglers' Association minutes, April 22, 1915, series IV, box 2, folder 27, MSS 213: Western Montana Fish and Game Association Records, Archives and Special Collections, Maureen and Mike Mansfield Library, University of Montana–Missoula [hereafter UMM].

22   Fred W. Chambers to Ira Lambert, April 17, 1911, box 2, letter book 4/12/1911–7/5/1911, series 1068: Fish and Game Commissioner, Correspondence Sent, Utah State Archives and Research Center, Salt Lake City.

23   W. H. Seebohm, *Biennial Report of the State Game Warden of Wyoming for the Two Years Ending September 30, 1914* (Cheyenne, WY: Labor Journal Publishing, 1914), 18.

24   Robert Grieve, *Biennial Report of the Wyoming Game and Fish Commissioner 1939–1940* (Cheyenne: Wyoming Game and Fish Department, [1941?]), 38.

25   This doctrine stemmed from the 1908 Supreme Court case *Winters v. United States*. For more information see David E. Wilkins and K. Tsianina Lomawaima, *Uneven Ground: American Indian Sovereignty and Federal Law* (Norman: University of Oklahoma Press, 2001), 130–31.

26   Photocopy, Robert Marshall to A. L. Wathen, July 22, 1936, box 13, folder 1, RS

26: Montana Governor's Office: Montana Indian Historical Jurisdiction Study Records, Montana Historical Society, Helena [hereafter MHS].

27 Walter W. McDonald to George Moon, October 12, 1964, series IV, box 4, folder 7, Western Montana Fish and Game Association Records, UMM.

28 Sharp, *Sixth Biennial Report*, 9.

29 Carter Tobey to Moses Alexander, August 11, 1916, box 4, folder 15, AR2/11: Governor Moses Alexander Records, ISHS.

30 Photocopy, L. W. Shotwell to the Commissioner of Indian Affairs, November 5, 1936, box 13, folder 1, Montana Governor's Office: Montana Indian Historical Jurisdiction Study Records, MHS.

31 Fiege, *Irrigated Eden*, 63, 49.

32 H. B. Cromar, *Biennial Report of the State Game and Fish Commissioner and the Commissioner of Hatcheries of Utah* (Ogden, UT: State Industrial School, 1908), 23.

33 Grieve, *Biennial Report*, 37.

34 Louis S. Pechacek, comp., *Summary of Fish from Cody Canal and Lakeview Canal*, November, 3–6, 1958, box 2, file M-122, RG 40: Game and Fish Department, Administration, 00.01 Attorney General Files (AS 5209), Wyoming State Archives, Cheyenne [hereafter WSA].

35 Clipping, "Game Fish Are Recovered from Lowell Canals," *Idaho Wildlife Review* 4, no. 3 (Jan.–Feb. 1952): 3, series II, box 15, folder 18, MSS 721: Bruce Bowler Papers, ISHS.

36 Worster, *Rivers of Empire*, 276.

37 Reisner, *Cadillac Desert*, 164–66.

38 Worster, *Rivers of Empire*, 260–61.

39 Resolution no. 7, Wyoming Division of the Izaak Walton League of America, August 12, 1939, sub-series 3, box 286, folder Fish Hatcheries, 1939 [no folder number], collection #275: Joseph C. O'Mahoney papers, AHC.

40 Dave Whitlock, "Dave Talks about Reichle," *River Rat*, Jan.–Feb. 1976, [no pagination].

41 Frank H. Dunkle to Cecil Gubser, March 10, 1965, series IV, box 5, folder 3, MSS 213: Western Montana Fish and Game Association Records, UMM.

42 LaFontaine, *Caddisflies*, 197.

43 Owens, "Blue-Ribbon Tailwaters," 2; Robert Behnke, "Tailwater Trout: Fish of Enormous Size," *Trout*, Spring 1996, 43.

44 Owens, "Blue-Ribbon Tailwaters," 3–4; Ed Engle, *Fly Fishing the Tailwaters* (Harrisburg, PA: Stackpole Books, 1991), 13–20; Helmer, "Float Trips," 68; and Behnke, "Tailwater Trout," 43.

45 Adrian A. Bantjes, "The Past and Present of Fly-Fishing in Jackson Hole,

Wyoming: An Interview with Jack Dennis," *Annals of Wyoming: The Wyoming History Journal* 76, no. 2 (Spring 2004): 21.

46 Ibid., 21.

47 Donald Pfitzer, "Tailwater Trout Fisheries with Special Reference to the Southern States," in *Proceedings of the Wild Trout Management Symposium at Yellowstone National Park, September 25–26, 1974*, ed. Willis King (N.p.: Trout Unlimited, 1975), 23.

48 Behnke, "Tailwater Trout," 43–44; Helmer, "Float Trips," 4.

49 Behnke, "Tailwater Trout," 44.

50 Quoted in John J. Brown, *The American Angler's Guide. Being a Compilation from the Works of Popular English Authors, from Walton to the Present Time; Together with the Opinions of Practices of the Best American Anglers: Containing Every Variety of Mode Adopted in Ocean, River, Lake and Pond Fishing; the Necessary Tackle and Baits Required; Manner of Making Artificial Flies, &c. &c. &c.; with Engravings on Wood*, 2nd ed. (New York: Burgress, Stringer, 1846), 108.

51 Owens, "Blue-Ribbon Tailwaters," 5.

52 Engle, *Fly Fishing*, 30.

53 For more information, see Gary LaFontaine, *Challenge of the Trout* (Missoula, MT: Mountain Press, 1976), 198–99. LaFontaine observed that "on Colorado streams, the art of the deep nymph is a cult akin to a religion. Anglers of the region are masters of the technique" (198).

54 Gary LaFontaine, "Sparring over Fly Lines and Tailwaters," *Trout*, Summer 1999, 59.

55 Engle, *Fly Fishing*, 33.

56 Behnke, "Tailwater Trout," 43.

57 Larry Peterson, "Comeback on the Miracle Mile," *Wyoming Wild Life* 30, no. 5 (May 1966): 6.

58 William O. Nord to Milward L. Simpson, October 29, 1963, series III, box 356, folder 11, collection #26: Milward L. Simpson senator's office files, AHC.

59 Idaho Fish and Game Department, *Twenty-ninth Biennial Report of the Fish and Game Department of the State of Idaho, July 1, 1960 to June 30, 1962* ([Boise, ID?], 1962), 63.

60 Pfitzer, "Tailwater Trout Fisheries," 27.

61 In 1965, the Montana Fish and Game Department took over responsibility for state parks and, in 1979, became known as Montana Fish, Wildlife and Parks, although the latter sometimes appeared earlier in publications. Both are used in the text, depending on what was listed in the sources used.

62 Helmer, "Float Trips," 61. Unsurprisingly, southern tailwaters relied more on

trout stocking than western ones because of the almost complete lack of natural reproduction. Pfitzer, "Tailwater Trout Fisheries," 26.

63   John Peters, *Southeast Montana Fishery Study, Job No. I, Inventory of the Waters of the Project Area, May 1, 1959–April 30, 1960*, Job Completion Report, F-20-R-4 (Montana Fish and Game Department, May 1, 1960), 2.

64   Patrick Marcuson and Clinton G. Bishop, *South Central Montana Fishery Study, Job No. IV-a, Bighorn Lake and Bighorn River Post-impoundment Study, March 1, 1975 through March 31, 1976*, Job Progress Report, F-20-R-20 (Montana Fish, Wildlife and Parks, March 1, 1976), 10.

65   Fred Quartarone, *Historical Accounts of Upper Colorado River Basin Endangered Fish* (n.p.: Recovery Program for Endangered Fish of the Upper Colorado River Basin, September 1995), 37–42.

66   Paul B. Holden and Clair B. Stalnaker, "Distribution and Abundance of Mainstream Fishes of the Middle and Upper Colorado River Basins, 1967–1973," *TAFS* 104, no. 2 (April 1975): 219.

67   See Anders Halverson, *An Entirely Synthetic Fish: How Rainbow Trout Beguiled America and Overran the World* (New Haven, CT: Yale University Press, 2010), ch. 8. For a different view, see Robert W. Wiley, "The 1962 Rotenone Treatment of the Green River, Wyoming and Utah, Revisited: Lessons Learned," *Fisheries* 33, no. 12 (Dec. 2008): 611–17.

68   Allen Binns, "The Lower Green—Rags to Riches Trout Stream," *Wyoming Wild Life* 30, no. 5 (May 1966): 12.

69   Holden and Stalnaker, "Distribution and Abundance," 217.

70   John Gierach, *Even Brook Trout Get the Blues* (New York: Simon and Schuster, 1992), 94–95.

71   William J. Hill, *Central Montana Fisheries Study, Job No. I-b, Fish Management Surveys, July 1, 1971 to June 30, 1972*, Job Progress Report, F-5-R-21 (Montana Fish, Wildlife and Parks, May 24, 1973), 14.

72   Fishery Management Investigations, Project Statement Amendment no. 2, Multi-species Management of the Lower Platte River System, Federal Aid in Fish and Wildlife Restoration, Project No. F-44-R, box 1, folder Fisheries Management Investigations—Project Amendments [no folder number], RG 40: Game and Fish Department, 00.16 Federal Aid Projects (AS 5019), WSA.

73   Karl F. Moffatt, "Fee for San Juan River Anglers Clears Hurdle," *Santa Fe New Mexican*, January 30, 2010, reprinted in "Legislature Considers San Juan Stamp to Generate Habitate Improvement Funds," January 31, 2010, http://karlfmoffatt.blogspot.com/2010/01/legislature-considers-san-juan-stamp-to.html (accessed July 15, 2014).

74   Megan Benson, "Damming the Bighorn: Indian Reserved Water Rights on the

Crow Reservation, 1900–2000" (PhD diss., University of Oklahoma, 2003), 177. For an in-depth study of the case and the Crow reaction, see Benson, ch. 5.

75 Peters, *Southeast Montana Fishery Study*, 2.

76 *Montana v. United States*, 450 U.S. 544, 101 S.Ct. 1245, 67 L.Ed.2d 493 (1981); Stephen L. Pevar, *The Rights of Indians and Tribes: The Authoritative ACLU Guide to Indian and Tribal Rights*, 3rd ed. (New York: New York University Press, 2004), 122.

77 *Montana v. United States*.

78 *Montana v. United States*.

79 Benson, "Damming the Bighorn," 208–10.

CHAPTER 6: WILD TROUT

1 Jack H. Dennis, Jr., *Western Trout Fly Tying Manual* (Jackson Hole, WY: Snake River Books, 1974), 140.

2 Doug Swisher and Carl Richards, *Selective Trout: A Dramatically New and Scientific Approach to Trout Fishing on Eastern and Western Rivers* (New York: Crown Publishers, 1971), 1. For more on Swisher, Richards, and their no-hackle flies, see Joe Brooks, *Trout Fishing* (New York: Outdoor Life, 1972), 272–80. For the growth of fly fishing during the 1970s, see Paul Schullery, *If Fish Could Scream: An Angler's Search for the Future of Fly Fishing* (Mechanicsburg, PA: Stackpole Books, 2008), 8–9.

3 Works on environmentalism and sport include Michael W. Childers, *Colorado Powder Keg: Ski Resorts and the Environmental Movement* (Lawrence: University Press of Kansas, 2012) and William Philpott, *Vacationland: Tourism and Environment in the Colorado High Country* (Seattle: University of Washington Press, 2013).

4 Barbara Novak, *Nature and Culture: American Landscape and Painting, 1825–1875* (New York: Oxford University Press, 1980), 3–38. See also Leo Marx, *The Machine in the Garden: Technology and the Pastoral Ideal in America* (New York: Oxford University Press, 1964).

5 Livingston Stone, *Domesticated Trout: How to Breed and Grow Them* (Boston: James R. Osgood, 1873), 3–4n.

6 Quoted in Paul Schullery, "Wild Trout IX—Closing Summary," in *Sustaining Wild Trout in a Changing World: Proceedings of the Wild Trout Symposium IX*, West Yellowstone, MT, October 9–12, 2007, ed. R. F. Carline and C. LoSapio (n.p.: 2007), 19, http://wildtroutsymposium.com/proceedings-9.pdf (accessed March 16, 2012) and Anders Halverson, *An Entirely Synthetic Fish: How Rainbow Trout Beguiled America and Overran the World* (New Haven, CT: Yale

University Press, 2010), 184. For more on Reed, see James A. Denton, *Rocky Mountain Radical: Myron W. Reed, Christian Socialist* (Albuquerque: University of New Mexico Press, 1997).

7   For instance, one US Bureau of Fisheries manager stated in 1931 that "it is the policy of all conservation organizations throughout the United States that the public waters shall be kept as well stocked as possible with game fishes because of the values of these fish in the recreational life of the people." Glen C. Leach, "Propagation and Distribution of Food Fishes, Fiscal Year, 1931," in US Bureau of Fisheries, *Report of the United States Commissioner of Fisheries for the Fiscal Year 1931 with Appendixes* (Washington, DC: GPO, 1932), 668, http://docs.lib.noaa.gov/rescue/cof/COF_1931.PDF (accessed January 30, 2011).

8   H. S. Davis, "Care and Diseases of Trout," in US Bureau of Fisheries, *Report of the United States Commissioner of Fisheries for the Fiscal Year 1929 with Appendixes* (Washington, DC: GPO, 1929), 134, http://docs.lib.noaa.gov/rescue/cof/COF_1929.PDF (accessed January 30, 2011).

9   Russell F. Lord, "Hatchery Trout as Foragers and Game Fish," *Transactions of the American Fisheries Society* 64, no. 1 (Jan. 1934): 339–43; 345 [hereafter *TAFS*].

10   Aldo Leopold, *A Sand County Almanac and Sketches Here and There* (1949; repr., New York: Oxford University Press, 1989), ix.

11   For a more in-depth history of ecology, see Donald Worster, *Nature's Economy: A History of Ecological Ideas*, 2nd ed. (New York: Cambridge University Press, 1994).

12   Ibid., 284.

13   Leopold, *Sand County Almanac*, 177–78.

14   Ibid., 169–70.

15   Arthur H. Carhart, *Fishing in the West* (New York: Macmillan, 1950), 124–34.

16   Wyoming Game and Fish Commission, *Report of the Wyoming Game and Fish Commission, for the Biennium 1947–1948* (Cheyenne, WY: Labor Journal, [1949?]), 64.

17   A. F. C. Greene to Milward L. Simpson, July 5, 1956, sub-series 2, box 187, folder 6, collection #00026: series II: Milward L. Simpson governor's office files, American Heritage Center, University of Wyoming, Laramie [hereafter AHC].

18   John D. Varley, "The Yellowstone Fishery," in *Proceedings of the Wild Trout Management Symposium at Yellowstone National Park, September 25–26, 1974*, ed. Willis King (N.p.: Trout Unlimited, 1975), 96, http://wildtroutsymposium.com/proceedings-1.pdf (accessed January 28, 2012).

19   Orthello L. Wallis, "Management of Sport Fishing in National Parks," *TAFS* 89, no. 2 (Apr. 1960): 235–36.

20 Ibid., 237.

21 Humphry Davy, *Salmonia: or, Days of Fly Fishing in a Series of Conversations with Some Account of the Habit of Fishes Belonging to the Genus Salmo*, 3rd ed. (London: John Murray, 1832), 25, http://www.archive.org/details/salmoni-aordaysof1832davy (accessed December 27, 2010). For a historical look at the present-day issues over fish pain and catch-and-release fishing, see Schullery, *If Fish Could Scream*, ch. 7. The title comes from an early nineteenth-century British story that has been handed down by generations of anglers, who now observe that "if fish could scream, a lot of things would be different" (167–68).

22 Lee Wulff, *Lee Wulff's Handbook of Freshwater Fishing* (New York: J. B. Lippincott, 1939), xv.

23 Ken Owens, "Fishing the Hatch: New West Romanticism and Fly-Fishing in the High Country," *Montana: The Magazine of Western History* 52, no. 2 (Summer 2002): 16.

24 May 17, 1930, and June 29, 1930, entries, Ted Trueblood notebook excerpts, series VI, box 21, MSS 89: Ted Trueblood Collection, Boise State University, Boise, Idaho.

25 Jennifer Corrinne Brown, "'The Gamest Fish That Swims': Management of the Big Hole River Fishery in Montana," *Pacific Northwest Quarterly* 97, no. 4 (Fall 2006): 176.

26 Norman Maclean to Nick Lyons, November, 10, 1976, in *The Norman Maclean Reader*, ed. O. Alan Weltzien (Chicago: University of Chicago Press, 2008), 236.

27 Samuel P. Hays, *Beauty, Health, and Permanence: Environmental Politics in the United States, 1955–1985* (New York: Cambridge University Press, 1987), 22–29. For the influence of conservationism on environmentalism, see Philpott, *Vacationland*, 189–221.

28 Rachel Carson, *Silent Spring* (1962; repr., Boston: Houghton Mifflin, 2002), 1–3.

29 Carson, however, faced critics from the chemical and agribusiness industries who regarded her as a subversive and, using gender ideas of the time, called her a "hysterical" woman in attempts to delegitimize her work. J. R. McNeill, *Something New under the Sun: An Environmental History of the Twentieth-Century World* (New York: W. W. Norton, 2000), 339. Nevertheless, Carson continued her work against DDT use before dying of breast cancer in 1964. As a result of continued protests and political activism, the US government banned DDT in 1972. For more on DDT and its eventual ban, see Thomas R. Dunlap, *DDT: Scientists, Citizens, and Public Policy* (Princeton, NJ: Princeton University Press, 1981).

30 Hays, *Beauty, Health*, 112–13.

31 George F. Grant, "Confessions of an Addict," *River Rat*, May–June 1975, no pagination.

32 Gardner L. Grant, "Wild Trout and the American Angler," in King, *Proceedings of the Wild Trout Management Symposium*, 82.

33 Gary LaFontaine, *Challenge of the Trout* (Missoula, MT: Mountain Press, 1976), 130.

34 David Quammen, "Jeremy Bentham, the Pieta, and a Precious Few Grayling," *Audubon* 84 (May 1982): 98.

35 Arnold Gingrich, *The Joys of Trout* (New York: Crown Publishers, 1973), 115–20. For criticisms of fishing stocking in Colorado and the successes of Trout Unlimited, see Philpott, *Vacationland*, 260–62.

36 Quoted in Dick Vincent, "The Catchable Trout," *Montana Outdoors* 3, no. 3 (May–June 1972): 25.

37 Charles E. Brooks, *The Living River: A Fisherman's Intimate Profile of the Madison River Watershed—Its History, Ecology, Lore, and Angling Opportunities* (Garden City, NY: Nick Lyons Books, 1979), 134.

38 H. G. Tapply, *The Sportsman's Notebook and Tap's Tips* (New York: Holt, Rinehart and Winston, 1964), 45.

39 Tom McGuane, *The Longest Silence: A Life in Fishing* (New York: Alfred A. Knopf, 1999), x.

40 Schullery, *If Fish Could Scream*, 160–66; 70–71. Emphasis in original.

41 Art Whitney, "Fish Stocking and the Wild Fish Concept," *Montana Outdoors* 2, no. 7 (July 1967): 1–4, http://www.archive.org/details/montanaoutdoors271967mont (accessed January 2, 2012).

42 E. Richard Vincent, "Effect of Stocking Catchable Trout on Wild Trout Populations," in King, *Proceedings of the Wild Trout Management Symposium*, 88. See also Vincent, "Catchable Trout," and Halverson, *Synthetic Fish*, ch. 9, esp. 118–22.

43 Brooks, *Living River*, 134–36.

44 See, for instance, Robert J. Domrose, *Northwest Montana Fishery Study, Job No. 1, Inventory of Waters of the Project Area, July 1, 1966 to June 30, 1967*, Job Completion Report, F-7-R-16 (Montana Fish and Game Department).

45 Vincent, "Effect of Stocking," in King, *Proceedings of the Wild Trout Management Symposium*, 88–89.

46 E. Richard Vincent, *Southwestern Fisheries Inventory, Job No. 1-a, Inventory and Survey of the Waters of the Project Area, February 1, 1975 through January 31, 1976*, Job Progress Report, F-9-R-24 (Montana Fish, Wildlife and Parks), 12.

47 Robert W. Wiley and James W. Mullan, "Philosophy and Management of the Fontenelle Green Tailwater Trout Fisheries," in King, *Proceedings of the Wild Trout Management Symposium*, 28.

48 Ray J. White, "In-Stream Management for Wild Trout," in King, *Proceedings of the Wild Trout Management Symposium*, 48.

49 Robert C. Averett, "Summary of Fish-Kills Occurring in Montana during Recent Years," Montana Fish and Game Department, May 9, 1960, box 10, folder Pollution-Water, 1958–1970 [no folder number], collection #08958: Wyoming Outdoor Council Records, AHC.

50 News release, US Department of Health, Education, and Welfare, April 23, 1962, box 14, folder Water Pollution, 1960–1972 [no folder number], Wyoming Outdoor Council Records, AHC.

51 Utah Fish and Game Commission, *Thirty-first Biennial Report of the State Fish and Game Commission of the State of Utah, July 1, 1952 to June 30, 1954* (n.p.: [1954?]), 58.

52 Peter Matthiessen, *Wildlife in America* (New York: Viking Press, 1959), 205–206. See also Peter Alagona, ed., "Fifty Years of Wildlife in America" forum, *Environmental History* 16, no. 3 (July 2011): 391–455.

53 Matthiessen, *Wildlife*, 210–11.

54 For more on interstate highway building and its powerful lobbyists, see Dolores Hayden, *Building Suburbia: Green Fields and Urban Growth, 1820–2000* (New York: Pantheon Books, 2003), 165–68.

55 Utah Department of Fish and Game, *Thirty-fifth Biennial Report, July 1, 1960 to June 30, 1962* (n.p.: [1962?]), 46.

56 Jack Sleight to E. G. Leipheimer, Jr., January 14, 1963, box 1, folder 1, collection 2441: Harry B. Mitchell Papers, Merrill G. Burlingame Special Collections, Montana State University, Bozeman [hereafter MSU].

57 North Central Montana Wildlife Federation Newsletter, April 1963, box 1, folder 5, Harry B. Mitchell Papers, MSU.

58 Harry Mitchell to William Browning, February 1, 1963, box 1, folder 1, Harry B. Mitchell Papers, MSU.

59 Radio speech transcript, "Fishing and Hunting," September 23, 1961, box 660, folder 4, MC 172: Lee Metcalf Papers, Montana Historical Society, Helena [hereafter MHS].

60 Radio speech transcript, "Trout vs. Roads," February 10, 1962, box 660, folder 3, Lee Metcalf Papers, MHS.

61 Montana Fish and Game Department, "Montana Trout Streams: Will We Have Tomorrow What We Have Today?" Box 1, folder 3, Harry B. Mitchell Papers, MSU.

62 Idaho Fish and Game Department, *Idaho and the . . . Vanishing Stream* (Boise: Idaho Fish and Game Department, [1970?]), no pagination.

63 For the importance of dam opposition in the growing wilderness movement of the twentieth century, see Mark W. T. Harvey, *A Symbol of Wilderness: Echo Park and the American Conservation Movement* (Albuquerque: University of New Mexico Press, 1994).

64 Statement Made before U.S. Senate Select Committee on National Water Resources, Billings, Montana, October 9, 1959, box 2, folder 40, RS 261: Montana Fisheries Division Records, MHS; and Frank H. Dunkle to Cecil Gubser, March 10, 1965, series IV, box 5, folder 3, MSS 213: Western Montana Fish and Game Association Records, Archives and Special Collections, Maureen and Mike Mansfield Library, University of Montana–Missoula [hereafter UMM]. The Montana Fish and Game Department developed a trout fishery rating system in the postwar era which considered the best trout streams "blue-ribbon." Other agencies later adopted this system.

65 Pat Munday, "'A Millionaire Couldn't Buy a Piece of Water as Good': George Grant and the Conservation of the Big Hole River Watershed," *Montana: The Magazine of Western History* 52, no. 2 (Summer 2002): 25–27.

66 Lester R. Rusoff to Chairman, Reichle Dam Hearing, Whitehall, Montana, November 9, 1965, series IV, box 5, folder 3, MSS 213: Western Montana Fish and Game Association Records, UMM.

67 David Quammen, *Wild Thoughts from Wild Places* (New York: Scribner, 1998), 20.

68 Schullery, "Closing Summary," in Carline and LoSapio, *Sustaining Wild Trout in a Changing World*, 21.

69 David James Duncan, *My Story as Told by Water: Confessions, Druidic Rants, Reflections, Bird-Watchings, Fish-Stalkings, Visions, Songs and Prayers Refracting Light, from Living Rivers, in the Age of the Industrial Dark* (San Francisco: Sierra Club Books, 2001), 101.

EPILOGUE

1 Epigraphs: Quoted in Lucy R. Lippard, *The Lure of the Local: Senses of Place in a Multicentered Society* (New York: Free Press, 1997), 290; Tom McGuane, *The Longest Silence: A Life in Fishing* (New York: Alfred A. Knopf, 1999), 110.

2 Paul Schullery, *If Fish Could Scream: An Angler's Search for the Future of Fly Fishing* (Mechanicsburg, PA: Stackpole Books, 2008), 55.

3 Anders Halverson, *An Entirely Synthetic Fish: How Rainbow Trout Beguiled America and Overran the World* (New Haven, CT: Yale University Press, 2010), 185–86.

4 For more on the whirling disease epidemic, see ibid., ch. 10.

5 "Poisoning Likely Over at Cherry Creek," *Billings Gazette*, September 15, 2010, http://billingsgazette.com/news/state-and-regional/montana/article_59519ab2-c0d9-11df-97e9-001cc4c002e0.html (accessed September 15, 2010). For California examples of native fish restoration projects, see Halverson, *Synthetic Fish*, ch. 12.

6   Samuel Snyder, "Why Restore? Cultural and Ecological Reasons for Native Trout Restoration," in *Conserving Wild Trout: Proceedings of the Wild Trout X Symposium*, West Yellowstone, MT, September 28–30, 2010, ed. R. F. Carline and C. LoSapio (Bozeman, MT: 2010), 332, http://www.wildtroutsymposium. com/proceedings-10.pdf (accessed March 14, 2012). See also Samuel Snyder, "Restoring Natives in New Mexico," *American Fly Fisher* 35, no. 3 (Summer 2009): 10–17.

7   Jim Robbins, "Along a Course of Purling Rivers, a Raw Divide," *New York Times*, December 11, 2010, http://www.nytimes.com/2010/12/12/us/12montana. html (accessed December 12, 2010). For more on the 1998 initiative, see David James Duncan, *My Story as Told by Water: Confessions: Druidic Rants, Reflections, Bird-Watchings, Fish-Stalkings, Visions, Songs and Prayers Refracting Light, from Living Rivers, in the Age of the Industrial Dark* (San Francisco: Sierra Club Books, 2001), ch. 9.

BIBLIOGRAPHY

ARCHIVAL COLLECTIONS

American Heritage Center, University of Wyoming, Laramie
Archives and Special Collections, Maureen and Mike Mansfield Library, University of Montana–Missoula
Idaho State Historical Society, Boise
Manuscripts, Archives, and Special Collections, Washington State University, Pullman
Merrill G. Burlingame Special Collections, Montana State University, Bozeman
Montana Historical Society, Helena
Special Collections and Archives, Boise State University
Utah State Archives and Research Center, Salt Lake City
Wyoming State Archives, Cheyenne

FEDERAL AND STATE DOCUMENTS

Alvord, William. *A History of Montana's Fisheries Division from 1890–1958*. Helena: Montana Fish, Wildlife and Parks, 1991.
Arbuckle, Charles H. *First Biennial Report of the State Fish and Game Warden of the State of Idaho, 1900*. Boise, ID: State Fish and Game Warden, December 20, 1900.
Binns, Allen. "The Lower Green—Rags to Riches Trout Stream." *Wyoming Wild Life* 30, no. 5 (May 1966): 10–14.
Chambers, Fred W. *Eighth Biennial Report of the Fish and Game Commissioner of the State of Utah, to the Governor and Members of the Ninth Legislature of the State of Utah, for the Years 1909–1910*. Salt Lake City, UT: Tribune-Reporter Printing, 1910.
———. *Ninth Biennial Report of the Fish and Game Commissioner of the State of Utah, to the Governor and Members of the Tenth Legislature of the State of Utah, for the Years 1911–1912*. Salt Lake City, UT: Arrow Press, 1913.
Clark, Frank N. "Disadvantage of Planting Small Fish." *Fishery Bulletin* 6, no. 1 (1886): 421–22. Accessed November 15, 2000. http://fisherybulletin.nmfs.noaa.gov/6-1/clark1.pdf.

Cook, N. B. *Biennial Report of the State Fish and Game Commission, July 1, 1938 to June 30, 1940*. N.p.: [1940?].

Cromar, H. B. *Biennial Report of the State Game and Fish Commissioner and the Commissioner of Hatcheries of Utah*. Ogden, UT: State Industrial School, 1908.

Cuch, Forrest S., ed. *A History of Utah's American Indians*. Salt Lake City: Utah State Division of Indian Affairs and the Utah State Division of History, 2000.

Curtis, J. E. "Fish in the National Park and Tributaries of Snake River—Propagation of Whitefish." *Fishery Bulletin* 4, no. 1 (1884): 335–36. Accessed November 14, 2010. http://fisherybulletin.nmfs.noaa.gov/4-1/curtis.pdf.

Domrose, Robert J. *Northwest Montana Fishery Study, Job No. 1, Inventory of Waters of the Project Area, July 1, 1966 to June 30, 1967*. Job Completion Report, F-7-R-16. Montana Fish and Game Department.

Erickson, Jon. *Summarization of Life History and Management Studies on the Rocky Mountain Whitefish in the Snake River Drainage*. Project 0166-23-5501. [Cheyenne?]: Wyoming Game and Fish Department, July 13, 1966.

Evermann, Barton W. "A Reconnaissance of the Streams and Lakes of Western Montana and Northwestern Wyoming." *Fishery Bulletin* 11, no. 1 (1891): 1–60. Accessed November 15, 2010. http://fisherybulletin.nmfs.noaa.gov/11-1/evermann.pdf.

———. "A Report upon Salmon Investigations in the Headwaters of the Columbia River, in the State of Idaho, in 1895, Together with Notes upon the Fishes Observed in That State in 1894 and 1895." *Fishery Bulletin* 16, no. 1 (1896): 149–202. Accessed November 17, 2010. http://fisherybulletin.nmfs.noaa.gov/16-1/evermann.pdf.

Evermann, Barton W., and Cloud Rutter. "The Fishes of the Colorado Basin." *Fishery Bulletin* 14, no. 1 (1894): 473–86. Accessed November 15, 2010. http://fisherybulletin.nmfs.noaa.gov/14-1/evermann1.pdf.

Gaffney, J. J. "Whitefish—The Rainbow's Country Cousin." *Montana Wildlife* 5, no. 1 (Winter 1955): 24–25.

Gay, John. "Colorado Trout and Whitefish." *Forest and Stream* 37, no. 15 (Oct. 29, 1891): 293.

Grieve, Robert. *Biennial Report of the Wyoming Game and Fish Commissioner 1939–1940*. Cheyenne: Wyoming Game and Fish Department, [1941?].

———. *Biennial Report of the Wyoming Game and Fish Commission 1941–1942*. Cheyenne: Wyoming Game and Fish Department, [1943?].

Hill, William J. *Central Montana Fisheries Study, Job No. I-a, Inventory and Survey of Waters in the Western Half of Region Four, July 1, 1974 to June 30, 1975*. Job Progress Report, F-5-R-24. Montana Fish, Wildlife and Parks, June 30, 1975.

———. *Central Montana Fisheries Study, Job No. I-b, Fish Management Surveys, July*

1, 1971 to June 30, 1972. Job Progress Report, F-5-R-21. Montana Fish, Wildlife and Parks, May 24, 1973.

Holton, George D. "Montana Grayling: The Lady of the Streams." *Montana Outdoors* 2, no. 5 (Sept.–Oct. 1971): 18–23.

Idaho Fish and Game Department. *Idaho and the . . . Vanishing Stream*. Boise: Idaho Fish and Game Department, [1970?].

———. *Mountain Whitefish Conservation and Management Plan for the Big Lost River Drainage, Idaho*. May 2007. Accessed August 13, 2011. https://research. idfg.idaho.gov/Fisheries%20Research%20Reports/Mgt-Grunder2003%20Moun-tain%20Whitefish%20Conservation%20and%20Management%20Plan%20 for%20the%20Big%20Lost%20River%20Drainage,%20Idaho.pdf.

———. *Twenty-ninth Biennial Report of the Fish and Game Department of the State of Idaho, July 1, 1960 to June 30, 1962*. [Boise?], 1962.

Idaho-Golden Gate International Exposition Commission. *It's a Privilege to Live in Idaho: A Balanced State*. N.p.: [1939?].

Jordan, David Starr. "A Reconnaissance of the Streams and Lakes of the Yellowstone National Park, Wyoming, in the Interest of the United States Fish Commission." *Fishery Bulletin* 9, no. 1 (1889): 41–63. Accessed November 15, 2010. http://fishery-bulletin.nmfs.noaa.gov/9-1/jordan1.pdf.

———. "Report of Explorations in Colorado and Utah during the Summer of 1889, with an Account of the Fishes Found in Each of the River Basins Examined." *Fishery Bulletin* 9, no. 1 (1889): 1–40. Accessed November 15, 2010. http://fishery-bulletin.nmfs.noaa.gov/9-1/jordan.pdf.

Juday, Chancey. "A Study of Twin Lakes, Colorado, with Special Consideration of the Food of the Trouts." *Fishery Bulletin* 26, no. 1 (1906): 147–78. Accessed November 17, 2010. http://fisherybulletin.nmfs.noaa.gov/26-1/juday1.pdf.

Judkins, William T. *Biennial Report of the State Game Warden of the State of Wyoming 1919–1920*. Laramie, WY: Laramie Printing Company, 1921.

Leonard, John R. *The Fish Car Era*. US Fish and Wildlife Service. Washington, DC: GPO, 1979.

Madsen, D. H. *Fourteenth Biennial Report of the Fish and Game Commissioner of the State of Utah, for the Years 1921 and 1922*. Salt Lake City, UT: Arrow Press, [1923?].

Marcuson, Patrick, and Clinton G. Bishop. *South Central Montana Fishery Study, Job No. IV-a, Bighorn Lake and Bighorn River Post-impoundment Study, March 1, 1975 through March 31, 1976*. Job Progress Report, F-20-R-20. Montana Fish, Wildlife and Parks, March 1, 1976.

Martin, Andrew J. *Biennial Report, State Game and Fish Department Wyoming, January 1, 1935–January 1, 1937*. Cheyenne, WY: Game and Fish Department, [1937?].

Mecham, J. Arthur. *Biennial Report of the [Utah] State Fish and Game Commissioner*,

1927 and 1928. Salt Lake City, UT: Arrow Press, [1929?].

Miller, Bill. "The Ling." *Montana Outdoors* 5, no. 6 (Nov.–Dec. 1974): 27–29.

Nelson, Wesley C. *High Lake Research and Management in Colorado*, special report no. 64, R-S-64–88. N.p.: Colorado Division of Wildlife, June 1988.

Nowlin, Bruce. *Biennial Report of the State Game and Fish Commissioner of the State of Wyoming 1927–1928*. Casper, WY: S. E. Boyer, [1929?].

Nowlin, D. C. *Report of the State Game Warden to the Governor of Wyoming*. Laramie, WY: Republic Book and Job Print, 1903.

Peters, John. *Southeast Montana Fishery Study, Job No. I, Inventory of the Waters of the Project Area, May 1, 1959–April 30, 1960, May 1, 1960*. Job Completion Report, F-20-R-4. Montana Fish and Game Department.

Peterson, Larry. "Comeback on the Miracle Mile." *Wyoming Wild Life* 30, no. 5 (May 1966): 5–6.

Peterson, Lawrence. *North Platte River Fisheries Restoration*, Job Completion Report, F-18-D-1. Wyoming Game and Fish Commission, January 15, 1958.

Quartarone, Fred. *Historical Accounts of Upper Colorado River Basin Endangered Fish*. N.p.: Recovery Program for Endangered Fish of the Upper Colorado River Basin, September 1995.

Rawley, Edwin V. *A Review of Utah Fish and Game Licensing and Financing, 1876–1972*. Publication no. 72–12. [Salt Lake City?]: State of Utah Division of Natural Resources, October 1972.

Rothweiler, Robert. "The Whitefish: A Worthwhile Adversary." *Montana Outdoors* 8, no. 1 (Jan.–Feb. 1977): 35–37.

Sanders, A. A. *Biennial Report of the State Game and Fish Commissioner of the State of Wyoming 1925–1926*. Cheyenne, WY: Labor Journal, [1927?].

Seebohm, W. H. *Biennial Report of the State Game Warden of Wyoming for the Two Years Ending September 30, 1914*. Cheyenne, WY: Labor Journal Publishing, 1914.

Sharp, John. *Fifth Biennial Report of the State Fish and Game Commissioner and the Commissioner of State Hatcheries, to the Governor and the Sixth Session of the State Legislature of Utah, for the Years 1903 and 1904*. Salt Lake City, UT: Star Printing, 1905.

———. *Fourth Biennial Report of the State Fish and Game Commissioner, to the Governor and the Fifth Session of the State Legislature of Utah, for the Years 1901 and 1902*. Salt Lake City, UT: Star Printing Company, 1903.

———. *Report of the State Fish and Game Warden, to the Governor and Third Session of the State Legislature of Utah, for the Years 1897 and 1898*. Salt Lake City, UT: Deseret News, 1899.

———. *Sixth Biennial Report of the State Fish and Game Commissioner and the Commissioner of State Hatcheries, to the Governor and the Seventh Session of the*

State Legislature of Utah, for the Years 1905 and 1906. Salt Lake City, UT: Deseret News, 1907.

————. *Third Biennial Report of the State Fish and Game Commissioner, to the Governor and the Fourth Session of the State Legislature of Utah, for the Years 1899 and 1900*. Salt Lake City, UT: Deseret News, 1901.

Sigler, William F., and Robert Rush Miller. *Fishes of Utah*. Salt Lake City: Utah State Department of Fish and Game, 1963.

Simon, James R. "The Whitefish—A Neglected Resource." *Wyoming Wild Life* 6, no. 9 (1941): 1–3.

Spangler, A. M. "The Decrease of Food-Fishes in American Waters, and Some of the Causes." *Fishery Bulletin* 13, no. 1 (1893): 21–35. Accessed November 15, 2010. http://fisherybulletin.nmfs.noaa.gov/13-1/spangler.pdf.

Stevens, W. N. *Annual Report of the [Idaho] Fish and Game Department, for the Year 1906*. Boise: [Idaho Fish and Game Department?], January 1, 1907.

Swan, J. S. *Biennial Report of the State Forest, Game and Fish Commissioner of the State of Colorado, for the Years 1897 and 1898*. Denver, CO: Smith-Brooks Printing, 1898. Accessed November 8, 2010. http://www.biodiversitylibrary.org/item/80520.

Thomas, R. E. *[Idaho] Department of Fish and Game, Biennial Report for 1923–4*. [Boise: Idaho Fish and Game Department?], January 1, 1925.

Tulian, E. A. "Acclimatization of American Fishes in Argentina." *Fishery Bulletin* 28, no. 2 (1908): 955–65. Accessed November 17, 2010. http://fisherybulletin.nmfs.noaa.gov/28-2/tulian.pdf.

US Bureau of Fisheries. *Report of the Commissioner of Fisheries for the Fiscal Year 1912 and Special Papers*. Washington, DC: GPO, 1914. Accessed January 25, 2011. http://docs.lib.noaa.gov/rescue/cof/COF_1912.PDF.

————. *Report of the United States Commissioner of Fisheries for the Fiscal Year 1919 with Appendixes*. Washington, DC: GPO, 1921. Accessed January 27, 2011. http://docs.lib.noaa.gov/rescue/cof/COF_1919.PDF.

————. *Report of the United States Commissioner of Fisheries for the Fiscal Year 1921 with Appendixes*. Washington, DC: GPO, 1922. Accessed January 27, 2011. http://docs.lib.noaa.gov/rescue/cof/COF_1921.PDF.

————. *Report of the United States Commissioner of Fisheries for the Fiscal Year 1929 with Appendixes*. Washington, DC: GPO, 1929. Accessed January 30, 2011. http://docs.lib.noaa.gov/rescue/cof/COF_1929.PDF.

————. *Report of the United States Commissioner of Fisheries for the Fiscal Year 1931 with Appendixes*. Washington, DC: GPO, 1932. Accessed January 30, 2011. http://docs.lib.noaa.gov/rescue/cof/COF_1932.PDF.

————. *Report of the United States Commissioner of Fisheries for the Fiscal Year 1935 with Appendixes.* Washington, DC: GPO, 1936. Accessed January 30, 2011. http://docs.lib.noaa.gov/rescue/cof/COF_1935.PDF.

US Commission of Fish and Fisheries. *Report of the Commissioner for 1872 and 1873.* Washington, DC: GPO, 1874. Accessed December 29, 2010. http://docs.lib.noaa.gov/rescue/cof/COF_1872–1873.PDF.

———. *Report of the Commissioner for the Year Ending June 30, 1893.* Washington, DC: GPO, 1895. Accessed January 22, 2011. http://docs.lib.noaa.gov/rescue/cof/COF_1893.PDF.

———. *Report of the Commissioner for the Year Ending June 30, 1897.* Washington, DC: GPO,1898. Accessed January 23, 2011. http://docs.lib.noaa.gov/rescue/cof/COF_1897.PDF.

———. *Report of the Commissioner for the Year Ending June 30, 1898.* Washington, DC: GPO, 1899. Accessed January 23, 2011. http://docs.lib.noaa.gov/rescue/cof/COF_1898.PDF.

———. *Report of the Commissioner for the Year Ending June 30, 1900.* Washington, DC: GPO, 1901. Accessed January 24, 2011. http://docs.lib.noaa.gov/rescue/cof/COF_1900.PDF.

Utah Department of Fish and Game. *Thirty-fifth Biennial Report, July 1, 1960 to June 30, 1962.* N.p.: [1962?].

———. *Thirty-third Biennial Report, July 1, 1956 to June 30, 1958.* N.p.: [1958?].

Utah State Fish and Game Commission. *Thirty-first Biennial Report of the State Fish and Game Commission of the State of Utah, July 1, 1952 to June 30, 1954.* N.p.: [1954?].

———. *Twenty-eighth Biennial Report of the State Fish and Game Commission of the State of Utah, July 1, 1946 to June 30, 1948.* N.p.: [1948?].

———. *Twenty-ninth Biennial Report of the State Fish and Game Commission of the State of Utah, July 1, 1948 to June 30, 1950.* N.p.: [1950?].

———. *Twenty-sixth Biennial Report of the State Fish and Game Commission of the State of Utah, July 1, 1944 to June 30, 1946.* N.p.: [1946?].

Vincent, E. Richard (Dick). "The Catchable Trout," *Montana Outdoors* 3, no. 3 (May–June 1972): 24–29.

———. *Southwestern Fisheries Inventory, Job No. 1-a, Inventory and Survey of the Waters of the Project Area, February 1, 1975 through January 31, 1976.* Job Progress Report, F-9-R-24. Montana Fish, Wildlife and Parks.

Walker, Deward E., Jr. *Lemhi Shoshone-Bannock Reliance on Anadromous and Other Fish Resources.* Idaho Bureau of Land Management Technical Bulletin no. 94–4. Boise, ID: Bureau of Land Management, April 1994.

Whitney, Art. "Fish Stocking and the Wild Fish Concept." *Montana Outdoors* 2, no. 7 (July 1967): 1–4. Accessed January 2, 2012. http://www.archive.org/details/montanaoutdoors271967mont.

Wiltzius, William J. *Fish Culture and Stocking in Colorado, 1872–1978.* Division Report no. 12, DOW-R-D-12–85. Denver: Colorado Division of Wildlife, June 1985.

Wyoming Travel Commission. *This Is BIG Wyoming.* Cheyenne: Wyoming Travel Commission, [1963–1967?].

———. *Wyoming Historical Handbook.* Cheyenne: Wyoming Travel Commission, 1950.

Wyoming Game and Fish Commission. *Annual Report 1952.* Cheyenne, WY: Pioneer Printing, [1953?].

———. *Report of the Wyoming Game and Fish Commission, for the Biennium 1947–1948.* Cheyenne, WY: Labor Journal, [1949?].

ARTICLES, BOOKS, AND OTHER PUBLICATIONS

Adams, Susan B., Christopher A. Frissell, and Bruce E. Rieman. "Geography of Invasion in Mountain Streams: Consequences of Headwater Lake Fish Introductions." *Ecosystems* 4, no. 4 (June 2001): 296–307.

Alagona, Peter, ed. "Fifty Years of Wildlife in America" forum. *Environmental History* 16, no. 3 (July 2011): 391–455.

Altherr, Thomas L. "The American Hunter-Naturalist and the Development of the Code of Sportsmanship." *Journal of Sport History* 5, no. 1 (Spring 1978): 7–22.

Anderson, Sheridan. *The Curtis Creek Manifesto: A Fully Illustrated Guide to the Strategy, Finesse, Tactics and Paraphernalia of Fly Fishing.* Portland, OR: Frank Amato, 1978.

Andrews, Thomas G. "'Made by Toile?' Tourism, Labor, and the Construction of the Colorado Landscape, 1858–1917." *Journal of American History* 92, no. 3 (Dec. 2005): 837–63.

Arlinghaus, Robert, Steven J. Cooke, Jon Lyman, David Policansky, Alexander Schwab, Cory Suski, Stephen G. Sutton, and Eva B. Thorstad. "Understanding the Complexity of Catch-and-Release in Recreational Fishing: An Integrative Synthesis of Global Knowledge from Historical, Ethical, Social, and Biological Perspectives." *Reviews in Fisheries Science* 15, nos. 1–2 (Jan.–June 2007): 75–167.

Arnold, David. *The Problem of Nature: Environment, Culture and European Expansion.* Oxford: Blackwell, 1996.

Arnold, David F. *The Fishermen's Frontier: People and Salmon in Southeast Alaska.* Seattle: University of Washington Press, 2008.

Bantjes, Adrian A. "Introduction: Bourdieu on the Bighorn? Or, Towards a Cultural History of Fly-Fishing in Wyoming and the Rocky Mountain West." *Annals of Wyoming: The Wyoming History Journal* 76, no. 2 (Spring 2004): 2–5.

———. "Nature, Culture, and the Fly-Fishing History of Wyoming and the Rocky Mountain West." *Annals of Wyoming: The Wyoming History Journal* 76, no. 2 (Spring 2004): 41–53.

———. "The Past and Present of Fly-Fishing in Jackson Hole, Wyoming: An Interview with Jack Dennis." *Annals of Wyoming: The Wyoming History Journal* 76, no. 2 (Spring 2004): 19–25.

Bederman, Gail. *Manliness and Civilization: A Cultural History of Gender and Race in the United States, 1880–1917.* Chicago: University of Chicago Press, 1995.

Behnke, Robert J. "Tailwater Trout: Fish of Enormous Size." *Trout*, Spring 1996, 43–44.

———. *Trout and Salmon of North America.* New York: Free Press, 2002.

Beinart, William, and Lotte Hughes. *Environment and Empire.* New York: Oxford University Press, 2007.

Biel, Alice Wondrak. *Do (Not) Feed the Bears: The Fitful History of Wildlife and Tourists in Yellowstone.* Lawrence: University Press of Kansas, 2006.

Binkley, Cameron. "'No Better Heritage Than Living Trees': Women's Clubs and Early Conservation in Humboldt County." *Western Historical Quarterly* 33, no. 2 (Summer 2002): 179–203.

Binnema, Theodore (Ted), and Melanie Niemi. "'Let the Line Be Drawn Now': Wilderness, Conservation, and the Exclusion of Aboriginal People from Banff National Park in Canada." *Environmental History* 11, no. 4 (Oct. 2006): 724–50.

Bjorn, Eugene E. "Preliminary Observations and Experimental Study of the Ling, *Lota maculosa* (LeSueur), in Wyoming." *Transactions of the American Fisheries Society* 69, no. 1 (Jan. 1940): 192–96.

Blacker, William. *Blacker's Art of Fly Making, &c, Comprising Angling, and Dyeing of Colours, with Engravings of Salmon and Trout Flies Shewing [sic] the Process of the Gentle Craft as Taught in the Pages. With Descriptions of Flies for the Season of the Year as They Come Out on the Water. Rewritten and Revised by the Author Blacker, Himself, Fishing Tackle Maker of 54, Dean St, Soho, London.* 1855. London, 1855.

Blum, Edward J. *Reforging the White Republic: Race, Religion, and American Nationalism 1865–1898.* Baton Rouge: Louisiana State University Press, 2005.

Blumin, Stuart M. *The Emergence of the Middle Class: Social Experience in the American City, 1760–1900.* New York: Cambridge University Press, 1989.

Bold, Christine. *The Frontier Club: Popular Westerns and Cultural Power, 1880–1924.* New York: Oxford University Press, 2013.

Booth, D. C. "Some Observations on Fish Culture." *Transactions of the American Fisheries Society* 55, no. 1 (Jan. 1925): 161–66.

Brooks, Charles E. *The Living River: A Fisherman's Intimate Profile of the Madison River Watershed—Its History, Ecology, Lore, and Angling Opportunities.* Garden City, NY: Nick Lyons Books, 1979.

Brooks, James P. "Introduction of Trout and the Planting of Eyed Eggs in Remote and Isolated Waters of Glacier National Park." *Transactions of the American Fisheries Society* 55, no. 1 (Jan. 1925): 149–53.

Brooks, Joe. *Trout Fishing*. New York: Outdoor Life, 1972.

Brown, Jennifer Corrinne. "'The Gamest Fish That Swims': Management of the Big Hole River Fishery in Montana." *Pacific Northwest Quarterly* 97, no. 4 (Fall 2006): 171–78.

Brown, John J. *The American Angler's Guide. Being a Compilation from the Works of Popular English Authors, from Walton to the Present Time; Together with the Opinions of Practices of the Best American Anglers: Containing Every Variety of Mode Adopted in Ocean, River, Lake and Pond Fishing; the Necessary Tackle and Baits Required; Manner of Making Artificial Flies, &c. &c. &c.; with Engravings on Wood*. 2nd ed. New York: Burgress, Stringer, 1846.

Brown, Larry R., and Peter B. Moyle. "The Impact of Squawfish on Salmonid Populations: A Review." *North American Journal of Fisheries Management* 1, no. 2 (April 1981): 104–11.

Byorth, John. "Trout Shangri-La: Remaking the Fishing in Yellowstone National Park." *Montana: The Magazine of Western History* 52, no. 2 (Summer 2002): 38–47.

Cambray, J. A. "Impact on Indigenous Species Biodiversity Caused by the Globalisation of Alien Recreational Freshwater Fisheries." *Hydrobiologia* 500, nos. 1–3 (June 2003): 217–30.

Campbell, Robert B. *In Darkest Alaska: Travel and Empire along the Inside Passage*. Philadelphia: University of Pennsylvania Press, 2007.

Carhart, Arthur H. *Fishing in the West*. New York: Macmillan, 1950.

Carline, R. F., and C. LoSapio, eds. *Conserving Wild Trout: Proceedings of the Wild Trout X Symposium*. West Yellowstone, MT, September 28–30, 2010. Bozeman, MT: 2010. Accessed March 14, 2012. http://www.wildtroutsymposium.com/proceedings-10.pdf.

———. *Sustaining Wild Trout in a Changing World: Proceedings of the Wild Trout Symposium IX*. West Yellowstone, MT, October 9–12, 2007. N.p.: 2007. Accessed March 16, 2012. http://wildtroutsymposium.com/proceedings-9.pdf.

Carson, Rachel. *Silent Spring*. 1962. Reprint, Boston: Houghton Mifflin, 2002.

Carter, Thomas. "Together for the Summer: Architecture and Seasonal Community on Idaho's Henry's Fork River." *Perspectives in Vernacular Architecture* 11 (2004): 71–89.

Catt, James. "Copper Sulphate in the Elimination of Coarse Fish." *Transactions of the American Fisheries Society* 64, no. 1 (Jan. 1934): 276–80.

Childers, Michael W. *Colorado Powder Keg: Ski Resorts and the Environmental Movement*. Lawrence: University Press of Kansas, 2012.

Clements, John. *Salmon at the Antipodes: A History and Review of Trout, Salmon and Char and Introduced Coarse Fish in Australasia*. N.p.: privately printed, 1988.

Coates, Peter. *American Perceptions of Immigrant and Invasive Species: Strangers on the Land*. Berkeley: University of California Press, 2006.

Cohen, Lizabeth. *A Consumers' Republic: The Politics of Mass Consumption in Postwar America*. New York: Vintage Books, 2003.

Coleman, Annie Gilbert. "The Rise of the House of Leisure: Outdoor Guides, Practical Knowledge, and Industrialization." *Western Historical Quarterly* 42, no. 4 (Winter 2011): 437–57.

———. *Ski Style: Sport and Culture in the Rockies*. Lawrence: University Press of Kansas, 2004.

Coleman, Jon T. *Vicious: Wolves and Men in America*. New Haven, CT: Yale University Press, 2004.

Colorado and Southern Railway. *Trouting in Colorado's Waters*. Denver, CO: Smith-Brooks Press, 1907.

Colpitts, George W. "Fish and Game Associations in Southern Alberta, 1907–1928." *Alberta History* 42, no. 4 (Autumn 1994): 16–26.

Cooke, Steven J., Christopher M. Bunt, Steven J. Hamilton, Cecil A. Jennings, Michael P. Pearson, Michael S. Cooperman, and Douglas F. Markle. "Threats, Conservation Strategies, and Prognosis for Suckers (*Catostomidae*) in North America: Insights from Regional Case Studies of a Diverse Family of Non-game Fishes." *Biological Conservation* 121, no. 3 (Feb. 2005): 317–31.

Crawford, Stephen S., and Andrew M. Muir. "Global Introductions of Salmon and Trout in the Genus *Oncorhynchus*: 1870–2007." *Reviews in Fish Biology and Fisheries* 18, no. 3 (Aug. 2008): 313–44.

Cronon, William. *Nature's Metropolis: Chicago and the Great West*. New York: W. W. Norton, 1991.

———. "The Trouble with Wilderness; or, Getting Back to the Wrong Nature." *Environmental History* 1, no. 1 (Jan. 1996): 7–28.

Crosby, Alfred W. *The Columbian Exchange: Biological and Cultural Consequences of 1492*. Westport, CT: Greenwood Press, 1972.

———. *Ecological Imperialism: The Biological Expansion of Europe, 900–1900*. New York: Cambridge University Press, 1986.

Crosby, W. W. *Some Western Fishing*. Baltimore, MD: Waverly Press, 1926.

Cross, C. Louise. "The Battle for the Environmental Provisions in Montana's 1972 Constitution." *Montana Law Review* 51, no. 2 (Summer 1990): 449–57.

Crowl, Todd A., Colin R. Townsend, and Angus R. McIntosh. "The Impact of Introduced Brown and Rainbow Trout on Native Fish: The Case of Australasia." *Reviews in Fish Biology and Fisheries* 2, no. 3 (Sept. 1992): 217–41.

Cumbler, John T. "The Early Making of an Environmental Consciousness: Fish, Fisheries Commissions and the Connecticut River." *Environmental History Review* 15, no. 4 (Winter 1991): 73–91.

Cutchins, Dennis, and Eric A. Eliason. *Wild Games: Hunting and Fishing Traditions in North America.* Knoxville: University of Tennessee Press, 2009.

Davis. H. S. "The Purpose and Value of Stream Improvement." *Transactions of the American Fisheries Society* 64, no. 1 (Jan. 1934): 63–67.

Davis, John W. *Wyoming Range War: The Infamous Invasion of Johnson County.* Norman: University of Oklahoma Press, 2010.

Davy, Humphry. *Salmonia: or, Days of Fly Fishing in a Series of Conversations with Some Account of the Habit of Fishes Belonging to the Genus Salmo.* 3rd ed. London: John Murray, 1832. Accessed December 27, 2010. http://www.archive.org/details/salmoniaordaysof1832davy.

Day, Francis. *Report of the Fresh Water Fish and Fisheries of India and Burma.* Calcutta: Office of the Superintendent of Government Printing, 1873. Accessed March 20, 2011. http://www.archive.org/details/reportonfreshwatooday.

Dennis, Jack H., Jr. *Western Trout Fly Tying Manual.* Jackson Hole, WY: Snake River Books, 1974.

Denton, James A. *Rocky Mountain Radical: Myron W. Reed, Christian Socialist.* Albuquerque: University of New Mexico Press, 1997.

Dill, William A., and Leo Shapovalov. "An Unappreciated California Game Fish, the Rocky Mountain Whitefish, *Prosopium williamsoni* (Girard)." *California Fish and Game* 25, no. 3 (July 1939): 226–27.

Dorman, Robert L. *Hell of a Vision: Regionalism and the Modern American West.* Tucson: University of Arizona Press, 2012.

Dowie, Mark. *Conservation Refugees: The Hundred-Year Conflict between Global Conservation and Native Peoples.* Cambridge, MA: MIT Press, 2009.

Draper, Malcolm. "Going Native? Trout and Settling Identity in a Rainbow Nation." *Historia* 48, no. 1 (May 2003): 55–94.

Duncan, David James. *My Story as Told by Water: Confessions, Druidic Rants, Reflections, Bird-Watchings, Fish-Stalkings, Visions, Songs and Prayers Refracting Light, from Living Rivers, in the Age of the Industrial Dark.* San Francisco: Sierra Club Books, 2001.

———. Writer and narrator. *Trout Grass.* DVD, directed by Ed George. Vashon, WA: Volcano Motion Pictures, 2007.

Dunlap, Thomas R. *DDT: Scientists, Citizens, and Public Policy.* Princeton, NJ: Princeton University Press, 1981.

———. *Nature and the English Diaspora: Environment and History in the United States, Canada, Australia, and New Zealand.* New York: Cambridge University Press, 1999.

————. *Saving America's Wildlife*. Princeton, NJ: Princeton University Press, 1988.

Egan, Michael. *Barry Commoner and the Science of Survival: The Remaking of American Environmentalism*. Cambridge, MA: MIT Press, 2007.

Engle, Ed. *Fly Fishing the Tailwaters*. Harrisburg, PA: Stackpole Books, 1991.

Ephemera [Edward Fitzgibbon]. *A Handbook of Angling: Teaching Fly-Fishing, Trolling, Bottom-Fishing, and Salmon-Fishing: With the Natural History of River Fish, and the Best Modes of Catching Them*. 3rd ed. London: Longman, Brown, Green, and Longmans, 1853.

Evenden, Matthew. *Fish versus Power: An Environmental History of the Fraser River*. New York: Cambridge University Press, 2004.

Farmer, Jared. *On Zion's Mount: Mormons, Indians, and the American Landscape*. Cambridge, MA: Harvard University Press, 2008.

Fiege, Mark. *Irrigated Eden: The Making of an Agricultural Landscape in the American West*. Seattle: University of Washington Press, 1999.

Forkey, Neil S. "Anglers, Fishers, and the St. Croix River: Conflict in a Canadian-American Borderland, 1867–1900." *Forest and Conservation History* 37, no. 4 (Oct. 1993): 179–87.

Fox, Stephen. *The American Conservation Movement: John Muir and His Legacy*. Madison: University of Wisconsin Press, 1985.

France, Lewis B. *Mountain Trails and Parks in Colorado*. 2nd ed. Denver, CO: Chain, Hardy, 1888.

————. *With Rod and Line in Colorado Waters*. Denver, CO: Chain, Hardy, 1884.

Francis, Francis. *A Book on Angling: Being a Complete Treatise on the Art of Angling in Every Branch with Explanatory Plates, Etc*. 3rd ed. London: Longmans, Green, 1872.

————. *Fish-Culture: A Practical Guide to the Modern System of Breeding and Rearing Fish*. London: Routledge, Warne, and Routledge, 1863.

Frank, Jerry J. *Making Rocky Mountain National Park: The Environmental History of an American Treasure*. Lawrence: University Press of Kansas, 2013.

Fritz, Harry W. "The 1972 Montana Constitution in a Contemporary Context." *Montana Law Review* 51, no. 2 (Summer 1990): 270–74.

Garlick, Theodatus. *A Treatise on the Artificial Propagation of Certain Kinds of Fish with the Description and Habits of Such Kinds as Are the Most Suitable for Pisciculture*. Cleveland, OH: Tho. Brown, 1857.

Gierach, John. *Even Brook Trout Get the Blues*. New York: Simon & Schuster, 1992.

————. *Sex, Death, and Fly-Fishing*. New York: Fireside Books, 1990.

Gillis, Peter R., and Thomas R. Roach. "The American Influence on Conservation in Canada: 1899–1911." *Journal of Forest History* 30, no. 4 (Oct. 1986): 160–74.

Giltner, Scott E. *Hunting and Fishing in the New South: Black Labor and White Leisure after the Civil War*. Baltimore, MD: Johns Hopkins University Press, 2008.

Gingrich, Arnold. *The Joys of Trout.* New York: Crown Publishers, 1973.

Gordon, Theodore. *The Complete Fly Fisherman: The Notes and Letters of Theodore Gordon.* Edited by John McDonald. New York: Charles Scribner's Sons, 1947.

Gottlieb, Robert. *Forcing the Spring: The Transformation of the American Environmental Movement.* Washington, DC: Island Press, 1993.

Grant, George F. "Confessions of an Addict." *River Rat,* May–June 1975, no pagination.

———. *Montana Trout Flies.* [Butte, MT?]: privately printed, 1972.

Great Northern Railway. *Shooting and Fishing along the Line of the Great Northern Railway.* 4th ed. Chicago: Poole Bros., 1901.

Griffiths, Tom, and Libby Robin, eds. *Ecology and Empire: Environmental History of Settler Societies.* Seattle: University of Washington Press, 1998.

Guha, Ramachandra. *How Much Should a Person Consume? Environmentalism in India and the United States.* Berkeley: University of California Press, 2006.

———. "Movement Scholarship." *Environmental History* 10, no. 1 (Jan. 2005): 40–41.

———. "The Paradox of Global Environmentalism." *Current History* 99, no. 640 (Nov. 2000): 367–70.

———. *The Unquiet Woods: Ecological Change and Peasant Resistance in the Himalaya.* 1989. Expanded edition, Berkeley: University of California Press, 2000.

Haak, Amy L., Jack E. Williams, Helen M. Neville, Daniel C. Dauwalter, and Warren T. Colyer. "Conserving Peripheral Trout Populations: The Values and Risks of Life on the Edge." *Fisheries* 35, no. 11 (Nov. 2010): 530–49.

Hahn, Steven. "Hunting, Fishing, and Foraging: Common Rights and Class Relations in the Postbellum South." *Radical History Review* 1982, no. 26 (Oct. 1982): 37–64.

Haig-Brown, Roderick L. *A River Never Sleeps.* 1946. Reprint, New York: Skyhorse Publishing, 2010.

Halford, Frederic M. *Dry Fly Entomology: A Brief Description of the Leading Types of Natural Insects Serving as Food for Trout and Grayling with 100 Best Patterns of Floating Flies and the Various Methods of Dressing Them.* 2 vols. London: Vinton, 1897.

———. *Floating Flies and How to Dress Them: A Treatise on the Most Modern Methods of Dressing Artificial Flies for Trout and Grayling with Fully Illustrated Directions and Containing Ninety Hand-Coloured Engravings of the Most Killing Patterns Together with a Few Hints to Dry-Fly Fishermen.* London: Sampson Low, Marston, Searle, and Rivington, 1886.

Halverson, Anders. *An Entirely Synthetic Fish: How Rainbow Trout Beguiled America and Overran the World.* New Haven, CT: Yale University Press, 2010.

Harris, Douglas C. *Fish, Law, and Colonialism: The Legal Capture of Salmon in British Columbia.* Toronto: University of Toronto Press, 2001.

Harris, William C. *The Angler's Guide Book and Tourists' Gazetteer of the Fishing Waters of the United States and Canada.* New York: American Angler, 1885.

Harvey, Mark W. T. *A Symbol of Wilderness: Echo Park and the American Conservation Movement.* Albuquerque: University of New Mexico Press, 1994.

Hatton, John H. "Trout Fishing in the National Forests." *Transactions of the American Fisheries Society* 55, no. 1 (Jan. 1925): 154–60.

Hayden, Dolores. *Building Suburbia: Green Fields and Urban Growth, 1820–2000.* New York: Pantheon Books, 2003.

Hays, Samuel P. *Beauty, Health, and Permanence: Environmental Politics in the United States, 1955–1985.* New York: Cambridge University Press, 1987.

———. "Comment: The Trouble with Bill Cronon's Wilderness." *Environmental History* 1, no. 1 (Jan. 1996): 29–32.

———. *Conservation and the Gospel of Efficiency: The Progressive Conservation Movement, 1890–1920.* Cambridge, MA: Harvard University Press, 1959.

Hazlett, Maril. "'Woman vs. Man vs. Bugs': Gender and Popular Ecology in Early Reactions to *Silent Spring.*" *Environmental History* 9, no. 4 (Oct. 2004): 701–29.

Henshall, James A. "Fish Protection." *Transactions of the American Fisheries Society* 19, no. 1 (Jan. 1890): 79–84.

———. "Food and Game Fishes of the Rocky Mountain Region." *Transactions of the American Fisheries Society* 31, no. 1 (Jan. 1902): 74–88.

———. "Indiscriminate and Inconsiderate Planting of Fish." *Transactions of the American Fisheries Society* 48, no. 3 (June 1919): 166–69.

———. "On the Protection of Fish in Inland Waters." *Transactions of the American Fisheries Society* 34, no. 1 (Jan. 1905): 139–47.

Herbert, Henry William. *Frank Forester's Fish and Fishing of the United States and British Provinces of North America.* New York: Stringer and Townsend, 1850. Accessed December 27, 2010. http://www.archive.org/details/frankforestersfi-00herb.

Her Majesty Montana Has a "Come-Hither" Look. Butte: Montana Standard Printers, 1940.

Herd, Andrew. *Angling Giants.* Ellesmere, UK: Medlar Press, 2010.

———. *The Fly.* Ellesmere, UK: Medlar Press, 2003.

Herr, F., E. Greselin, and C. Chappel. "Toxicology Studies of Antimycin, a Fish Eradicant." *Transactions of the American Fisheries Society* 96, no. 3 (July 1967): 320–26.

Hoffman, Richard C. "Economic Development and Aquatic Ecosystems in Medieval Europe." *American Historical Review* 101, no. 3 (June 1996): 631–69.

Hogan, Austin S. *American Sporting Periodicals of Angling Interest: A Selected Check List and Guide.* Manchester, VT: Museum of American Fly Fishing, 1973.

Holden, Paul B., and Clair B. Stalnaker. "Distribution and Abundance of Mainstream Fishes of the Middle and Upper Colorado River Basins, 1967–1973." *Transactions of the American Fisheries Society* 104, no. 2 (April 1975): 217–31.

Hoover, Herbert Clark. *A Remedy for Disappearing Game Fishes.* New York: Huntington Press, 1930.

Jackson, Wes. *Becoming Native to This Place.* Lexington: University Press of Kentucky, 1994.

Jacobs, Margaret G. *White Mother to a Dark Race: Settler Colonialism, Maternalism, and the Removal of Indigenous Children in the American West and Australia, 1880–1940.* Lincoln: University of Nebraska Press, 2009.

Jacobson, Matthew Frye. *Whiteness of a Different Color: European Immigrants and the Alchemy of Race.* Cambridge, MA: Harvard University Press, 1998.

Jacoby, Karl. *Crimes against Nature: Squatters, Poachers, Thieves, and the Hidden History of American Conservation.* Berkeley: University of California Press, 2001.

Jelks, Howard L., Stephen J. Walsh, Noel M. Burkhead, Salvador Contreras-Balderas, Edmundo Díaz-Pardo, Dean A. Hendrickson, John Lyons, et al. "Conservation Status of Imperiled North American Freshwater and Diadromous Fishes." *Fisheries* 33, no. 8 (Aug. 2008): 372–407.

Johnson, Benjamin Heber. "Conservation, Subsistence, and Class at the Birth of Superior National Forest." *Environmental History* 4, no. 1 (Jan. 1999): 80–99.

Jones, Peter N. "Identity through Fishing: A Preliminary Analysis of Impacts to the Nez Perce as a Result of the Damming of the Clearwater and Snake Rivers." *Cultural Dynamics* 17, no. 2 (July 2005): 155–92.

Jones, Susan. "Becoming a Pest: Prairie Dog Ecology and the Human Economy in the Euroamerican West." *Environmental History* 4, no. 4 (Oct. 1999): 531–52.

Jordan, David Starr, and Barton Warren Evermann. *American Food and Game Fishes: A Popular Account of All the Species Found in America North of the Equator, with Keys for Ready Identification, Life Histories and Methods of Capture.* New York: Doubleday, Page, 1902.

Judd, Richard W. *Common Lands, Common People: The Origins of Conservation in Northern New England.* Cambridge, MA: Harvard University Press, 1997.

———. *The Untilled Garden: Natural History and the Spirit of Conservation in America, 1740–1840.* New York: Cambridge University Press, 2009.

Kelson, Geo. M. *The Salmon Fly: How to Dress It and How to Use It.* London: privately printed, 1895. Accessed February 29, 2011. http://www.archive.org/details/salmonflyhowtodookelsgoog.

Kemmis, Daniel. *Community and the Politics of Place.* Norman: University of Oklahoma Press, 1990.

King, Willis, ed. *Proceedings of the Wild Trout Management Symposium at Yellowstone National Park, September 25–26, 1974.* N.p.: Trout Unlimited, 1975. Accessed January 28, 2012. http://wildtroutsymposium.com/proceedings-1.pdf.

Kinsey, Darin. "'Seeding the Water as the Earth': The Epicenter and Peripheries of a Western Aquacultural Revolution." *Environmental History* 11, no. 3 (July 2006): 527–66.

Kiser, R. W., John R. Donaldson, and Paul R. Olson. "The Effect of Rotenone on Zooplankton Populations in Freshwater Lakes." *Transactions of the American Fisheries Society* 92, no. 1 (Jan. 1963): 17–24.

Klingle, Matthew. *Emerald City: An Environmental History of Seattle.* New Haven, CT: Yale University Press, 2009.

———. "Spaces of Consumption in Environmental History." *History and Theory* 42, no. 4 (Dec. 2003): 94–110.

Knapp, Roland A., Paul Stephen Corn, and Daniel E. Schindler. "The Introduction of Nonnative Fish into Wilderness Lakes: Good Intentions, Conflicting Mandates, and Unintended Consequences." *Ecosystems* 4, no. 4 (June 2001): 275–78.

Knight, William. "Samuel Wilmot, Fish Culture, and Recreational Fisheries in Late 19th Century Ontario." *Scientia Canadensis: Canadian Journal of the History of Science, Technology and Medicine* 30, no. 1 (2007): 75–90.

Kohrman, Robert. "Checklist of Angling Pseudonyms." *American Fly Fisher* 13, no. 4 (Fall 1987): 22–26.

Lackey, Bertram D. *Outwitting Trout with a Fly: Letters of a Western Angler.* Los Angeles: Phillips Printing, 1929.

LaFontaine, Gary. "The Bighorn River: As You Like It." *Trout* (Spring 1998): 59–61.

———. *Caddisflies.* Guilford, CT: Lyons Press, 1981.

———. *Challenge of the Trout.* Missoula, MT: Mountain Press, 1976.

———. "Sparring over Fly Lines and Tailwaters." *Trout* (Summer 1999): 57–59.

Lang, William. "Saving the Yellowstone." *Montana: The Magazine of Western History* 85, no. 4 (Autumn 1985): 87–90.

Langston, Nancy. *Where Land and Water Meet: A Western Landscape Transformed.* Seattle: University of Washington Press, 2003.

Leach, Glen C. "Co-operative Fish Culture," *Transactions of the American Fisheries Society* 55, no. 1 (Jan. 1925): 102–14.

Leach, William. *Land of Desire: Merchants, Power, and the Rise of a New American Culture.* New York: Vintage Books, 1993.

Lears, Jackson. *Fables of Abundance: A Cultural History of Advertising in America.* New York: Basic Books, 1994.

Leeson, Ted. *Inventing Montana: Dispatches from the Madison Valley.* New York: Skyhorse Publishing, 2009.

Leopold, Aldo. *A Sand County Almanac and Sketches Here and There.* 1949. Reprint, New York: Oxford University Press, 1989.

———. "Mixing Trout in Western Waters." *Transactions of the American Fisheries Society* 47, no. 3 (June 1918): 101–102.

Lessner, Richard. "How Meriwether Lewis's Cutthroat Trout Sealed Custer's Fate at the Little Bighorn." *American Fly Fisher* 36, no. 4 (Fall 2010): 16–19.

Lever, Christopher. *They Dined on Eland: The Story of Acclimatisation Societies.* London: Quiller Press, 1992.

Lichatowich, Jim. *Salmon without Rivers: A History of the Pacific Salmon Crisis.* Washington, DC: Island Press, 1999.

Limerick, Patricia Nelson. *The Legacy of Conquest: The Unbroken Past of the American West.* New York: W. W. Norton, 1987.

Linderman, Frank B. *Montana Adventure: The Recollections of Frank B. Linderman.* Edited by H. G. Merriam. Lincoln: University of Nebraska Press, 1968.

Lipin, Lawrence M. *Workers and the Wild: Conservation, Consumerism, and Labor in Oregon, 1910–30.* Chicago: University of Illinois Press, 2007.

Lippard, Lucy R. *The Lure of the Local: Senses of Place in a Multicentered Society.* New York: Free Press, 1997.

Locke, S. B. "The National Forests of the West and the Fish Supply." *Transactions of the American Fisheries Society* 58, no. 1 (Jan. 1928): 201–204.

Loo, Tina. *States of Nature: Conserving Canada's Wildlife in the Twentieth Century.* Seattle: University of Washington Press, 2006.

Lord, Russell F. "Hatchery Trout as Foragers and Game Fish." *Transactions of the American Fisheries Society* 64, no. 1 (Jan. 1934): 339–45.

———. "Rearing a Brood Stock of Blackspotted Trout." *Transactions of the American Fisheries Society* 60, no. 1 (Jan. 1930): 164–66.

Louter, David. *Windshield Wilderness: Cars, Roads, and Nature in Washington's National Parks.* Seattle: University of Washington Press, 2006.

Lowe, S., M. Browne, S. Boudjelas, and M. De Poorter. *100 of the World's Worst Invasive Alien Species: A Selection from the Global Invasive Species Database.* Auckland, New Zealand: IUCN/SSC Invasive Species Specialist Group, November 2004. Accessed September 26, 2011. http://www.issg.org/pdf/publications/worst_100/English_100_worst.pdf.

Lowerson, John. "Brothers of the Angle: Coarse Fishing and English Working-Class Culture, 1850–1914." In *Pleasure, Profit, Proselytism: British Culture and Sport at Home and Abroad, 1700–1914,* edited by J. A. Mangan, 105–27. London: Frank Cass, 1988.

———. *Sport and the English Middle Classes, 1870–1914.* Manchester, UK: Manchester University Press, 1993.

Lucas, Clarence R. "Game Fish Management." *Transactions of the American Fisheries Society* 68, no. 1 (Jan. 1939): 67–75.

Lyons, Nick, ed. *In Praise of Wild Trout: On the Pleasure, Biology, and Preservation of Wild Trout.* New York: Lyons Press, 1998.

Macchi, P. J., V. E. Cussac, M. F. Alonso, and M. A. Denegri. "Predation Relationships between Introduced Salmonids and the Native Fish Fauna in Lakes and Reservoirs in Northern Patagonia." *Ecology of Freshwater Fish* 8, no. 4 (Dec. 1999): 227–36.

MacCrimmon, Hugh R. "World Distribution of Rainbow Trout (*Salmo gairdneri*)." *Journal of the Fisheries Research Board of Canada* 28, no. 5 (June 1971): 663–704.

———. "World Distribution of Rainbow Trout (*Salmo gairdneri*): Further Observations." *Journal of the Fisheries Research Board of Canada* 29, no. 12 (Dec. 1972): 1788–91.

MacCrimmon, Hugh R., and J. Scott Campbell. "World Distribution of Brook Trout, *Salvelinus fontinalis*." *Journal of the Fisheries Research Board of Canada* 26, no. 7 (July 1969): 1699–725.

MacCrimmon, Hugh R., Barra L. Gots, and J. Scott Campbell. "World Distribution of Brook Trout, *Salvelinus fontinalis*: Further Observations." *Journal of the Fisheries Research Board of Canada* 28, no. 3 (Apr. 1971): 452–56.

MacCrimmon, Hugh R., and T. L. Marshall. "World Distribution of Brown Trout, *Salmo trutta*." *Journal of the Fisheries Research Board of Canada* 25, no. 12 (Dec. 1968): 2527–48.

MacCrimmon, Hugh R., T. Larry Marshall, and Barra L. Gots. "World Distribution of Brown Trout, *Salmo trutta*: Further Observations." *Journal of the Fisheries Research Board of Canada* 27, no. 4 (May 1970): 811–18.

MacDowell, Syl. *Western Trout.* New York: Alfred A. Knopf, 1948.

MacKenzie, John M. *The Empire of Nature: Hunting, Conservation and British Imperialism.* Manchester: Manchester University Press, 1988.

———, ed. *Imperialism and the Natural World.* Manchester: Manchester University Press, 1990.

Maclean, Norman. *A River Runs Through It, and Other Stories.* Chicago: University of Chicago Press, 1976.

MacPhee, Craig, and Richard Ruelle. "A Chemical Selectively Lethal to Squawfish (*Ptychocheilus oregonensis* and *P. umpquae*)." *Transactions of the American Fisheries Society* 98, no. 4 (Oct. 1969): 676–84.

Madsen, David H. "Protection of Native Fishes in the National Parks." *Transactions of the American Fisheries Society* 66, no. 1 (Jan. 1937): 395–97.

Mangan, J. A., ed. *Pleasure, Profit, Proselytism: British Culture and Sport at Home and Abroad, 1700–1914.* London: Frank Cass, 1988.

Manley, J. J. *Notes on Fish and Fishing*. London: Sampson Low, Marston, Searle, and Rivington, 1877.

Marbury, Mary Orvis. *Favorite Flies and Their Histories*. 1892. Reprint, Guilford, CT: Lyons Press, 2001.

Marsh, George Perkins. *Man and Nature*. 1864. Reprint, Seattle: University of Washington Press, 2003.

Marx, Leo. *The Machine in the Garden: Technology and the Pastoral Ideal in America*. New York: Oxford University Press, 1964.

Matthiessen, Peter. *Wildlife in America*. New York: Viking Press, 1959.

McClay, William. "Rotenone Use in North America (1988–2002)." *Fisheries* 30, no. 4 (April 2005): 29–31.

McDowall, R. M. "Crying Wolf, Crying Foul, or Crying Shame: Alien Salmonids and a Biodiversity Crisis in the Southern Cool-Temperate Galaxioid Fishes?" *Reviews in Fish Biology and Fisheries* 16, nos. 3–4 (Nov. 2006): 233–422.

———. "Impacts of Introduced Salmonids on Native Galaxiids in New Zealand Upland Streams: A New Look at an Old Problem." *Transactions of the American Fisheries Society* 132, no. 2 (March 2003): 229–38.

McEvoy, Arthur F. *The Fisherman's Problem: Ecology and Law in the California Fisheries, 1850–1980*. New York: Cambridge University Press, 1986.

McGuane, Tom. *The Longest Silence: A Life in Fishing*. New York: Alfred A. Knopf, 1999.

McMurray, David. "'The Charm of Being Loose and Free': Nineteenth-Century Fisherwomen in the North American Wilderness." *International Journal of the History of Sport* 30, no. 8 (2013): 826–52.

———. "Rivaling the Gentleman in the Gentle Art: The Authority of the Victorian Woman Angler." *Sport History Review* 39, no. 2 (Nov. 2008): 99–126.

McNeill, J. R. *Something New under the Sun: An Environmental History of the Twentieth-Century World*. New York: W. W. Norton, 2000.

McPhail, J. D., and P. Troffe. "The Mountain Whitefish (*Prosopium williamsoni*): A Brief Review of the Distribution, Biology, and Life History of a Neglected Recreational Species." In *Bull Trout II*, edited by M. K. Brewin, A. J. Paul, and M. Monita, 17–21. Calgary: Trout Unlimited Canada, 2001.

Merchant, Carolyn. "George Bird Grinnell's Audubon Society: Bridging the Gender Divide in Conservation." *Environmental History* 15, no. 1 (Jan. 2010): 3–30.

———. "Women of the Progressive Conservation Movement: 1900–1916." *Environmental Review* 8, no. 1 (Spring 1984): 57–85.

Mercier, Laurie. *Anaconda: Labor, Community, and Culture in Montana's Smelter City*. Chicago: University of Illinois Press, 2001.

Meyer, Kevin A., F. Steven Elle, and James A. Lamansky, Jr. "Environmental Factors

Related to the Distribution, Abundance, and Life History Characteristics of Mountain Whitefish in Idaho." *North American Journal of Fisheries Management* 29, no. 3 (June 2009): 753–67.

Mighetto, Lisa. "Sport Fishing on the Columbia River." *Pacific Northwest Quarterly* 87, no. 1 (Winter 1995–96): 5–15.

———. *Wild Animals and American Environmental Ethics.* Tucson: University of Arizona Press, 1991.

Miller, Char. *Ground Work: Conservation in American Culture.* Durham, NC: Forest History Society, 2007.

Miller, Robert R. "Is Our Native Underwater Life Worth Saving?" *National Parks Magazine* 37, no. 188 (May 1963): 4–9.

Milner, Clyde A., II, and Carol A. O'Connor. *As Big as the West: The Pioneer Life of Granville Stuart.* New York: Oxford University Press, 2009.

Mitchell, Finis. *Wind River Trails: A Hiking and Fishing Guide to the Many Trails and Lakes of the Wind River Range in Wyoming.* Salt Lake City, UT: Wasatch Publishers, 1975.

Mittlefehldt, Sarah. *Tangled Roots: The Appalachian Trail and American Environmental Politics.* Seattle: University of Washington Press, 2013.

Monnett, John H. *Cutthroat and Campfire Tales: The Fly-Fishing Heritage of the West.* Boulder: University Press of Colorado, 2001.

———. "Lewis B. France: Pioneer Outdoor Writer of Colorado." *Colorado Heritage*, Summer 1993, 16–21.

———. "Mystery of the Bighorns: Did a Fishing Trip Seal Custer's Fate?" *American Fly Fisher* 19, no. 4 (Fall 1993): 2–5.

Montana v. United States, 450 U.S. 544, 101 S.Ct. 1245, 67 L.Ed.2d 493 (1981).

Muir, John. *Our National Parks.* Boston: Houghton Mifflin, 1901.

Mundahl, C. M. *Line Fishing.* Papers of the Conferences Held in Connection with the Great International Fisheries Exhibition, London, 1883. London: William Clowes and Sons, 1883. Accessed May 16, 2011. http://www.archive.org/details/linefishingoomund.

Munday, Pat. "'A Millionaire Couldn't Buy a Piece of Water as Good': George Grant and the Conservation of the Big Hole River Watershed." *Montana: The Magazine of Western History* 52, no. 2 (Summer 2002): 20–37.

———. *Montana's Last Best River: The Big Hole and Its People.* Guilford, CT: Lyons Press, 2001.

Nash, Roderick. *Wilderness and the American Mind.* 3rd ed. New Haven, CT: Yale University Press, 1982.

Neel, Susan Rhoades, ed. "Tourism and the American West." Special issue, *Pacific Historical Review* 65, no. 4 (Nov. 1996).

Nelson, Joseph S., Edwin J. Crossman, Hector Espinosa-Perez, Carter R. Gilbert, Robert N. Lea, and James D. Williams. "Recommended Changes in Common Fish Names: Pikeminnow to Replace Squawfish (*Ptychocheilus* spp.)." *Fisheries* 23, no. 9 (Sept. 1998): 37.

Newell, Dianne. *Tangled Webs of History: Indians and the Law in Canada's Pacific Coast Fisheries.* Toronto: University of Toronto Press, 1993.

Nicholas, Liza, Elaine M. Bapis, and Thomas J. Harvey, eds. *Imagining the Big Open: Nature, Identity, and Play in the New West.* Salt Lake City: University of Utah Press, 2003.

Nichols, Jeffrey. "'These Waters Were All Virgin': Finis Mitchell and Wind River." *Annals of Wyoming: The Wyoming History Journal* 76, no. 2 (Spring 2004): 26–35.

Norris, Thaddeus. *The American Angler's Book: Embracing the Natural History of Sporting Fish, and the Art of Taking Them. With Instructions in Fly-Fishing, Fly-Making, and Rod-Making; and Directions for Fish-Breeding.* Philadelphia: E. H. Butler, 1864.

———. *American Fish-Culture, Embracing All the Details of Artificial Breeding and Rearing of Trout: The Culture of Salmon, Shad and Other Fishes.* Philadelphia: Porter & Coates, 1868.

Northcote, T. G., and G. L. Ennis. "Mountain Whitefish Biology and Habitat Use in Relation to Compensation and Improvement Possibilities." *Reviews in Fisheries Science* 2, no. 4 (1994): 347–71.

Novak, Barbara. *Nature and Culture: American Landscape and Painting, 1825–1875.* New York: Oxford University Press, 1980.

Nugent, Walter. *Crossings: The Great Transatlantic Migrations, 1870–1914.* Indianapolis: Indiana University Press, 1992.

O'Connor, Sue, Rintaro Ono, and Chris Clarkson. "Pelagic Fishing at 42,000 Years before the Present and the Maritime Skills of Modern Humans." *Science* 334, no. 6059 (Nov. 25, 2011): 1117–21.

Osborne, Michael A. "Acclimatizing the World: A History of the Paradigmatic Colonial Science." *Osiris* 15 (2000): 135–51.

———. *Nature, the Exotic, and the Science of French Colonialism.* Indianapolis: Indiana University Press, 1994.

Ott, Cindy. *Pumpkin: The Curious History of an American Icon.* Seattle: University of Washington Press, 2012.

Owens, Ken. "Blue-Ribbon Tailwaters: The Unplanned Role of the U.S. Bureau of Reclamation in Western Fly Fishing." *American Fly Fisher* 33, no. 2 (Spring 2007): 2–10.

———. "Fishing the Hatch: New West Romanticism and Fly-Fishing in the High Country." *Montana: The Magazine of Western History* 52, no. 2 (Summer 2002): 10–19.

———. "While Custer Was Making His Last Stand: George Crook's 1876 War on Trout in the Bighorn Country." *Montana: The Magazine of Western History* 52, no. 2 (Summer 2002): 58–61.

Painter, Nell Irvin. *The History of White People.* New York: W. W. Norton, 2010.

———. *Standing at Armageddon: The United States, 1877–1919.* New York: W. W. Norton, 1989.

Palmer, T. S. "Licenses for Hook and Line Fishing." *Transactions of the American Fisheries Society* 41, no. 1 (Jan. 1912): 91–97.

Pardo, R., I. Vila, and J. J. Capella. "Competitive Interaction between Introduced Rainbow Trout and Native Silverside in a Chilean Stream." *Environmental Biology of Fishes* 86, no. 2 (Oct. 2009): 353–59.

Parenteau, Bill. "A 'Very Determined Opposition to the Law': Conservation, Angling Leases, and Social Conflict in the Canadian Atlantic Salmon Fishery, 1867–1914." *Environmental History* 9, no. 3 (July 2004): 436–63.

Patten, B. G., and D. T. Rodman. "Reproductive Behavior of the Northern Squawfish, *Ptychocheilus oregonensis.*" *Transactions of the American Fisheries Society* 98, no. 1 (Jan. 1969): 108–11.

Payne, Darwin. *Owen Wister: Chronicler of the West, Gentleman of the East.* Dallas, TX: Southern Methodist University Press, 1985.

Pettit, Stephen W., and Richard L. Wallace. "Age, Growth, and Movement of Mountain Whitefish, *Prosopium williamsoni* (Girard), in the North Fork Clearwater River, Idaho." *Transactions of the American Fisheries Society* 104, no. 1 (1975): 68–76.

Pevar, Stephen L. *The Rights of Indians and Tribes: The Authoritative ACLU Guide to Indian and Tribal Rights.* 3rd ed. New York: New York University Press, 2004.

Philpott, William. *Vacationland: Tourism and Environment in the Colorado High Country.* Seattle: University of Washington Press, 2013.

Pisani, Donald J. "Fish Culture and the Dawn of Concern over Water Pollution in the United States." *Environmental Review* 8, no. 2 (Summer 1984): 117–31.

———. *Water and the American Government: The Reclamation Bureau, National Water Policy, and the West, 1902–1935.* Berkeley: University of California Press, 2002.

———. *Water, Land, and Law in the West: The Limits of Public Policy, 1850–1920.* Lawrence: University Press of Kansas, 1996.

Pister, Edwin P. "Wilderness Fish Stocking: History and Perspective." *Ecosystems* 4, no. 4 (June 2001): 279–86.

Pochin, W. F. *Angling and Hunting in British Columbia.* Vancouver, BC: Sun Directories Limited, 1946.

Pomeroy, Earl. *In Search of the Golden West: The Tourist in Western America.* New York: Alfred A. Knopf, 1957.

Price, Jennifer. *Flight Maps: Adventures with Nature in Modern America*. New York: Basic Books, 1999.

Prince, E. E. "Irrigation Canals as an Aid to Fisheries Development in the West." *Transactions of the American Fisheries Society* 52, no. 1 (Jan. 1923): 157–65.

Quammen, David. "Jeremy Bentham, the Pieta, and a Precious Few Grayling." *Audubon* 84 (May 1982): 96–103.

———. *Wild Thoughts from Wild Places*. New York: Scribner, 1998.

Radcliffe, William. *Fishing from the Earliest Times*. London: John Murray, 1921. Accessed March 20, 2011. http://www.archive.org/details/fishingfromearliooradc.

Red Collar Steam Ship Line. *Lake and River Excursions via Red Collar S. S. Line in the Panhandle of Idaho*. N.p.: Red Collar Steam Ship Line, 1910.

Reeves, Peter. "Inland Waters and Freshwater Fisheries: Issues of Control, Access and Conservation in Colonial India." In *Nature, Culture, Imperialism: Essays on the Environmental History of South Asia*, edited by David Arnold and Ramachandra Guha, 260–92. New York: Oxford University Press, 1995.

Reiger, John F. *American Sportsmen and the Origins of Conservation*. 3rd ed. Corvallis: Oregon State University Press, 2001.

Reisner, Marc. *Cadillac Desert: The American West and Its Disappearing Water*. Rev. ed. New York: Penguin, 1993.

Renk, N. F. "Off to the Lakes: Vacationing in North Idaho during the Railroad Era, 1885–1915." *Idaho Yesterdays* 34, no. 2 (Summer 1990): 2–15.

Richardson, John. *Fauna Boreali-Americana; or, The Zoology of the Northern Parts of British America: Containing Descriptions of the Objects of Natural History Collected on the Late Northern Land Expeditions under Command of Captain Sir John Franklin, R. N., Part Third. The Fish*. London: Richard Bentley, 1836. Accessed December 30, 2010. http://www.archive.org/details/faunaborealiamer-03rich.

Rico, Monica. *Nature's Noblemen: Transatlantic Masculinities and the Nineteenth-Century American West*. New Haven, CT: Yale University Press, 2013.

Riley, Glenda. *Women and Nature: Saving the "Wild" West*. Lincoln: University of Nebraska Press, 1999.

Ritvo, Harriet. *The Animal Estate: The English and Other Creatures in the Victorian Age*. Cambridge, MA: Harvard University Press, 1987.

Robbins, William G. *Colony and Empire: The Capitalist Transformation of the American West*. Lawrence: University Press of Kansas, 1994.

Rodgers, Daniel T. *Atlantic Crossings: Social Politics in a Progressive Age*. Cambridge, MA: Harvard University Press, 1998.

Roediger, David. *The Wages of Whiteness: Race and the Making of the American Working Class*. Rev. ed. London: Verso, 1999.

Rome, Adam. *The Bulldozer in the Countryside: Suburban Sprawl and the Rise of American Environmentalism.* New York: Cambridge University Press, 2001.

———. "'Give Earth a Chance': The Environment Movement and the Sixties." *Journal of American History* 90, no. 2 (Sept. 2003): 525–54.

Roosevelt, Robert Barnwell. *Game Fish of the Northern States of America, and British Provinces.* New York: Carleton, 1862. Accessed August 12, 2013. http://archive.org/details/gamefishofnortheoooroos.

Roosevelt, R. Barnwell, and Seth Green. *Fish Hatching and Fish Catching.* Rochester, NY: Union and Advertiser Co.'s Book and Job Print, 1879.

Rothman, Hal K. *Devil's Bargains: Tourism in the Twentieth-Century American West.* Lawrence: University Press of Kansas, 1998.

Rushton, W. "Fresh Water Fishery Problems of the British Isles." *Transactions of the American Fisheries Society* 66, no. 1 (Jan. 1937): 383–91.

Sanders, Jeffrey Craig. *Seattle and the Roots of Urban Sustainability: Inventing Ecotopia.* Pittsburgh, PA: University of Pittsburgh Press, 2010.

Sandlos, John. "From the Outside Looking in: Aesthetics, Politics, and Wildlife Conservation in the Canadian North." *Environmental History* 6, no. 1 (Jan. 2001): 6–31.

Schmitt, Peter J. *Back to Nature: The Arcadian Myth in Urban America.* New York: Oxford University Press, 1969.

Schullery, Paul. *American Fly Fishing: A History.* New York: Lyons Press, 1987.

———. *Cowboy Trout: Western Fly Fishing As If It Matters.* Helena: Montana Historical Society Press, 2006.

———. "Fly Fishing's Three-Century Saga of Silkworm Gut." *American Fly Fisher* 32, no. 2 (Spring 2006): 2–9.

———. "Frontier Fly-Fishing in the New West." *Montana: The Magazine of Western History* 52, no. 2 (Summer 2002): 2–9.

———. *If Fish Could Scream: An Angler's Search for the Future of Fly Fishing.* Mechanicsburg, PA: Stackpole Books, 2008.

———. *Searching for Yellowstone: Ecology and Wonder in the Last Wilderness.* Helena: Montana Historical Society Press, 2004.

———. "Their Numbers Are Perfectly Fabulous: Sport, Science, and Subsistence in Yellowstone Fishing, 1870." *Annals of Wyoming: The Wyoming History Journal* 76, no. 2 (Spring 2004): 6–18.

Schwiebert, Ernest. *Trout.* 2 vols. New York: E. P. Dutton, 1978.

Scott, Genio C. *Fishing in American Waters.* New York: Harper & Brothers, 1869.

Sears, John F. *Sacred Places: American Tourist Attractions in the Nineteenth Century.* 1989. Reprint, Amherst: University of Massachusetts Press, 1998.

Shaffer, Marguerite S. *See America First: Tourism and National Identity, 1880–1940.* Washington, DC: Smithsonian Institution Press, 2001.

Shellenbarger, Melanie. *High Country Summers: The Early Second Homes of Colorado, 1880–1940*. Tucson: University of Arizona Press, 2012.

Sigler, William F. "The Life History and Management of the Mountain Whitefish *Prosopium williamsoni* (Girard) in Logan River Utah." Bulletin 347. Logan: Utah State Agricultural College, May 1951.

Sigler, William F., and John W. Sigler. *Fishes of the Great Basin: A Natural History*. Reno: University of Nevada Press, 1987.

Slotkin, Richard. *Gunfighter Nation: The Myth of the Frontier in Twentieth-Century America*. New York: Atheneum, 1992.

Smalley, Andrea L. "'Our Lady Sportsmen': Gender, Class, and Conservation in Sport Hunting Magazines." *Journal of the Gilded Age and Progressive Era* 4, no. 4 (Oct. 2005): 355–80.

Smith, M. W. "Copper Sulphate and Rotenone as Fish Poisons." *Transactions of the American Fisheries Society* 69, no. 1 (Jan. 1940): 141–57.

Smith, Michael B. "Silence, Miss Carson! Science, Gender, and the Reception of *Silent Spring*." *Feminist Studies* 27, no. 3 (Fall 2001): 733–52.

Smith, Sherry L. *Reimagining Indians: Native Americans through Anglo Eyes, 1880–1940*. New York: Oxford University Press, 2000.

Snyder, Gary. "The Rediscovery of Turtle Island." In *A Place in Space: Ethics, Aesthetics, and Watersheds*, 236–51. Washington, DC: Counterpoint, 1995.

Snyder, Samuel. "Restoring Natives in New Mexico." *American Fly Fisher* 35, no. 3 (Summer 2009): 10–17.

Spackman, W. H. *Trout in New Zealand: Where to Go and How to Catch Them*. Wellington, NZ: George Didsbury, 1892.

Spence, Mark David. *Dispossessing the Wilderness: Indian Removal and the Making of the National Parks*. New York: Oxford University Press, 1999.

Stegner, Wallace. *Beyond the Hundredth Meridian: John Wesley Powell and the Second Opening of the West*. 1954. Reprint, New York: Penguin, 1992.

———. *The Sound of Mountain Water: The Changing American West*. 1969. Reprint, New York: Penguin Books, 1997.

Steinberg, Ted. *Down to Earth: Nature's Role in American History*. New York: Oxford University Press, 2002.

Stickney, Robert R. *Aquaculture in the United States: A Historical Survey*. New York: John Wiley and Sons, 1996.

Stone, Livingston. *Domesticated Trout: How to Breed and Grow Them*. Boston: James R. Osgood, 1873.

Stuart, Granville. *Forty Years on the Frontier As Seen in the Journals and Reminiscences of Granville Stuart, Gold-Miner, Trader, Merchant, Rancher and Politician*. Edited by Paul C. Phillips. 2 vols. Cleveland, OH: Arthur H. Clark, 1925.

Sutter, Paul S. *Driven Wild: How the Fight against Automobiles Launched the Modern Wilderness Movement.* Seattle: University of Washington Press, 2002.

———. "When Environmental Traditions Collide: Ramachandra Guha's *The Unquiet Woods* and U.S. Environmental History." *Environmental History* 14, no. 3 (July 2009): 543–50.

Swisher, Doug, and Carl Richards. *Selective Trout: A Dramatically New and Scientific Approach to Trout Fishing on Eastern and Western Rivers.* New York: Crown Publishers, 1971.

Synnestvedt, Harold. "The Work of the Western Food and Game Fish Protective Association." *Transactions of the American Fisheries Society* 58, no. 1 (Jan. 1928): 78–79.

Szylvian, Kristin M. "Transforming Lake Michigan into the 'World's Greatest Fishing Hole': The Environmental Politics of Michigan's Great Lakes Sport Fishing, 1965–1985." *Environmental History* 9, no. 1 (Jan. 2004): 102–27.

Tapply, H. G. *The Sportsman's Notebook and Tap's Tips.* New York: Holt, Rinehart and Winston, 1964.

Taylor, Joseph E., III. "American Pastoral." *Environmental History* 12, no. 2 (April 2007): 378–80.

———. *Making Salmon: An Environmental History of the Northwest Fisheries Crisis.* Seattle: University of Washington Press, 1999.

———. "The Many Lives of the New West." *Western Historical Quarterly* 35, no. 2 (Summer 2004): 141–65.

———. "Master of the Seas? Herbert Hoover and the Western Fisheries." *Oregon Historical Quarterly* 105, no. 1 (Spring 2004): 40–61.

Taylor, Matthew. "Editorial—Sport, Transnationalism, and Global History." *Journal of Global History* 8, no. 2 (July 2013): 199–208.

Thomas, Henry Sullivan. *The Rod in India: Being Hints How to Obtain Sport, with Remarks on the Natural History of Fish, Their Culture, and Value; and Illustrations of Fish and Tackle.* 2nd ed. London: Hamilton, Adams, 1881.

Thompson, E. P. *Whigs and Hunters: The Origin of the Black Act.* London: Allen Lane, 1975.

Thompson, W. T. "Is Irrigation Detrimental to Trout Culture?" *Transactions of the American Fisheries Society* 41, no. 1 (Jan. 1912): 103–14.

Thoms, J. Michael. "A Place Called Pennask: Fly-fishing and Colonialism at a British Columbia Lake." *BC Studies*, no. 133 (Spring 2002): 69–98.

Titcomb, John W. "The Use of Copper Sulphate for the Destruction of Obnoxious Fishes in Ponds and Lakes." *Transactions of the American Fisheries Society* 44, no. 1 (Dec. 1914): 20–26.

Todd, Kim. *Tinkering with Eden: A Natural History of Exotics in America.* New York: W. W. Norton, 2001.

Towle, Jerry C. "Authored Ecosystems: Livingston Stone and the Transformation of California Fisheries." *Environmental History* 5, no. 1 (Jan. 2000): 54–74.

Trachtenberg, Alan. *The Incorporation of America: Culture and Society in the Gilded Age*. New York: Hill and Wang, 1982.

Trotter, Patrick. *Cutthroat: Native Trout of the West*. 2nd ed. Berkeley: University of California Press, 2008.

Tvedt, Terje. "'Water Systems,' Environmental History and the Deconstruction of Nature." *Environment and History* 16, no. 2 (May 2010): 143–66.

Tyrrell, Ian. *True Gardens of the Gods: Californian-Australian Environmental Reform, 1860–1930*. Berkeley: University of California Press, 1999.

Union Pacific Railroad. *Union Pacific Outings: Fishing in Colorado and Wyoming*. N.p.: Union Pacific Railroad, 1909.

United States v. Winans, 198 U.S. 371, 25 S.Ct. 662, 49 L.Ed. 1089 (1905).

Vance, Norman. "Imperial Rome and Britain's Language of Empire 1600–1837," *History of European Ideas* 26, nos. 3–4 (2000): 211–24.

Varley, John D., and Paul Schullery. *Freshwater Wilderness: Yellowstone Fishes and Their World*. Yellowstone National Park: Yellowstone Library and Museum Association, 1983.

Vinson, Mark R., Eric C. Dinger, and Deanna K. Vinson. "Piscicides and Invertebrates: After 70 Years, Does Anyone Really Know?" *Fisheries* 35, no. 2 (Feb. 2010): 61–71.

Vogel, Eve. "Defining One Pacific Northwest among Many Possibilities: The Political Construction of a Region and Its River during the New Deal." *Western Historical Quarterly* 42, no. 1 (Spring 2011): 29–53.

von Brandt, Andres. *Fish Catching Methods of the World*. Rev. ed. London: Fishing News, 1972.

Waite, Thornton. *Union Pacific: Montana Division, Route of the Butte Special*. Idaho Falls, ID: Brueggenjohann/Reese and Thornton Waite, 1998.

Wallis, Orthello L. "Management of Sport Fishing in National Parks." *Transactions of the American Fisheries Society* 89, no. 2 (Apr. 1960): 234–38.

Ward v. Race Horse, 183 U.S. 504, 16 S.Ct. 1076, 41 L.Ed. 244 (1896).

Warren, Julianne Lutz. "Weaving a Wider Net for Conservation: Aldo Leopold's Water Ethic." *Organization and Environment* 23, no. 2 (2010): 220–32.

Warren, Louis S. *The Hunter's Game: Poachers and Conservationists in Twentieth-Century America*. New Haven, CT: Yale University Press, 1997.

Weltzien, O. Alan, ed. *The Norman Maclean Reader*. Chicago: University of Chicago Press, 2008.

West, Elliott. *The Contested Plains: Indians, Goldseekers, and the Rush to Colorado*. Lawrence: University Press of Kansas, 1998.

————. *The Last Indian War: The Nez Perce Story*. New York: Oxford University Press, 2009.

Wheatley, Harriet. *Lady Angler: Fishing, Hunting, and Camping in Wilderness Areas of North America*. San Antonio, TX: Naylor, 1952.

White, G. Edward. *The Eastern Establishment and the Western Experience: The West of Frederic Remington, Theodore Roosevelt, and Owen Wister*. New Haven, CT: Yale University Press, 1968.

White, Richard. "'Are You an Environmentalist or Do You Work for a Living?': Work and Nature." In *Uncommon Ground: Toward Reinventing Nature*, edited by William Cronon, 171–85. New York: W. W. Norton, 1995.

————. *"It's Your Misfortune and None of My Own": A History of the American West*. Norman: University of Oklahoma Press, 1991.

————. "The Nationalization of Nature." *Journal of American History* 86, no. 3 (Dec. 1999): 976–86.

————. *The Organic Machine: The Remaking of the Columbia River*. New York: Hill and Wang, 1995.

Whitehouse, Francis C. *Sport Fishes of Western Canada, and Some Others*. 2nd ed. Vancouver, BC: privately printed, 1945.

Whittlesey, Lee H. "Of Fairies' Wings and Fish: Fishery Operations and the Lake Fish Hatchery in Yellowstone." *Yellowstone Science* 14, no. 2 (Spring 2006): 13–19.

Wiley, Robert W. "The 1962 Rotenone Treatment of the Green River, Wyoming and Utah, Revisited: Lessons Learned." *Fisheries* 33, no. 12 (Dec. 2008): 611–17.

Wilkins, David E., and K. Tsianina Lomawaima. *Uneven Ground: American Indian Sovereignty and Federal Law*. Norman: University of Oklahoma Press, 2001.

Wiltzius, William. "William Radcliffe and the Grand Mesa Lake Feud." *American Fly Fisher* 13, no. 1 (Winter 1986): 23–26.

Worster, Donald. *Nature's Economy: A History of Ecological Ideas*. 2nd ed. New York: Cambridge University Press, 1994.

————. *Rivers of Empire: Water, Aridity, and the Growth of the American West*. New York: Oxford University Press, 1985.

Wrobel, David M. *Global West, American Frontier: Travel, Empire, and Exceptionalism from Manifest Destiny to the Great Depression*. Albuquerque: University of New Mexico Press, 2013.

Wrobel, David M., and Patrick T. Long, eds. *Seeing and Being Seen: Tourism in the American West*. Lawrence: University Press of Kansas, 2001.

Wrobel, David M., and Michael C. Steiner, eds. *Many Wests: Place, Culture, and Regional Identity*. Lawrence: University Press of Kansas, 1997.

Wulff, Lee. *Lee Wulff's Handbook of Freshwater Fishing*. New York: J. B. Lippincott, 1939.

Wyckoff, William. *Creating Colorado: The Making of a Western American Landscape, 1860–1940*. New Haven, CT: Yale University Press, 1999.

THESES AND DISSERTATIONS

Benson, Megan Kathleen. "Damming the Bighorn: Indian Reserved Water Rights on the Crow Reservation, 1900–2000." PhD diss., University of Oklahoma, 2003.

Blaisdell, James P. "A History of the Conservation Effort in Wyoming and the Wyoming Game and Fish Commission to 1950." MA thesis, University of Wyoming, 1964.

Borgelt, Bryon. "Flies Only: Early Sport Fishing Conservation on Michigan's Au Sable River." PhD diss., University of Toledo, 2009.

DosSantos, Joseph Michael. "Comparative Food Habits and Habitat Selection of Mountain Whitefish and Rainbow Trout in the Kootenai River, Montana." MA thesis, Montana State University, 1985.

Helmer, Joel William. "Float Trips, Dams, and Tailwater Trout: An Environmental History of the White River of Northern Arkansas, 1870–2004." PhD diss., Oklahoma State University, 2005.

Kinsey, Darin. "Fashioning a Freshwater Eden: Elite Anglers, Fish Culture, and State Development of Quebec's 'Sport' Fishery." PhD diss., University of Quebec, 2008.

Liebelt, James Edward. "Studies on the Behavior and Life History of the Mountain Whitefish (*Prosopium williamsoni* Girard)." PhD diss., Montana State University, 1970.

Snyder, Samuel. "Casting for Conservation: Religion, Popular Culture, and Environmental Politics of River Restoration." PhD diss., University of Florida, 2008.

Whiteley, Andrew Robert. "Effects of Historical and Contemporary Factors on Genetic Diversity in the Mountain Whitefish (*Prosopium williamsoni*)." PhD diss., University of Montana, 2005.

INDEX

greenheart rods, 29

Green River, 124, 128

Grey, Zane, 77

Grinnell, George Bird, 170n5

guddling or tickling, 22, 165n45

H

habitat degradation and protection, 147–50

Haig-Brown, Roderick, 11, 184n9

Halford, Frederic, 32, 32–33, 33

Hallock, Charles, 97

A Handbook of Angling (Fitzgibbon), 15

Handbook of Freshwater Fishing (Wulff), 140

hatchery system: additional hatcheries,
77–78, 82, 84; Booth's call for efficiency,
78; criticisms of hatchery trout, 135–36,
138, 144; decline of, 136, 145; disease and
parasites in, 136; historical background,
41–42; individual promoters, 43–45;
planting larger fish, 78–79, 90; production methods, 42–43; railroads and, 50;
rearing ponds of sporting clubs, 79, 82,
84, 89; state hatcheries, 45–47; transnational exchanges and, 50–51; trout,
choice of, 51–52; US Fish Commission
enterprise, 45

Hauser, Samuel T., 36

Henshall, James A., 51, 71, 72, 117–18, 155

Herbert, Henry William, 96–97, 108

Hessel, Rudolph, 50–51

highway building, 148–49

"hogs," 124

Holter Dam, 129

hook-and-line laws, 34–37, 58

hooks, 15, 31, 141

Hoover, Herbert, 79

horsehair lines, 29

hybridization, 71, 73

I

Idaho: advertising by, 76–77; canal rescue
operations, 120; game wardens in, 56, 115;
regulations, 58; Sunbeam Dam, 61–62

Idaho Fish and Game Department, 109, 115

If Fish Could Scream (Schullery), 197n21

imperialism, 12–13, 25, 35

India, 35

industrialization, 12, 24

Interstate Highway Defense Act (1956), 148

irrigation canals: collection of fish from
canals and fields, 119; fish losses through,
116–19; fish screens for, 117–18; on Indian
reservations, 118–19; Montana access bill
debate, 112–13; prior appropriation water
rights doctrine and dewatering, 114–16;
state salvage operations, 119–21

Izaak Walton League, 79, 122

J

Jackson, William Henry, 46

Japan, 15

the Jock Scott (fly), 25, 25

Joe's Valley Reservoir, 143

Johnson County War (Wyoming), 44

Jordan, David Starr, 44, 52, 60, 101–2, 103,
108, 115, 116

K

Keeler, Greg, 109

Kipling, Rudyard, 13–14, 15

L

Lackey, Bertram D., 77

LaFontaine, Gary, 113–14, 122, 124, 127, 142

lake trout, 49, 159n8

laws and regulations: in British colonies, 35;
catch limits and creel limits, 58; coarse
fish and, 98; community-centered angling
rules, 37; complaints over state laws,
61–63; early angling laws in Massachusetts, 34; fishing seasons, 58–59; game
wardens and enforcement of, 55–56; hook-
and-line laws, 34–37, 58; irrigation screen
laws, 117–18; pollution laws, 61, 176n83;
resistance to, 58–60; subsistence fishing,
accommodation of, 57–58